1/11/89

To John Rowe
with warmest regards

Leonard Sagan

THE HEALTH
OF NATIONS

True Causes of
Sickness and Well-Being

LEONARD A. SAGAN

Basic Books, Inc., Publishers   New York

Table 7.1 on p. 134 is reprinted with permission of The Free Press, a Division of Macmillan, Inc. from *Social Origins of Depression* by George W. Brown and Tirril Harris. Copyright © 1978 by George W. Brown and Tirril Harris.

Figure 8.2B on p. 168 is reprinted by permission of the Kinsey Institute for Research in Sex, Gender, and Reproduction, Inc., from Alfred C. Kinsey et al., *Sexual Behavior in the Human Male*, p. 354. Philadelphia: W. B. Saunders, 1948.

Library of Congress Cataloging-in-Publication Data

Sagan, Leonard A.
  The health of nations.

  Bibliography.
  Includes index.
  1. Public health. 2. Life expectancy. 3. Health
behavior. 4. Social medicine. 5. Public health—United
States. 6. Life expectancy—United States. 7. Health
behavior—United States. 8. Social medicine—United
States. I. Title. [DNLM: 1. Health. 2. Life
Expectancy. 3. Social Environment. WA 30 S129h]
RA425.S165 1987   362.1   87-47518
ISBN 0-465-02893-4

Contents

The Health of Nations

Introduction: The Search for Health

THIS IS A BOOK about health, about its meaning, and about its sources. We place a high value on health, yet we know little about the psychological, biological, and behavioral characteristics of healthy people. Nor do we understand fully why it is that modernization has produced dramatic improvements in human health—the average life-span increasing by as much as forty years—truly one of the most remarkable events in human history. What can we as individuals learn about health by examining why it is that we are now so much healthier and live so much longer?

A second objective of this inquiry is to examine the health experience of the United States in the postmodern* period. We shall consider, in particular, the troubling recent evidence of the failure of U.S. mortality rates to keep pace with those of other modernized countries and the fact that there has been an actual increase in morbidity and disability rates. Why is it that in this country, which boasts the finest medical system in the world and which has the second highest per-capita expenditure on

* Since "modern," "premodern," and "postmodern" are terms that are used differently, let me specify my meaning. I use "modern" to refer to, among other things, the adoption of science and technology, increased productivity, an emphasis on individualism, gender equality, and educational achievement, urbanization, and the rise of the nation state, conditions that first began to emerge in parts of Europe and North America in the eighteenth century. Societies that are largely agricultural, authoritarian, preliterate, and without an industrial base, I refer to as "premodern." Many parts of the world today, particularly in Africa and southeast Asia, remain premodern.

I use "postmodern" to refer to societies where the process of modernization has fully matured. Physical and social security will be widely, but not necessarily universally, available. One of the major characteristics of the postmodern society is the decline of a lifelong commitment to a stable nuclear family. The end of World War II is a convenient benchmark for the appearance of the postmodern era in North America and western Europe.

3

medical care in the world (following Sweden), our life expectancy trails that of eighteen other nations, including Greece, Spain, and Italy? Although the United States led the decline in death rates in the earlier part of this century, we have begun to slip over the past few decades. In fact, not only has the decline slowed, but it shows signs of coming to a complete halt. Adult mortality rates were declining rapidly in the United States throughout the early 1900s, a trend that continued through the 1960s. In the 1970s, the decline in mortality rates began to slow, and from 1979 to 1981, changes in mortality have been very small.

There is much additional evidence of a decline in health in the United States.

1. In New York City, where deaths among those aged fifteen through sixty-four were declining through the year 1982, the trend has now reversed; deaths are now increasing and are predicted to continue to grow (Kristal 1986).

2. Suicide rates are increasing, and suicide is the third leading cause of death among teenagers and young adults. Of all suicides, 20 percent are committed by persons under twenty-five.

3. In 1950 the rate of suicides among young people was only about 20 percent of what it was in 1977. It is estimated that some 5 million Americans have made one or more suicide attempts and that 10 percent of this group will succeed. Some estimates are that the actual suicide rate is actually three times higher than the reported rate.

4. The decline in infant mortality rates in the United States, in comparison with other modernized countries, is also flagging. In 1950 through 1954, the United States was seventh lowest in infant mortality rates among the nations of the world; in 1960 through 1964, eleventh; in 1970 through 1974, sixteenth; and in 1982, seventeenth.

5. Although mortality from heart disease is declining, the prevalence of heart disease and other chronic conditions, such as high blood pressure, are increasing, not decreasing (Feinleib and Wilson 1985).

6. The frequency of hospitalization and the limitation of activity due to disability is increasing. For reasons not at all clear, disability among children has doubled in the last two decades (Newachek, Budetti, and McManus 1984). Could it be that, as some observers claim, the health of Americans is now worsening (Verbrugge 1984)?

7. Not only are direct measures of health declining, so too are those health habits that have been shown to be important determinants of health. In the 1970s several health habits were shown to influence morbidity and mortality rates: never smoking, drinking fewer than five alcoholic beverages at one sitting, maintaining desirable weight, sleeping

seven to eight hours per night, exercising, eating breakfast regularly, and avoiding snacks (Breslow and Endstrom 1980). Comparison of data collected systematically in 1977 and 1983 demonstrate that overall, American health habits are worsening, not improving. Prevalence rates for four of the seven measures increased more than 10 percent; only cigarette smoking showed a favorable trend. There was more obesity, less exercise, more drinking, and less sleep (Schoenborn 1986).

8. Of greatest concern for the future of American health is the fact that certain social conditions known to be associated with poor health outcomes are rapidly increasing. As we shall see later in this book, the prevalence of illiteracy, divorce, teenage pregnancy, and homelessness, all of which are associated with increased morbidity and mortality, are on the increase in the United States.

These recent decades of apparent health decline are the very years during which our health expenditures have been growing most rapidly. In 1950 we spent only $12.7 billion for health, 4.4 percent of our gross national product (GNP). By 1984 those costs grew to $392.7 billion, more than 11 percent of our GNP—more than a billion dollars a day! Much of that money is spent for the spectacular: 326,000 organ transplants, 50,000 coronary bypass operations, 500,000 cardiac catheterizations, and 60,000 dialysis patients. Just how effective is this medical strategy for achieving and maintaining health? Is our emphasis on disease detection and treatment as likely to prolong life as is a strategy directed toward understanding and enhancing health? What is the relationship between health and disease? Is health no more than the absence of disease?

Our Disease Paradigm

All cultures create their own theories of disease and death. Although there are variants, theories generally fall into two categories—those that emphasize behavioral factors (health-oriented theories) and those that emphasize the importance of environmental factors (disease-oriented theories). During the thousand years prior to the modern period, western medicine focused on behavior; illness was seen as evidence of a disordered physiology, which was in turn seen as the result of unhealthy or immoral behavior. Even as recently as the nineteenth century, cholera epidemics, which affected the poor almost exclusively, were viewed as divine punishment of those who were considered slothful (Rosenberg 1962). Consistent with this person-oriented theory of disease, physicians prescribed diet, medications, or a change in location to restore health.

With the onset of the Enlightenment and the appearance of Newtonian physics, a paradigmatic shift in medical theory appeared. Just as defendants were considered innocent until proven guilty, individuals were assumed to be healthy until proven sick. Medical attention largely moved from the individual to the environment as the source of illness and disease. Just as the motions of the earth and stars could be explained by the action of physical forces acting upon them, so too could all biology and behavior be explained as the result of exposure to environmental factors. Human beings were no more than large machines, somewhat like complicated clocks. Because the major causes of death in the premodern period were the infectious diseases, the discovery of bacteria and their insect vectors appeared to substantiate the environmental source of disease. Tuberculosis, for example, was "caused" by the tubercle bacillus. In the twentieth century, we continue to place major emphasis on external agents of disease and ignore behavioral factors in health.

One important consequence of this newer view of disease is the schism between the domains of physical and mental health. Enlightenment scientists, willing to accept the movements of stars and other foreign bodies as under the control of universal and knowable physical forces, remained profoundly theistic. They were unwilling to accept the mind (they preferred "soul") as mere object, to be studied, dissected, and experimented upon. The Cartesian compromise was adopted—the mind was removed from the medical sphere. And thus we now have diseases presided over by physicians while the psyche and its illnesses has become the realm of psychiatrists and psychologists. The distinction between the demonstrable reality of the bodily *diseases* and the ephemeral and subjective nature of mental *illnesses* is reflected in the terms disease and illness. "Disease" denotes pathology that has some objective manifestation, whereas "illness" refers to malaise or symptoms as experienced by the patient. It is sometimes said that illness is what patients have on the way to the doctor's office ("I don't feel well") while disease is what they have on the way home ("I have the flu"). It is the diseases of the body—that is, the "organic" diseases—that are considered to determine the length of life. While certain limited elements of lifestyle are recognized as influencing mortality rates (as with those "health habits" just described), that association has, at least until recently, attracted very little attention.

6

Moreover, "lifestyle" as it relates to health has far greater complexity than is captured by those seven poor health habits. The definition of lifestyle adopted here represents much more than behavior that is merely the final expression of basic values and attitudes. It includes, "the general pattern of assumptions, motives, cognitive styles, and coping techniques that characterize the behavior of an individual and give it consistency" (Coleman 1964, p. 664).

When we do consider characteristics of health, we place by far the greatest emphasis on what is more properly called fitness. The implicit model is the "body as machine." Many people feel that they are "taking good care of themselves" if they take vitamins, avoid cholesterol-containing foods, and jog regularly. How they feel about themselves and how they are able to relate to others, how fulfilling their work is, are factors that may be considered important, but they are not considered relevant to health nor able to influence the onset or course of disease.

The common wisdom regarding good health envisions a program of regular physical exercise, preferably of a vigorous nature ("aerobic"), a near-vegetarian diet, protection from stress, abstinence from addictive drugs, and protection from industrial chemicals. Yet these are the very conditions that have existed for human populations throughout history. People living in agricultural communities have engaged in vigorous physical activity daily, most often farming; they have eaten little or no meat; they have used no addictive drugs; they have no time clocks to punch, no bills to pay; and their environment was free from fertilizers, pesticides, food additives, and air pollution—so why did they die by the age of thirty-five?

We also have the notion that people living in small, closely knit farming communities who are free of the stresses of modern living are free of mental disease. Yet the evidence does not support that view. Studies of the membership of the Hutterite church, who live communally and who determinedly follow traditional agricultural practices, and whose lives are supposedly simple, austere, free of commercialism and greed, and who own property in common, show that their frequency of mental disease is not markedly different from that of more conventional modern communities (Eaton and Weil 1955).

In contrast with our notions of health, which is perceived as at least partly a matter of personal responsibility, disease is seen as striking at random—the patient is viewed as victim. Just as with other external enemies, we make "war" on disease: a "war on cancer," a "fight against multiple sclerosis," a "March of Dimes." The conquest of specific infectious diseases such as malaria and typhoid through environmental control is seen as the glory of medical science and the model for our attack on the modern diseases. The decline in mortality rates is viewed as the result of a decline in disease rates rather than an improvement in health. Are those lower death rates the consequence of a better environment, or are they the result of our having become better animals—that is, healthier?

Who Are the Healthy People?

Physicians reach conclusions regarding health when they find that disease is absent; health, then, is a diagnosis by exclusion. For example, patients undergoing a yearly checkup are likely to be told that they are in excellent health if their weight, blood pressure, electrocardiogram, and so on are normal and there is no anatomical evidence of disease. If no evidence of disease is found, a physician is likely to reassure the patient complaining of symptoms.

While the absence of disease may be necessary to good health, clearly health implies more than an absence of disease. Most would agree that an element critical to health is a sense of subjective well-being, happiness, joy, or exuberance—in other words, health is not an objective entity but a highly subjective one, reflecting the individual's cultural and personal values. Such entities are difficult to define and measure.

The World Health Organization (WHO) of the United Nations defines health as "a state of complete physical, mental and social well-being and not simply the absence of disease or infirmity" (WHO 1958). This definition provides a useful starting point, particularly in its emphasis on health as a positive and meaningful entity that has dimensions of its own. But the definition creates other problems: for example, who is to decide whether a state of well-being exists? Presumably judgments of "well-being" are subjective judgments of the individuals themselves. If this is the case, how do we identify persons with good health other than by asking them? If psychotic individuals tell us in their manic exuberance that they are in excellent health, are we willing to accept that judgment? If those who are very elderly but in apparent good health tell us that they are in good health, are we to assign them to the same category to which we assign the young and vigorous? What of the individual with transient disability, say, a skier with a fractured bone; is such a person in good health? And what of the WHO inclusion of "social well-being"? This suggests that the individual's characteristics alone are not sufficient to establish and maintain health, but that a salutary environment, both psychological and economic, must also be present.

Clearly, the concept of health, just as the concept of disease, is value-laden and subjective. So if health is largely subjective in nature, how are we to identify and study healthy populations? The brilliant psychologist Abraham Maslow simply selected those whom he considered "healthy" without defining his selection criteria. They were healthy because he said they were healthy (Maslow 1950).

One indisputable characteristic of healthy people is their resistance to disease. As a consequence, healthy people, given an adequate socioeconomic environment, will live long lives. One assumption of this book then will be that healthy people will have low morbidity rates and low death rates. It is a plausible assumption; populations that experience high mortality rates also experience high disease rates. One example that we shall examine in some detail in chapter 8 is the correspondence between high morbidity and mortality rates among members of "lower" social classes. Still another example is the high prevalence of chronic disease, especially infectious disease, among members of underdeveloped societies that characteristically manifest high mortality rates.

Still, the congruence is not perfect—some individuals who appear to be in excellent health die at young ages, whereas some who appear to be chronically ill live very long lives. Women tend to have higher morbidity rates, as measured by doctor visits, sickness absences, and hospital admissions, than do men; yet their mortality rates at all ages are lower than are those of men. Clearly then, as illustrated by this example of the sexes, one should not expect to find high degrees of correlation between illness and death rates. Nevertheless, to assume a relationship between length of life and health appears to be, overall, plausible and generally consistent with available data. Therefore, in the absence of any other objective measure of health, a study of the characteristics of those who live long lives cannot help but broaden our understanding of health.

Some factors are widely recognized as appearing to be associated with long life. One of these is sex; as mentioned, females clearly have the advantage (as we shall see later, this has not always been the case historically). Another is social class—those of higher social class have the advantage over those of lower social class. Education is still another factor influencing mortality rates. Some attention is directed to all of these factors in subsequent chapters; however, by far the most powerful factor influencing life expectancy is modernization. Because of its dramatic influence on life-span, a major portion of this book is devoted to understanding what it is about modernization that so powerfully reduces death rates and contributes to health. A second objective, as noted earlier, is to better understand why we in the United States appear to be backsliding in our historical movement toward better health.

A Note on Causation

In the following chapters we shall examine the role of various factors on the development of modern life expectancy. The objective is to understand whether each of these is or is not an important antecedent— that is, something that "causes" good health. The issue of causation consumes the interest of philosophers; it is not simple to understand the cause of things. Many people confuse a simple association of two phenomena with causation, which may operate in either direction in the relationship, or may not directly link the two at all. As an extreme example, it would clearly be an error for the farmer to assume that the crowing of the rooster is responsible for the rising of the sun.

When two phenomena such as modernization and increased life expectancy are closely associated, a common error is to assume that one causes the other—to assume, that is, that one is a risk factor for the other. For example, it might be concluded that modernization (or medical care, or improved nutrition) "causes" increased life expectancy. Yet there are other possibilities that may explain this association—each member of the pair may influence the other, or both may be influenced by some third, possibly unrecognized factor. For example, does modernization produce changes in health, or do changes in health lead to changes in population dynamics that in turn stimulate modernization, or do both of these occur simultaneously as a result of some other factor? It is the difficulty of unraveling causation that permits tobacco companies to claim that cigarettes are not a risk factor for lung cancer, but rather that those who are susceptible to lung cancer are more prone to smoke cigarettes.

With complex biological phenomena such as human disease, multiple causative factors may play some role, each of which may be necessary, but no one of which is sufficient to produce disease. For this reason, questions related to the causal role of specific microorganisms or insect carriers in the appearance of infectious diseases led pathologists of the nineteenth century to certain rules that became known as "Koch's Postulates."*

The underlying assumption was that each specific disease is the result of exposure to a specific agent: "one germ, one disease." These criteria were quickly recognized, even by Koch, as being far too rigid and simplistic. We now know that one agent, whether it be bacterial, viral, or chemical, may produce different diseases under different environmental conditions. For example, the Epstein-Barr virus (EBV) is known to be associated in the United States with a rather benign disease common to college students, infectious mononucleosis. In Africa the same virus is associated with a malignant tumor of children known as Burkitt's lymphoma. In China the same virus has been identified with the otherwise uncommon nasopharyngeal cancer. It has also been found in association with several other cancer types (Leyvraz et al. 1985). Finally, many people carry the virus without any evidence of harm. This pattern is not unique to EBV; most infectious agents produce this same chameleon effect, appearing in each person in a different guise and often being present harmlessly.† The virus may be necessary to the development of a particular "named disease," but it will not be sufficient to produce that disease. Obviously the notion of "one germ, one disease," is inadequate. More appropriate is the notion of a "web of causation" in which multiple factors, personal and environmental, interact to result in disease.

Newer information makes it appear that the acquired immune deficiency syndrome (AIDS) fits this same pattern. The virus is not transmitted easily. Multiple exposures are required and personal behavior patterns (sexual practices, drug use) strongly predispose to infection. Still, many people are apparently carrying the virus harmlessly—that is, they are infected, yet they do not have disease. Among those with the virus who do become ill, personal or other characteristics will combine, in the presence of the virus, to produce a wide spectrum of individual diseases. The final appearance of disease, then, is a reflection of all of the indi-

---

* Robert Koch, 1843–1910, won the Nobel Prize in 1910 for his discovery of the tubercle bacillus, the organism associated with tuberculosis.

† The streptococcus, that organism which creates so much anxiety in parents when found in the throats of their children ("strep throat"), can be found in the throats of as high as 90 percent of apparently healthy people, if searched for diligently enough.

11

vidual's past experiences, exposures, and genetic predisposition.*

How can the appearance of this new disease, AIDS, be explained? Not only does the human population change in its behavior and its susceptibility to diseases, but so too do disease-producing organisms. As a consequence, new diseases constantly appear and old ones disappear. For example, typhus does not occur historically until the sixteenth century—it was then a new disease (Zinsser 1935). There are no historical records of polio, a disease that because of its dramatic clinical features is likely to have attracted clinical attention, before the nineteenth century. In this century leprosy has almost disappeared and smallpox has been obliterated, but we now have AIDS and Legionnaire's disease. Certain cancer types, such as stomach cancer, are rapidly decreasing while others, such as lung cancer, are increasing, sometimes for reasons that are partially known, sometimes for totally unknown reasons.

Just as the appearance of disease represents the consequence of a web of causation, so too does health undoubtedly reflect the operation of a number of factors that are social, psychological, environmental, and genetic. In the same way that the antecedents of disease are difficult to identify and quantify, the antecedents of health are likely to be elusive.

How then shall we proceed? If association alone provides traps in understanding causation, what tests shall we apply in our search for health? Reasonable tests are:

1. Relationships in time. Is there a consistent association between the availability or abundance of postulated causal factors and improvements in health as societies modernize? For example, did the introduction of antibiotics or other medical therapeutic agents occur sufficiently early in the course of the decline of infectious disease to have been influential therein? If so, the role of medical care in the decline of infectious disease mortality is strengthened; if not, some doubt is cast on the influence of antibiotics.

2. Consistency of the association. Does the association of health with the postulated causal factor exist consistently among populations? For example, is the association of education and health found among all populations at various levels of modernization?

3. Experimental evidence. In the modern period, many efforts have

* Clearly there are important genetic or inherited differences among individuals that influence their response to disease agents, whether microbiological, chemical, psychological, or physical. Throughout this book those differences will be ignored, since there is no evidence that healthy modern populations differ genetically from premodern populations where mortality rates are high. That is, while genetic differences may explain some portion of the variability in disease among individuals, they probably do not play an important role in understanding how modern populations differ in their health experiences from premodern populations.

been made to introduce specific changes into populations with high mortality rates; do mortality rates fall as a result? We shall examine the effects of the controlled introduction of nutritional supplements and/or medical care or sanitary water supplies. Such efforts provide a useful backdrop against which to check observations made from historical data.

4. Animal studies. Does evidence from animal studies support the importance to health of a postulated factor, such as improved nutrition?

5. Plausibility. Does the relationship between a certain factor and health "make sense" biologically? Are the known facts consistent with other information? For example, it is not plausible to interpret the association of telephone use with life expectancy as evidence that the former "causes" the latter.

In this book, we first examine those factors that are commonly assumed to be important in explaining modern health and life expectancy. These include sanitation, nutrition, and medical care (see chapters 1 to 4). Then we examine several other factors that have not generally been considered as important as determinants of health. These are principally directed toward changes in behavior and "life skills" that characterize modern people. Chapter 5 opens with a discussion of the modern nuclear family which, because of its influence on life skills and behavior, I consider fundamental to an understanding of health in modern society. In chapter 6 we shall examine the difficult concept of stress, the mechanisms with which we cope with stress, and the consequences for health of the inability to cope with stress. From a consideration of the value of personal coping skills, we move on in chapter 7 to a consideration of social support systems and health. Here I will suggest that, contrary to the common wisdom, social support systems increase with modernization and provide some explanation for modern life expectancy. In chapter 8 we then examine social class differences in health. To what extent can the differences in health and morbidity noted among social classes also be explained by the same factors that explain differences in health noted among nations at different stages of modernization? Chapter 9 examines the consistent and powerful relationship between educational achievement and health. Nowhere is the direction of causation more difficult to unravel than here; do healthy people seek more education, or does education contribute to health? If so, then how? Chapter 10 presents conclusions on the causes of both the rise as well as the apparent recent decline in U.S. health experience and suggests some remedies.

1 The Rise of Modern Life Expectancy

> The decline in rates of certain diseases, correlated roughly with improving socioeconomic circumstances, is merely the most important happening in the history of the health of man, yet we have only the vaguest and most general notions about how it happened and by what mechanisms socioeconomic improvement and decreased rates of certain diseases run in parallel.
>
> —E. H. Kass, 1971

GIVEN THAT life expectancy from birth has risen greatly for modern populations as a whole, have all segments of society benefited equally? In this chapter we shall examine some differences in health improvement that may provide us with some clues to this process of improving health. The questions we shall ask are:

1. When did the decline in mortality rates begin?

2. Have all age groups benefited equally from the decline in death rates, or have some age groups benefited more than others?

3. Have all social classes benefited to the same degree from the decline in mortality rates?

4. How have the two sexes differed, if at all, in the decline of modern death rates? If there are differences, what explains these differences?

FIGURE 1.1.

Probability of Survival, Order of the Golden Fleece

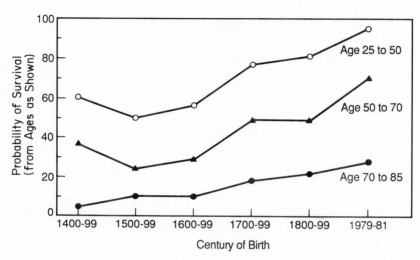

NOTE: Reprinted, by permission of the publisher, from J. Vandenbroucke, "Survival and Expectation of Life from the 1400's to the Present," *American Journal of Epidemiology* 122 (1985): 1012.

When Did the Decline in Mortality Rates Begin?

It is sometimes said, at least as an approximation, that in Shakespeare's time life expectancy from birth was thirty-five years. We do know that the first two children born to Shakespeare's parents died in childhood. William himself died at age fifty-three. His brother died at age forty-seven.

With a very few exceptions, reliable data on the life expectancy of populations does not exist prior to the middle of the nineteenth century—governments simply did not collect birth and death information with sufficient consistency to permit calculations of the average length of life. Data on the privileged and the nobility do exist, however. This historical record allows us to examine the early history of the rise of modern life expectancy. What those data show is that the increase in life-span—that is, the decline in death rates—began well before the rise of the sanitary movement of the nineteenth century. For example, a study of the survival of members of the Order of the Golden Fleece, a very exclusive knighthood consisting of the ruling members of the empires and kingdoms of Europe, began to increase in the sixteenth century (see figure 1.1). Later

TABLE 1.1

Average Life Expectancy at Birth for
Six European Countries and
One State in the United States,
1840–1965 (Both Sexes)

Year	Life Expectancy	Decennial Increase Between Two Successive Dates
1840	41.0	
1850	41.5	0.5
1860	42.5	0.7
1870	43.5	1.3
1880	45.2	1.7
1890	47.1	2.0
1900	50.5	3.4
1910	54.3	3.8
1920	58.3	4.0
1930	61.7	3.4
1940	64.6	2.9
1950	69.8	5.2
1960	72.0	2.2
1965	72.3	0.3

SOURCE: United Nations, "The Determinants and Consequences of Population Trends," *Population Studies* 50 (1973): 111.

in this chapter I shall return to the issue of whether the lower social classes shared in this increase in health.

In the middle of the nineteenth century, data for national populations first became available. These permit comparisons of mortality experience as well as some examination of the rate of rise of life expectancy. For example, during the period 1840 to 1900, life expectancy from birth was increasing from about forty years to fifty years (see table 1.1). This information is derived from six European nations for which data is available, as well as from the state of Massachusetts.* The increase in life expectancy began slowly, rising by only half a year between 1840 and 1850, and then more rapidly until the rate of increase reached a peak in 1920, only to begin a long period of slow growth beginning with the Depression years. An increase reappeared following World War II and now shows signs of reaching a plateau, particularly in the United States.

For reasons not entirely understood, modernization appeared at different times in different countries, first in Scandinavia, England, and North America. Most of the world today remains premodern. Illustrative

*The only U.S. state for which there is an adequate historical record.

of this is the fact that more than half of the world's population still exists today with a per-capita annual income of less than $120; fewer than a billion persons, or less than a fifth of the world's population, have an annual income of greater than $2,000.

What is the meaning of this remarkable phenomenon, "merely the most important happening in the history of the health of man"? Clearly this rapid and dramatic change in the probability of survival to the latter part of the biological human life-span presents an opportunity for us to study those factors that contribute to good health.

Which Age Groups Have Benefited Most from Modernization?

More than any other age group, the health of the infant is sensitive to its social and physical environment. For that reason, infant mortality rates often serve as the most sensitive index of socioeconomic conditions. In the United States, for example, infant mortality rates have fallen from just less than 200 per thousand live births in 1900 to 10.9 per thousand in 1983 (Metropolitan Life 1984), a fall of almost 2000 percent. Many premodern countries of the world today still have infant mortality rates that exceed those of the United States some eighty years ago.

This extreme sensitivity of the very young to modernization is reflected in figure 1.2, which graphically shows a rapid rise in expectation of life at birth in 1900, with only small absolute changes in life expectancy for those at older age groups.

Differences in death rates among premodern and modern nations may be even greater among older children than among infants. The reason is that while children's death rates fall to very low levels after their first year of life in the modern community, they remain high throughout the childhood years in premodern societies. For example, in one Mexican village studied in the early 1980s, infant mortality rates of 124/1,000 were six times higher than those in the United States, while death rates among children aged two through five (126 per thousand) were more than one hundred times higher than those in the United States (1 per thousand) (Millard 1985).

Further improvements in infant mortality rates are increasingly dif-

FIGURE 1.2.

Expectation of Life at Selected Ages, United States, 1900–1984

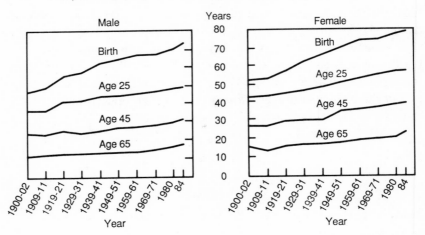

NOTE: Reprinted, by permission of the publishers, from Metropolitan Life Insurance Company, "Gains in U.S. Life Expectancy," *Statistical Bulletin* Jul./Sept. (1984): 20.

ficult to achieve as rates approach ten per thousand live births (in the United States they were 10.9 in 1983). As childhood death rates begin to plateau, so too will life expectancy, and that is now happening as the number of childhood deaths approaches the unavoidable minimum due to accident, congenital malformations, and so on. For example, the slight increases in life expectancy from birth that have occurred in the last few years do not compare in magnitude with those of the first half of the century.

While older people have not benefited from modernization to the same spectacular degree as have infants and children, they nevertheless have benefited. Measured as a percentage of life expectancy rates in 1900, those at older ages have benefited to almost the same extent as the very young. For example, while life expectancy has increased from 49.2 in 1900 to 74.7 in 1984—or 51 percent—the life expectancy for those who are eighty-five years old has increased from 4.0 years to 6.3 years, or 57 percent (see table 1.2).

Furthermore, the relative gains for the elderly are now increasing, whereas those for children are reaching a plateau. During the last thirty years, life expectancy for the thirty-five-year-old male increased by an average of 0.1 years annually, whereas during the first fifty years of the century, this age group improved their life expectancy by only 0.08 years

18

TABLE 1.2
Life Expectancy, United States, 1900–02 to 1984

Sex and Age	1900–02	1949–51	1969–71	1982	1983	1984
		Expectation of Life (in Years)				
Both Sexes: 0	49.2	68.1	70.7	74.6	74.7	74.7
25	39.1	46.6	48.4	51.3	51.3	51.4
45	24.8	28.5	30.1	32.7	32.7	32.7
65	11.9	13.8	15.0	16.8	16.8	16.9
85	4.0	4.7	5.3	6.3	6.1	6.3
Male: 0	47.9	65.5	67.0	70.9	71.0	71.1
25	38.4	44.4	45.1	47.9	48.0	48.1
45	24.1	26.6	27.2	29.6	29.7	29.8
65	11.5	12.7	13.0	14.5	14.5	14.5
85	3.8	4.4	4.7	5.3	5.1	5.3
Female: 0	50.7	71.0	74.6	78.2	78.3	78.3
25	39.9	49.0	51.8	54.6	54.6	54.6
45	25.4	30.6	33.1	35.6	35.5	35.5
65	12.2	15.0	16.8	18.8	18.8	18.8
85	4.1	4.9	5.6	6.8	6.6	6.9

NOTE: Reprinted, by permission of the publisher, from Metropolitan Life Insurance Company, "Slight Gains in U.S. Longevity," *Statistical Bulletin* Jul./Sept. (1985): 21.

annually (Metropolitan Life 1984). To a large extent, this experience has been the result of a decline in cardiovascular disease among middle-aged males.

Which Social Class Has Benefited Most from Modernization?

The influence of social class on mortality rates within countries is so pervasive that an entire chapter (chapter 8) is devoted to an examination of factors that may explain this phenomenon. Although health data segregated by social class do not exist in abundance prior to the twentieth century, the best evidence is that differences in health did not exist among social classes prior to the late phases of modernization (Antonovsky 1967). Illustrative of this evidence are studies of mortality rates among the ruling families of Europe beginning in the sixteenth century. These studies,

19

including those of the members of the Order of the Golden Fleece cited earlier, show clearly that even among those who could command unlimited housing and food, mortality rates existed that would be considered unacceptable today (Peller 1965). Among members of the British aristocracy, life expectancy during the seventeenth and eighteenth centuries varied between 30.0 and 38.8 years for males and 33.7 and 38.3 years for females. Only at the end of the eighteenth century does this group begin to achieve a life expectancy greater than that of the rest of the population (Hollingsworth 1977).

Which Sex Has Benefited More from Modernization?

Although it is sometimes said that it is a man's world, the advantage with respect to death rates is clearly with the female. Increased male death rates and greater female life expectancy are found among essentially all species, including insects, birds, reptiles, as well as mammals (Hamilton 1948). At almost every stage of life, males have a greater risk of death than do females. On the very first day of life, approximately 125 boys will die for every 100 girls. Fifty percent more sudden infant deaths ("crib deaths") occur among boys than among girls (Arneil et al. 1985). Both childhood incidence and mortality from a great variety of infectious diseases as well as from accident are greater among males (Washburn, Medearais, and Childs 1965). This female advantage in survival continues at every age throughout life (Metropolitan Life 1985). As a result, life expectancy for women considerably exceeds that for men. For example, for the year 1983, life expectancy from birth for U.S. males was 70.9, whereas for women it was 78.3 years (Metropolitan Life 1984).

One might reasonably conclude from the consistency of these observations that some basic biological phenomena are operating to produce these differences in survival. There is some sound evidence of this. For example, the immune system of the female is more efficient than that of the male. This phenomenon has been demonstrated in both animal and human populations. Why is this? There has been some speculation that the immune mechanism may be partly controlled by genes on the X chromosome, of which females have twice as many as males. Other speculation is that the effect is controlled by hormonal mechanisms; estrogens seem to potentiate the immune mechanism (Cyeyinka 1984). Many other physiological/biochemical differences between the sexes may underlie the difference in mortality rates. Gastrointestinal absorption, enzymatic activation, and tissue distribution of administered drugs differ in the two sexes (Calabrese 1985). Men are approximately 2.5 times more likely to develop lung cancer as a result of smoking cigarettes than are women (Haenzel and Tauber 1964). In sum, women are more resistant to toxic exposures than are men.

Whereas lower female death rates may indeed reflect fundamental biological superiority, there are also reasons to conclude that psychosocial and other environmental factors may play an important role in altering the relative mortality rates of the sexes (Verbrugge 1985). These factors may operate even within the womb of the pregnant woman; there is an inverse relationship between social class and fetal mortality rates (Chase 1967). Women of the American middle and upper classes have an 8 to 9 percent greater chance of having a male child than do working-class women (Teitelbaum and Mantel 1971). There is also evidence from historical studies of a strong environmental factor operating on the ratio of male-female death rates—the female advantage appears to be widening. In 1900 the ratio of male deaths to female deaths was 1.1, and there was little difference in death rates between the sexes at all ages (see figure 1.3). Today the ratio is 1.8.* This experience is not peculiar to the United States; it is the same in several other western countries (Wingard 1984). As shown in the figure, the female advantage is not constant at all ages. The major advantage falls to young women in the fifteen-to-twenty-four-year age group. Since accidental deaths predominate at this age, the sex differential is very likely to be strongly influenced by the greater frequency of accidental deaths among males than females. However, other causes are also undoubtedly operating; for example, declining maternal death rates and the known sex differential in cigarette smoking that formerly prevailed also influence these data (Wingard 1984).

The important scientific issue here is not whether females have greater biological vigor than males; we have already noted that such a biological superiority is consistently found throughout the animal world. The more intriguing issue is why that advantage was not expressed in human populations until very recently. Although high maternal mortality rates contribute to high female death rates, maternal mortality is only a small part of the explanation of the relatively high female death rates seen in premodern society—death rates even among prepubertal girls

---

* The mortality ratio between males and females is the age-adjusted ratio of male deaths per 100,000 males to that of female deaths per 100,000. In 1980, the ratio was 733/433, or 1.79.

FIGURE 1.3.
Sex Mortality Ratio (M/F), United States, 1900–1980

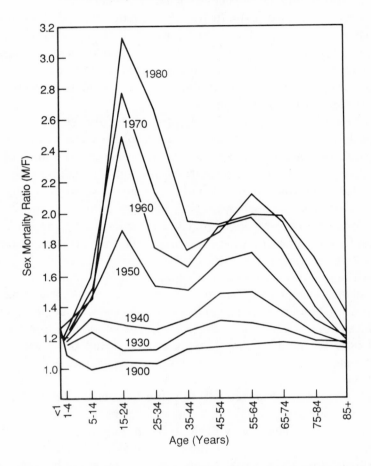

are high relative to boys. Indeed, in primitive populations the excess of female deaths above those of males is dramatic. In some 600 tribes, the ratio of boys to girls was consistently more than 150 to 100 (Divale 1972). We must search further for explanations. One intriguing explanation is the influence of sexism that is so prevalent in premodern societies. That influence first manifests itself at birth, where the preference for male offspring often results in either overt infanticide or, more commonly, covert infanticide through neglect (Poffenburger 1981). In Southeast Asia, where the male child is considered far more valuable, the female childhood death rate is 59 percent higher than among male

22

children. Studies show that the male child is given priorities in food and medical care and that the female is the object of benign neglect. While the incidence of illness among children of both sexes is the same, recovery from illness is far greater among males, whose illnesses are tended to (Koenig and D'Souza 1986). It is almost universal in premodern societies that boys, who are viewed as having higher productive value and are the ones who can inherit and transmit property, are almost always preferred over girls. As a consequence, discrimination against women from infancy onward, often ruthless and extreme, exists throughout the premodern world. Men almost universally receive the lion's share of the available food; women are usually served last and receive the least desirable portions. Education is commonly denied to women. Under conditions of deprivation, such treatment cannot help but influence morbidity and mortality rates. For example, among young women of northern Italy at the beginning of this century, deaths from pellagra, a disease associated with malnutrition, were two to three times more frequent than among young men (Livi-Bacci 1986).

In societies where women are held in contempt, they are also more frequently the victims of physical abuse. Historian Edward Shorter finds support for the prevalence of such treatment in such folk sayings as, "If the cow kicks off, mighty cross. If the wife kicks off, no big loss." "Got a dead wife? No big deal. Got a dead horse? How you squeal" (Shorter 1982).

A Psychosocial View of Modernization

Many people think of modernization as predominantly the result of changes in the means of production. In this view, improvements in health are seen largely as flowing from the increased availability of goods and services. Yet the social and psychological changes associated with modernization are even more profound than are changes in the productive process. Above all, the consistent feature of premodern societies, one that explains much of their high mortality rates, is grinding poverty together with the inevitable ignorance, superstition, apathy, and fatalistic attitude toward disease, disaster, and death. Poverty ensures not only a daily struggle for survival—which is bad enough—but a continual dread of catastrophe, whether it be a personal family tragedy or a natural disaster.

> When the peasant speaks of *la miseria*, he refers first to his hard physical labor, to his patched rags, and to the bread that is often all that he has to eat. Cruel as it is, however, his poverty does not account entirely for his chronic melancholy. . . . In part, the peasant's melancholy is caused by worry. Having no savings, he must always dread what is likely to happen. What for others are misfortunes are for him calamities. When their hog strangled on its tether, a laborer and his wife were desolate. The woman tore her hair and beat her head against the wall while the husband sat mute and stricken in a corner. The loss of the hog meant that they would have no meat that winter, no grease to spread on bread, nothing to sell for cash to pay taxes, and no possibility to acquire a pig the next spring. Such blows may fall at any time. Fields may be washed away in a flood. Hail may beat down the wheat. Illness may strike. To be a peasant is to stand helpless before these possibilities. [Banfield 1958, pp. 62–63]

How do people cope with such cruelty and deprivation? Almost universally, the social adjustment to poverty and helplessness has been the adoption of a fatalistic, authoritarian world view: "These events are out of our hands, they are in the hands of God." Children are taught that bad outcomes are the result of forces beyond their control, that life must be lived in the present, since, in an incalculable world, individual effort counts for naught. Such a belief system is not irrational in a culture of scarcity; on the contrary, in a society where there are inadequate resources with which to defend against stressors, a very useful psychological defense is to view circumstances as uncontrollable and oneself as without responsibility.

This pervading sense of helplessness dominated the human condition throughout history—until the Enlightenment. The Enlightenment encouraged the attitude that all natural phenomena operate in conformance with universal physical-chemical principles and are predictable, not the result of whimsical divine forces. If men could understand those principles, they could control their environment and their destiny. These were heady and revolutionary thoughts, unique in human history.

If the Enlightenment invoked a new view of the operation of the universe, it also invoked a new view of the proper relationships among people, best expressed on the banners of the French Revolution—Liberty, Equality, and Fraternity—and in the Declaration of Independence— "We hold these Truths to be self-evident, that all Men are created equal, that they are endowed by their Creator with certain unalienable Rights, that among these are Life, Liberty, and the Pursuit of Happiness . . ."

24

Still another significant attribute of modern populations is their firm belief in the possibility of progress.

> These differences in the extent of man's control over his environment reflect differences in his fundamental attitudes toward, and expectations from, his environment. The contrast between modern man and traditional man is the source of the contrast between modern society and traditional society. Traditional man is passive and acquiescent: he expects continuity in nature and society and does not believe in the capacity of man to change or control either. Modern man, in contrast, believes in both the possibility and the desirability of change, and has confidence in the ability of man to control change so as to accomplish his purposes. [Huntington 1976, pp. 28–29]

Finally, modernization implies certain characteristics in the personality structure of modern people. Sociologist Alex Inkeles has conducted lengthy interviews with more than six thousand men in Argentina, Chile, India, Israel, Nigeria, and Pakistan. The interviews were conducted by native interviewers, usually social workers or college students whose social origins were similar to those they were interviewing. On the basis of these interviews, Inkeles concluded that the characteristics of modern people everywhere are essentially the same no matter where they live:

> The modern man's character may be summed up under four major headings. He is an informed participant citizen; he has a marked sense of personal efficacy; he is highly independent and autonomous in his relations to traditional sources of influence, especially when he is making basic decisions about how to conduct his personal affairs; and he is ready for new experiences and ideas, that is, he is relatively open-minded and cognitively flexible. [Inkeles 1974, p. 290]

Inkeles sought the sources of these modern qualities; what environmental or social factors seemed to most strongly enhance the growth of these modern qualities? He concluded that

> In all six diverse countries, education emerged as unmistakably the most powerful force in shaping the modernity score. Indeed, judged by the number of points gained on the modernity scale for each year of schooling, education was generally two or three times as powerful as any other input. In this, our conclusions are not new but rather confirm findings in several other studies of modernity. [Inkeles 1974, p. 304]

As we shall see in chapter 9, not only does education enhance modernity, it is also powerfully influences health.

Another quality of modern people that Inkeles identified was their

25

sense of trust. The traditional person existing in an environment of scarcity is legitimately distrustful of others, particularly strangers, bureaucrats, or anyone not a member of his or her kinship group. In such an environment parenting behavior, often detached and authoritarian, reinforces this sense of distrust. Modernization is associated with an increase in trust—necessarily so since we have become so interdependent. A complex technical society cannot exist unless there is trust—trust of the other driver, of the many implicit contracts each of us makes with manufacturers and vendors, with government both nationally and locally. I emphasize the growth of trust because, as I shall show in chapter 7, strong social networks contribute in an important way to our improved modern health.

However, there is reason to believe that the level of trust among Americans has recently begun to decline. Commitments to others are in general deteriorating while the level of contentiousness and distrust appears to be on the rise (Lipset 1983). Witness, for example, the increase in divorce rates; the increasing use of marital contracts; the law suits brought against manufacturers, governments, physicians, and other professionals. I take all of these to be evidence of decreased trust. To the extent that trust in others contributes to the growth of modern health, then, to some extent this decline in trust explains the failure of American health to progress.

Summary

Modernization has been associated with a steep decline in mortality. That decline began slowly in the eighteenth and nineteenth centuries, first in Sweden, the United Kingdom, and North America, and then more rapidly in other more recently modernizing countries. The decline in death rates was particularly marked during the early part of the twentieth century, most notably among the youngest age group from birth through early childhood. Females have benefited more than males. As will be shown in more detail in chapter 8, those in higher social classes were the first to benefit, and that advantage has persisted to this day.

What do these observations tell us with respect to the factors that contribute to human life expectancy? Which of the many changes associated with modernization are producing these remarkable advances? Is it true, as noted in the epigraph, that "we have only the vaguest and most general notions" of the factors contributing to these observations, or does our prevailing disease model prevent us from recognizing some important insights into human health that this history reveals? This question is one that we shall explore in subsequent chapters.

2 The Decline of Infectious Disease: Better Environment or Better Animals?

AS NOTED in the last chapter, modern improvements in mortality rates have been most remarkable among infants, children, and young adults, among whom the commonest diseases are infectious. For example, during the past 120 years, deaths from infectious disease in the United Kingdom fell from 13,000 to 714 per million per year, one-twentieth of the former rate. As a percentage of all deaths, those due to infectious diseases fell from more than half to about 13 percent (McKeown 1976).

The same has been true in the United States; from 1900 to 1935, tuberculosis death rates fell by 77 percent, deaths from communicable diseases among children fell by 82 percent, and those from influenza and pneumonia fell by 53 percent (Winslow 1980).

Among the most common of the infectious diseases of the nineteenth and early twentieth centuries was tuberculosis, known at the time as the "white plague." In some communities as many as 25 percent of deaths were attributed to this disease, as dreaded then as is cancer now. Indeed, tuberculosis took a considerably greater toll in human misery than does cancer in the twentieth century. The median age at death from tuber-

FIGURE 2.1.

Mortality from Pulmonary Tuberculosis, 1857–1926, in Massachusetts

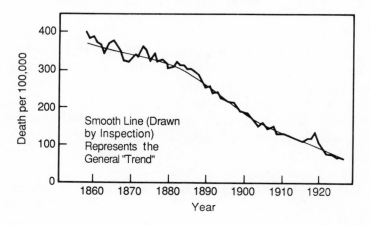

NOTE: Reprinted, by permission of the publisher, from E. Sydenstricker, "The Declining Death Rate from Tuberculosis," in *The Challenge of Facts: Selected Public Health Papers of Edgar Sydenstricker*, ed. R. Kasius, p. 358. New York: Prodist, 1974, copyright Milbank Memorial Fund.

culosis was midlife, unlike cancer, which occurs most frequently among the elderly. As shown in figure 2.1, the decline in the mortality rate from this disease began in the mid-nineteenth century and has been persistent to the present time. Among the general population, it is now an infrequent cause of death.

The causes of tuberculosis were entirely unknown in the early nineteenth century, but there was considerable speculation about a predisposing personality pattern; the disease was considered to be more common among those with romantic qualities. When Robert Koch first demonstrated the existence of the tubercle bacillus in the tissues of persons dying with the disease, debate about the role of personal and psychological elements came to an end. It was concluded that personal qualities were unimportant; exposure to the organism was a sufficient "explanation" of the disease. Public health efforts were mounted to sanitize the environment. Campaigns were waged to prohibit spitting, widely thought to be the source of environmental contamination. Stop the spitting and the disease would disappear, or so it was thought. We now know that such thinking is naive.

Sanitary Conditions During Early Modernization

Because the decline in infectious diseases occurred in parallel with improvements in sanitation, it is widely concluded that the former is the result of the latter. There is strong support for such a conclusion. Sanitation in premodern rural communities is generally appalling; the squalor and filth, defecation in the streets, animals and families sharing the same living spaces, the absence of running water, garbage piled on the doorstep, swarms of flies noisily plying back and forth among the animals and the food are likely to be repulsive to modern travelers.

City life during the early period of industrialization was not much better. Consider a physician's observation of mid-nineteenth-century London:

> Upon this street refuse and garbage are continually being thrown. All the slops of this, and, I might almost say the majority of this district, are thrown upon the streets: these remain on the surface, and become thoroughly incorporated with the mud, forming a thick, semipultaceous black fetid mass. When the streets are cleaned, this matter is swept into the middle of the street, to remain in a heap until the cart shall come, into which it is to be thrown. As the streets are very imperfectly paved, a very considerable portion of this putrid refuse still remains on the surface, and in the hollows between the boulder-stones. The first shower of rain washes this mud up, and renders the streets as filthy as if they had not been swept for months. The odor of these streets is always most offensive and disgusting. [Gavin 1848, p. 50]

Identical conditions were found in all of the world's large cities of the time. In New York City, shoppers passed among carts of "putrid vegetables and week-old fish, and stepped around the heads of sheeps, and the hoofs of cattle, blood and offals strewn in the gutters. . . . Numerous stables, shambles, tanneries, and overflowing backyard privies gave off a noisome effluvia, and foul smelling miasmas" (Mohl 1971, p. 11).

Environmental filth generally has its counterpart in a lack of personal hygiene. In premodern Europe, bathing was rare even among the gentry. No undergarments were worn and clothes went unwashed. Bedsheets might be washed once a year. Samuel Pepys was a successful bureaucrat, a business associate of London nobles and courtiers of the 1660s.

> Yet, he regarded it as a matter of course that he should have lice in his hair, for which his maid regularly combed him, and he only expressed

surprise when one day his wife found no fewer than twenty of them. He hardly ever washed his body until February 1664 when his wife suddenly went to a bathhouse, temporarily discovered the pleasures of cleanliness and refused to allow him into her bed until he too had washed. After holding out for three days, he finally gave way to her whim and bathed in hot water. [Stone 1977, p. 304]

Such conditions are found universally in premodern society, whether it be in seventeenth-century European capitals or in the cities of the lesser developed countries of today.

The argument, then, that a better environment explains the fall in infectious disease deaths has a high degree of plausibility; however, there are also reasons for skepticism regarding this explanation and powerful evidence supporting the alternative explanation, namely that improvements in the environment are less important than improvements in human resistance to disease. These two possibilities are, of course, not mutually exclusive, and I shall argue that both have likely played a role in the extension of modern life expectancy.

I am skeptical about the role of environmental sanitation in bringing about the decline in infectious disease deaths because most of the decline in deaths over the past two hundred years has not been from those "named" infections such as typhoid and cholera, but rather have been the result of a decline in the diarrheas and pneumonias of infants and children. These are not the result of exposure to organisms brought into the household by contaminated water or food but are the result of infection with viruses that are omnipresent; these organisms are not susceptible to water or food purification. In addition, efforts to introduce sanitation, particularly piped water, into premodern communities have largely failed to produce improvements in health. Some examples of this will be cited here; others will be cited in chapter 4.

Before proceeding with those arguments, however, it is necessary to briefly review some of the elements of infection—how infection is transmitted and something of our biological defense against infection.

The Transmission of Infection

The appearance of infectious disease in a human being is the result of several interacting factors: exposure to an infectious agent that is sufficiently potent and in sufficient dosage to produce disease in a vulnerable person. Clearly, if no exposure occurs, no infection can result. Some microorganisms even in small quantities will produce disease in most people who are exposed. Other agents—those with low virulence—will rarely produce disease, even in vulnerable individuals. The commonly held belief is that infectious disease has declined because our exposure to disease-producing bacterial and viral agents has decreased.

While it is true that improvements in water and food sanitation have undoubtedly reduced exposure to certain disease agents primarily transmitted through these media, such efforts alone can explain only part of the decline in infection. One reason for skepticism regarding the primary importance of sanitary efforts is that diseases transmitted from person to person through droplets (that is, through coughing, sneezing, and so on)—diseases that are not affected by sanitation—declined as rapidly as did those that are transmitted through water and food. Droplet-spread diseases include such important infectious diseases as tuberculosis, measles, mumps, diphtheria, and chicken pox. These diseases are highly contagious—the great majority of people who are exposed to infected persons will become infected, but not necessarily ill. For example, a single patient with open pulmonary cavitary disease can and will infect the great majority of those with whom he or she comes into contact (Sachs et al., 1985). Even persons who use the same rooms but with whom there is no personal contact will become infected.*

These diseases are extremely difficult to control through public health efforts; isolation or quarantine is relatively ineffective because there are in the apparently healthy population carriers who will unknowingly continue to infect others. As early as 1893 Koch published a paper on the existence of cholera organisms in normal and apparently healthy persons. Shortly afterward, it was found that at least 1 percent of the healthy population of New York City harbored virulent diphtheria organisms in their throats. The existence of typhoid carriers was discovered soon after (Winslow 1980, p. 337).

Second, the decline in infectious disease deaths appears to have preceded, rather than followed, improvements in sanitation and to have occurred long before the decline in infection. That is, there is evidence that exposure to infectious organisms continued long after the decline in death rates from those organisms had declined. As sanitary conditions were worsening in cities, mortality rates were in decline. From the decade

* An important distinction must be made between "infection" and "disease." The former refers to the presence of organisms in the body but those organisms do not produce significant damage or symptoms. "Disease," on the other hand, refers to a pathological response accompanied by tissue destruction and often the development of symptoms. For example, people may be "healthy carriers" of the typhoid bacteria; they are "infected," but they are not "diseased."

TABLE 2.1

Rate of Persons Infected with Tuberculosis,
as Determined by Tuberculin Skin-testing,
United States, 1940

Age	Infected (%)	Deaths per 100,000 Infected Persons
0–1	0.5	4,920
1–9	18	71
10–19	40	40
20–29	60	89
30–39	80	71
40–4	90	69
45–9	95	66
50–4	95	73
55–9	95	79
60–4	95	81
65–9	95	82
70–4	95	89
75 and over	95	82

NOTE: Reprinted, by permission of the publisher, from W. Pagel, F. Simmonds, and N. Macdonald, *Pulmonary Tuberculosis: Pathology, Diagnosis, Management and Prevention*, p. 663. New York: Oxford University Press, 1953.

of 1841–50 to 1891–1900, London death rates declined by over 12 percent in the zero- to four-year-old group, by over 50 percent in the five- to twenty-four-year-old group, and by almost 38 percent in the thirty-five- to forty-four-year-old group (Wohl 1983). Again, the evidence from the history of tuberculosis is pertinent. Table 2.1 shows the prevalence of people with positive skin tests in 1940, by which time tuberculosis mortality had already fallen dramatically. Note that the great majority of people reaching adulthood had in fact been exposed, as evidenced by their immune status. The table also depicts the mortality rate among infected persons. From their extremely low rate of mortality, it is clear that it was the rare person who died from exposure and that personal factors must have been of primary importance in determining who lived and who died, not the presence or virulence of the organism. Although the organism's characteristics may determine the nature of the pathology, it is primarily the status of the patient's resistance that determines the disease extent and outcome. If the tissues of persons dying or dead with tuberculosis are found to be teeming with the tubercle bacillus, are such deaths "caused" by the bacillus, or is the bacillus simply taking advantage of a defenseless host to flourish? As we shall see later in this chapter, the role of the tubercle bacillus in the disease tuberculosis illustrates what commonly occurs with most infectious disease: the patient's resistance primarily determines whether he or she lives or dies.

The experience with tuberculosis is not unique—it is typical. The decline in death rates from measles in modern countries parallels the tuberculosis story: exposure to the organism did not decline; rather the fatality rate per case declined. The attack rates for measles between 1900 and 1930, the very period during which death rates from the disease were rapidly declining, were constant (Hedrich 1933). In other words, the frequency of measles was not declining; death from measles was declining as personal resistance to the disease was increasing. There is no plausible reason to think that the organism changed, as evidenced by the continued high death rates from measles among children in still-developing countries. Death rates among those with this disease are two hundred times greater in the developing countries than in the modernized countries (Latham 1975). In other words, the child with measles in a modernized country is almost certain to survive, whereas the child in an underdeveloped country has a significant risk—about 15 percent—of dying of the disease.

Why is it that our primary dependence on the immune system in the preservation of our health is not more generally recognized? To a large extent, it is due to our conviction that disease has its origins in the environment. We interpret the growth of a bacterial agent in the tissues of the ill person as the *explanation* of the disease. We ignore the role of personal factors. Illustrative of this was the epidemic of Legionellosis, or Legionnaire's disease, that occurred in 1976 during an American Legion convention in Philadelphia. Thirty-four deaths and considerable morbidity occurred; at the time they were considered to be the result of a mysterious pneumonia for which no identifying organism could be found. Much later, the elusive organism that produces the disease, Legionella Pneumophila, was finally cultured and identified. Many considered the mystery solved. But was it? Since then the organism has been found to be widespread and can be cultured from almost any pool of stagnant water; it must have been in the air-conditioning system of the Philadelphia hotel that had been the convention headquarters. Now that we can culture the organism and recognize the disease, it turns out to be a fairly common form of pneumonia. Could the stress of travel and the excitement of the convention have contributed to the seriousness of the epidemic? None of the hotel employees developed the disease. Why then did an outbreak occur among the Legionnaires during the convention? It has subsequently been learned that 20 to 30 percent of the members of the general population have antibodies in their blood to the Legionnaire's organism.

Again, that which at first appeared to be a rare disease, largely explained by an unfortunate exposure to a rare organism, later comes to be recognized as a common, rather benign, organism that flourishes and becomes virulent only when exploiting a particularly vulnerable victim. In one study of sixty-five cases, sixty-one had significant preexisting disease; many were being treated with immune suppressive therapy. Only four were previously healthy (Kirby et al. 1980). Why the Legionnaires at the Philadelphia convention in 1976 were so terribly vulnerable is still not known. The most plausible explanation is that an elderly group of men under some stress were subjected to a massive exposure of the organism growing in a heavily contaminated air-conditioning system.

Although we take some comfort in assuring ourselves that the infectious diseases have been conquered or vanquished, such a conclusion is largely illusory. What have largely disappeared are the epidemic or "named" diseases such as typhoid fever and cholera. Although these epidemic diseases produced waves of mortality, they were responsible, over the long term, for only a small percentage of deaths. Frequently these epidemics occurred in the wake of war or other political upheaval, as did the flu epidemic of 1918–19. The vast majority of infectious disease deaths throughout history as well as in the underdeveloped world today are not from these epidemic diseases, but rather are the consequence of opportunistic infections with agents, principally viruses, that are ubiquitous. As evidence of the predominant role of personal immunity in the defense against infection, consider the relative immunity of those millions of Americans who have, as soldiers, missionaries, or tourists, visited or lived unharmed in geographical regions where very high infectious disease rates prevail. This is only to a very small extent the consequence of immunization, which is not available for those large groups of diseases, the pneumonias and diarrheas, which are the major infectious diseases of both premodern and modern populations.

How Important, Then, Is Clean Water?

The importance of clean water to health has been recognized for literally thousands of years. Hippocrates drew attention to the need to boil water. Proof of the importance of clean water, however, did not occur until late in history. Early in this century, experiments in a number of cities demonstrated that filtering and then, later, chlorination of water were significantly associated with a reduction in the incidence of certain diseases, notably typhoid fever (Safe Drinking Water Committee 1977). For such reasons, the provision of access to clean water is widely considered to be a major factor in explaining mortality decline. Yet the matter is far from proven. For example, when clean water is introduced into a highly contaminated environment where filth, illiteracy, and infectious diseases are highly prevalent, the anticipated improvement in mortality rates is frequently disappointing. Diarrheal diseases, those transmitted through the fecal-oral route, can and are transmitted as often through food contamination or from water contaminated after it arrives in the home. In such impoverished communities, it is common to have farm animals in or near the home, there is no sanitary means for disposing of feces, there are no insect barriers, and often night soil is used for fertilizer; it will be almost impossible to prevent food from being contaminated with fecal material either from fingers or flies. To reduce the level of contamination in the home requires not only a clean water source, but also the use of soap and water, clean hands, personal hygiene, safe disposal of feces, and, finally, the conviction that these measures are important, are useful, and will make a difference (Schneider, Shiffman, and Faigenblum 1978). Critical to such behavior is education, without which a clean water supply is generally useless.

Because of the high prevalence of cholera in Bangladesh, thousands of community wells have been drilled in order to provide an uncontaminated source of drinking and cooking water. Comparisons show that the use of these wells has had little effect on the prevalence of the disease (Schneider 1976; Levine 1976). Infection is undoubtedly spread through other routes. Studies in Africa reveal the same result—there is no relationship between the cleanliness of the water supply and mortality rates from infectious disease (Feachem et al. 1978).

One factor that does consistently produce a fall in cholera rates is unrelated to the physical environment, but rather reflects personal behavior, namely education (Levine et al. 1976). In a study that attempted to quantify the relative importance of clean water and characteristics of the individuals consuming that water, the investigator found that piped water did play some role in the decline of infant mortality rates in Brazil, but the water source was only about one-fifth as important as the increased prevalence of parental education in explaining the significant change in the infant mortality from 1970 to 1976 (Merrick 1985).

These observations should not be interpreted as suggesting that clean water is of no importance. Rather, I would like to emphasize that environmental sanitation alone is insufficient to explain decreased infectious disease death rates.

Waterborne illnesses in the United States are not rare; our sanitary system is hardly perfect. Between 1971 and 1978 there were 224 outbreaks of waterborne disease, which were responsible for almost 50,000 individual cases of illness (Safe Drinking Water Committee 1982). Generally these result from cross-connections between the water and sewer systems or are the consequence of a failure of the chlorination system. These illnesses rarely lead to death.

The degree of contamination of the environment almost certainly has been reduced, and since the risk of infection is related to the number of organisms (or "dose"), the risk of disease is also reduced. Yet, as noted earlier with the example of tuberculosis, the environment was until quite recently sufficiently contaminated to infect most vulnerable individuals. The evidence is that improvements in health preceded rather than followed improvements in environmental sanitation.

There are, then, sources of infection in the community beyond the control of the sanitary engineer. The importance of sanitation as a means of ridding the environment of pathologic organisms and thus "explaining" the decline of infectious diseases has been oversold. Again, I do not mean to imply that sanitation is of no importance, but only that its importance has been exaggerated.

If our environment continues to harbor potentially harmful agents, then how do we explain the decline of deaths from infectious disease?

Resistance to Infection

Because we cannot see microorganisms, we maintain the illusion that our clean modern world is sanitized. In fact, however, every shining surface, the air we breathe, the food we eat is crawling with an enormous variety of microorganisms, including bacteria, viruses, fungi, and, in some cases, parasites. Although the visual filth of the rural peasant village is repulsive to us, our own environment is nearly as contaminated as is theirs. Our bodies crawl with an enormous variety of organisms with which most of us live in perfect harmony unless our immune system, for any one of a variety of reasons, becomes compromised. Streptococci and staphylococci can be found on the skin of all healthy persons. Those with boils or acne are those whose skin is unable to resist these organisms. The older patient with cancer, particularly if being treated with immunosuppressive drugs, the alcoholic, the malnourished need not be exposed to pathogenic organisms in order to develop a flagrant pneumonia; whatever organisms that normally exist peacefully in his or her upper respiratory tree are available to become the "old man's friend," the fatal pneumonia.

What is truly remarkable is that we are able to remain healthy in such an environment. Why is that? It is because healthy people have extremely effective defense systems, including an immune system that, when functioning normally, is able to protect against infectious disease. The immune system is composed of both proteins (antibodies) and white blood cells. Antibodies are thought to coat bacteria or other foreign materials, preparing them for engulfment and disposal by the white cells. The fact that our immune systems also protect our bodies from developing cancer is now fairly well established (Herberman 1983). Just as bacteria can be recognized and destroyed by specific antibodies, so too can cancer cells.

Just a few decades ago, only a few types of white cells were recognized, based on the characteristics that could be recognized under the microscope. Today, with much more sophisticated techniques of differentiation, many new types of white cells have been recognized. There are T cells, B cells, and yet others known as "helper T cells," "killer cells," all of which were once known simply as lymphocytes.

Effective defense against infection requires more than the circulating cells and antibodies just described. While still a medical student, I carried out an experiment that provided me with an early insight into the natural resistance of healthy tissues. The experiment is still as illustrative as ever. Laboratory rats were injected with a common bacterial organism. Healthy animals survived without harm. Their immune systems were well able to destroy the injected organisms. In the follow-up experiment, similar animals were anesthetized, the abdomen was opened, and the ureter (the tube that carries urine from the kidney to the bladder) from one kidney was partially occluded, restricting urine outflow. The animal was allowed to recuperate and then was injected with the identical amount of bacteria. The obstructed kidney became infected, the animal suffering from a disease called pyelonephritis. The point of this little exercise is straightforward; while healthy tissues are resistant to infection, tissues that are damaged or otherwise compromised become vulnerable to infection.

In clinical practice, physicians frequently see analogous situations. For example, in patients in whom there is arterial disease, as in diabetics, blood supply to tissues becomes marginal and the affected tissues are notoriously susceptible to infection. Infection frequently follows surgical procedures. Why? The preexisting illness itself, the effects of the anaesthesia, the inevitable damage to tissues, the use of antibiotics and other medications that suppress the immune system, the prolonged inactivity, all leave the postoperative patient susceptible to infection. These infections are usually the result of the invasion of omnipresent common bacteria, which produce "opportunistic" infections that are often difficult to treat. Many conditions are known that impair immunity, including certain congenital diseases; treatment with certain drugs, including the adrenal steroids, chemotherapeutic agents, and immunosuppressants; premature birth; severe malnutrition; promiscuous male homosexuality (Goedert et al. 1985); and many chronic disease conditions, including cancer.

The Influence of Stress on the Immune System

In addition to the conditions just cited, there is now extensive evidence that psychological stress can also depress the immune system and lead to an increased frequency of many diseases. Clinicians have long recognized that emotional factors can influence the onset of disease (see chapter 6). Many perceptive laypeople also recognize that disease, particularly infections, is more likely when they are undergoing psychological stress.

We now have a much better understanding of just how psychological factors affect the immune system and thus influence disease. For example, in a number of retrospective studies of human populations with infectious diseases, patients have been queried regarding stressful conditions preceding the onset of illness. In many such studies a high frequency of stressful experiences have been found to apparently trigger the illness. Streptococcal infections are known to be associated with the development of rheumatic fever. This association has been interpreted as demonstrating a causative role of the streptococcus in rheumatic fever. Yet school surveys have repeatedly shown that the streptococcus can be found in the throats of many children who are asymptomatic and otherwise well. In one

39

survey, 29.8 percent of schoolchildren were found to be harboring the organism (Cornfeld and Hubbard 1961).

Why is it only the rare child that becomes seriously ill and perhaps permanently crippled? One factor is the level of stress within the family. Family stress was measured over a period of a year through both interviews and the use of a family diary. By any measure, whether it was simply the presence of the streptococcal organism in the throat, the number of streptococcal illnesses, or the antibody response to the organism, the children of families with a higher level of chronic stress had higher frequencies of streptococcal disease than did those with low levels of chronic stress (Hagerty 1980).

The evidence is that for tuberculosis and for certain viral illnesses stress is not only a precipitating factor, but also prolongs both the illness and convalescence (Jemmot and Locke 1984).

Animal studies have been conducted in which rodents are subjected to stressful experiences such as electric shock or swimming to the point of exhaustion. Such stressed animals, when exposed to pathogenic organisms, manifest a reduced resistance to disease (Ader 1979).

Last, there are direct studies of immune mechanisms among human populations undergoing stress. Examples are persons who are bereaved (Bartrop and Schleifer 1984), clinically depressed (Schleifer et al. 1985), and medical students during final examinations (Kiecolt-Glaser et al. 1984).

Could stress be an unrecognized factor in explaining the decreased resistance of premodern populations to infection and death? We greatly underestimate the stress associated with the poverty and uncertainty of premodern society—the reduced coping ability of the illiterate and hopeless, the acquiescence and fatalism that mark members of traditional societies. Is it not plausible to speculate that widespread disease was closely linked to stress, apathy, and hopelessness, to depression of the immune system, and to increased mortality rates? The functions of the immune system are by no means limited to protection against infection and cancer; many so-called chronic diseases are now thought to be mediated to some degree by the operation of the immune system. These include diabetes, certain diseases of the heart and nervous system, and particularly the autoimmune diseases, those disease entities that are thought to represent damage of an organ or organ system as a result of attack by the body's own immune system.

The Decline of Infectious Disease

Summary

Improvements in sanitation of food and water supply have undoubtedly produced benefits to health; yet these benefits are likely to have been small compared to the benefits associated with the increased resistance of the human population. Several lines of evidence support this judgment:

1. The decline in mortality rates began prior to the great sanitary movement of the nineteenth century.

2. It was not a decline in infection that caused the decline in mortality rates but rather a decline in death rates of those who were infected. High rates of infection persisted until very recent decades.

3. The majority of deaths among infants are not due to microbiological agents transmitted through the food and water supply but rather are from microbiological agents commonly present in the environment; the deaths are the result of infection with viruses and other ubiquitous organisms, which will inevitably result among infants with lowered resistance.

4. The decline in mortality from infectious diseases has been as dramatic among those diseases that are spread from person to person, such as tuberculosis, where sanitation efforts are ineffective, as among those that are spread through the food and water supply or through insect vectors.

5. Finally, there is another explanation for the decline in deaths from infectious diseases, namely, an improvement in human resistance. In subsequent chapters we shall further examine the possibility that psychosocial factors played a critical role in strengthening immunity and reducing death rates.

3   The Role of Nutrition in the Rise of Modern Life Expectancy

> Currently fashionable is the view that nutritional improvements account for the decline in mortality from common infections and that nutritional inadequacy is a major factor in explaining the present predilection of the poor for certain communicable disorders. In fact, there is little evidence to support this view.
>
> —E. H. Kass, 1971

MANY PEOPLE BELIEVE that improvements in the availability, purity, and variety of the food supply have been a powerful determinant of our prolonged life expectancy. They assume that through improvements in the quantity and quality of the food supply, famines as well as lesser degrees of malnutrition that predispose to infection have been overcome, resulting in a major reduction in mortality rates.

In this chapter I challenge that view and argue that while the relationship between food supply and health is complex and not fully understood, food supplies per se have probably had a small effect on health in comparison with changes in our use of food—that is, our food *behavior*.

This should not be taken to mean that malnutrition did not occur in premodern populations. It means rather that under premodern conditions, malnutrition will prevail, not only because of scarcity but primarily because low priorities are attached to health, nutrition, and survival. As we shall see, this is particularly true of infant and toddler nutrition under the common condition of high fertility and high mortality—the norm in premodern society. Likewise, we shall see that under modern conditions, where high values are placed on health and survival, malnutrition occurs only under the most desperate of circumstances.

The British physician Thomas McKeown has argued that in the absence of other convincing explanations, improved nutrition must therefore be the condition principally responsible for our greater life expectancy. Yet there is no convincing evidence with which to prove the point. We do know that great excesses (leading to obesity) are harmful, just as is gross undernutrition or starvation; between these extremes, the evidence suggests that humans can tolerate a great variety of diets without harm or benefit. Clearly the decline in famines and the reduction in starvation was beneficial, but it was achieved relatively early in modernization. The United States has not experienced famine throughout its history. Highly monotonous diets limited in variety can produce vitamin or mineral deficiencies that in turn can lead to serious symptoms and even death. The conditions necessary to reproduce such deficiencies, however, are produced only with difficulty, even in the laboratory. This is because of the wide distribution of necessary vitamins and minerals in a variety of foodstuffs. Such deficiencies occur rarely in modern populations. When, for example, scurvy is found, it is generally in elderly people with highly eccentric diets (Reuler, Broudy, and Cooney 1985). Rickets are occasionally seen in patients in large city hospitals, these days not as a result of poverty but among cultists following exotic vegetarian diets.

More contentious than the effects of gross starvation on health are the effects of so-called hidden hunger.* By "hidden hunger" is meant malnutrition that is not detectable through clinical examination and does not lead directly to death, but that may contribute as a secondary cause of death, primarily by predisposing to infection. The definition of hidden hunger is vague and evidence for its significance to health is highly speculative.

In contrast with hidden hunger, there is stronger evidence regarding the health significance of obesity. As will be discussed, beneficial changes in the diet have not paralleled the decline in death rates; indeed, it appears that improvements in health during this century have occurred in spite of, rather than as a result of, changes in the American diet.

---

* The words hunger and malnutrition are often used interchangeably and without precision. By "hunger" I mean a subjective desire for food, a desire that may be quite unrelated to nutritional need. By "malnutrition" I mean a deficit in either the quantity or quality of food that has demonstrable clinical significance to the health of the individual. There is no necessary relationship between the two.

Hidden Hunger in Modernizing Societies

The "hidden hunger" theory holds that high levels of mortality during early and middle periods of modernization can be explained by marginal nutritional conditions that were sufficient to prevent overt malnutrition and starvation but nevertheless left people vulnerable to infectious disease and death. Advocates of this theory offer two kinds of evidence: one is the association between grain prices and mortality rates in premodern societies, and the other is the observation of high mortality rates from infectious disease among impoverished and undernourished populations in the modern world, with the implication that these "must" be the result of malnutrition.

The first of these arguments is based on studies of historical data from a number of European countries, including France and Scandinavia. These data demonstrate a strong relationship among crop yield, grain prices, and mortality. For example, wheat prices and death rates both tripled and even quadrupled in parts of France in 1693–94 (Meuret 1965). In eighteenth-century Denmark and Finland, death rates are three to four per thousand lower after years with good agricultural conditions (Gille 1949). These relationships weaken in the nineteenth century. The weaknesses in this argument lie in the use of correlations as evidence of causation and in the assumption that grain prices are an adequate indication of food consumption. Changes in mortality rates accompanying economic cycles can still be detected in the United States today (Brenner 1984). No one suggests that hidden hunger explains this association; rather, a common interpretation is that the effect is due to economic and psychosocial stress (Brenner 1984). Stress may also explain, at least in part, the historical association of grain prices and mortality rates.

The second argument is based on the observation of high death rates and poor growth rates among grossly impoverished and grossly undernourished populations, such as those of Southeast Asia and Africa. Yet when measures of nutrition, including caloric intake, percent of calories of animal origin, and per-capita intake of protein are studied in developing countries and compared with mortality rates, no significant relationships are found (Pendleton and Yang 1985). In addition to such correlational studies, there are also observations of direct intervention where supplemental food has been provided to pregnant women and young children living in conditions of great deprivation. While a decline in infant and child mortality rates can sometimes be demonstrated, the magnitude of that decline is small. Attempts to demonstrate such benefits in populations where mortality rates are more moderate usually have failed.

Nor is it at all clear that the undernourished child is more vulnerable to death from infection during outbreaks of disease than the well-nourished child. As mentioned earlier (chapter 2), the risk of death among children with infectious diseases is many times greater among those living in the less modernized countries. Yet nutrition does not appear to be an important cause of these differences. Several studies show that in epidemics, the well-nourished child is as likely to die of the disease as is the poorly nourished child (Aaby et al. 1984). The last major worldwide epidemic, the influenza pandemic of 1918–19, was by no means limited to undernourished populations. In the United States, deaths were more frequent among young adults, presumably the most robust sector of the population (Britten 1932). The poor were not more vulnerable than the rich. The contribution of undernutrition to infectious disease deaths, then, is not nearly so demonstrable as is widely thought.

The Counterargument

A number of counterarguments to the hidden hunger theory exist. These include:

1. The highest death rates in premodern societies are among infants and toddlers whose survival is less dependent on available food supplies than on the culturally determined practices of breast feeding and weaning. Mother's milk, unless the mother is grossly malnourished or attempting to nurse several children simultaneously, will be adequate for the survival of the great majority of children, whereas in the absence of wholesome and sanitary food, early weaning can be disastrous. Millions of babies have died from inadequate nutrition where an adequate food supply was no farther than the mother's breast.

2. Not all premodern societies experience nutritional deprivation. Death rates are as high among those populations where food is abundant, as in those that are deprived.

3. Among modern societies deprived of adequate nutrition, as during

wartime, death rates remain low and may actually decline unless food supplies are severely depressed.

4. In animal studies where nutritional and other conditions can be controlled, severe dietary limitation interfering with normal growth increases life-span and reduces death rates.

Let us now examine these arguments.

Infant Mortality and Infant Nutrition

Since our extended life expectancy in modern society is largely the result of a decline in childhood mortality, we must focus our study of the influence of nutrition on mortality on these early years of life.

Mother's milk is pure, and in the absence of severe inadequacies in her health, a woman's milk supply will be adequate to feed her child. Nature gives priority to the nutrition of the young, even at the expense of the mother's health. If children are maintained on breast milk, they have an excellent chance of surviving their first year. Why, then, are there such high infant mortality rates in premodern communities? The paramount reason is that pressures arise, whether from economic necessity in working classes or from the dictates of fashion in the upper classes, to wean* the infant early in infancy.

There are two alternatives to mother's milk, and mothers have resorted to both throughout at least the past few thousand years. These two are "hand nursing," or the use of animal milk or other food as a substitute for mother's milk; and "wet nursing," or the substitution of the milk of a woman other than that of the mother. Throughout history artificial nipples and other devices have been fashioned with which to introduce the milk into the infant's mouth. Such devices have been found in the tombs of ancient Greek and Roman children (Wickes 1953).

As the mother begins to wean the child, she introduces into the diet a variety of foods, principally those that are available and culturally approved for the purpose. These "paps" generally consist of gruel, or bean

* The word wean may be used to refer to the time at which the child is finally removed from the breast permanently or the time at which foods other than maternal milk are offered.

juice, or vegetables or meat that have first been masticated by the mother or nurse.

Yet historically milk substitutes have been unsatisfactory. One reason is that these thin gruels often have had little nutritious value and may also be grossly contaminated. Infections that occur in weanlings often appear in epidemic proportions in the summertime, an occurrence that attests to the contamination of these foods.

Animal milk, although not in every respect equal to human milk, should be a good substitute. The difficulty has always been that milk animals have not been available, and where they have been available, there have not been means for storing the milk properly or under sanitary conditions. The milk animals themselves are often infected, or the milk may be contaminated during the milking process or during storage. For example, a modern writer recalls the following from his own boyhood:

> The women in Kansas at that time were convinced that if a baby were fed cow's milk it should surely die. Their belief was woefully justified. If you could go back with me and see our cows, or barn, the milk pails and cans, and our lack of facilities for keeping milk cold, you would doubtless have been convinced that no baby could survive such unsanitary milk. It is my belief that I could have survived being fed on milk contaminated with stable filth. It was the cloth strainer which a baby could not compete with by his defense mechanisms. We rinsed the strainer after pouring the morning's milk through it, and then hung it up to dry. In summer fifty or more flies would alight on it within a minute and feed upon the milk residues, speckling it with fly specks. In the evening, the fresh milk was poured through this fly-excrement-laden cloth. A baby could scarcely ever fail, when fed such contaminated milk, to suffer from diarrheal infection and die. [McCollum 1958, p. 124]

On the face of it, a wet nurse who is caring and loving should do as well for her charge as the biological mother. The unfortunate fact is that wet nursing was often a commercial enterprise, with the overburdened nurse taking on far more charges than she could properly feed or care for. As a consequence, she would often wean the child as quickly as possible, using the gruels just described. Another apparently common practice was for the nurse to sedate the child with opiates, which were freely available and commonly used for the purpose in centuries past (Wickes 1953). These children, then, often suffered not only from malnutrition but from isolation and neglect as well.

Children given out to wet nurses often experienced very high mortality rates. A British physician, Walter Harris, describes the situation in Kent in the eighteenth century. The local minister told him that:

TABLE 3.1
*Mortality Rates to Age 1 Year in Breast-fed and
Artificially Fed Infants*

| Study area | Date | Mortality (per 1000) | |
		Breast-fed	Artificially fed
Berlin, Germany	1895–96	57	376
Barmen, Germany	1905	68	379
Hanover, Germany	1912	96	296
Boston, Mass.	1911	30	212
Eight U.S. cities	1911–16	76	255
Paris, France	1900	140	310
Cologne, Germany	1908–09	73	241
Amsterdam, Holland	1904	144	304
Liverpool, England	1905	84	134
Eight U.S. cities	1911–16	76	215
Derby, England	1900–03	70	198
Chicago, Ill.	1924–29	2	84
Liverpool, England	1936–42	10	57
Great Britain	1946–47	9	18

NOTE: Reprinted, by permission of the publisher, from J. Knodel, "Breast-feeding and Population Growth," *Science* 198 (1977): 1113.

his parish was, when he first came to it, filled with infants from London, and yet, in the space of one year, he buried them all except two; and that the same number of small infants being soon supplied, according to the usual custom with hireling nurses, from the very great and almost inexhaustible city he had committed them all to their parent earth in the very same year. [Harris, quoted in Wickes 1953, p. 235]

In a study carried out in Berlin, Germany, in 1895–96, the death rate among artificially fed infants was more than six times as great as among children who were breast-fed throughout the first year of life. Of those who were artificially fed, about a third failed to survive the first year of life. As shown in table 3.1, the benefits of breast feeding as opposed to artificial feeding have been demonstrated in a number of cities. With the passage of time, differences in mortality rates between breast-fed and artificially fed children have fallen; the difference in modern societies is very small. However, in premodern societies where sanitation is poor, where superstitious practices abound, and where milk substitutes are not available, the advantages afforded by ample and sanitary milk supply from the breast are great. Given this natural and available source of nutrition, why have infants historically died in such prodigious numbers? The answer is that the majority of mothers did not breast-feed their children. Why not?

The Role of Nutrition in the Rise of Modern Life Expectancy

In western Europe of the seventeenth and eighteenth centuries, early separation of the child from the mother was widely practiced and encouraged. One estimate is that by the end of the eighteenth century, only 5 percent of babies born in Paris each year were fed by their own mothers. Another 5 percent were fed by wet nurses brought into the home. Ten to 15 percent were sent into the nearby countryside; the remainder were sent greater distances (McManners 1981). Among the working classes, there were economic incentives for putting the newly born child out for nursing. The new mother had to care for her older children, maintain the household, and return to work quickly. She simply did not have the time to adequately breast-feed and care for still another child and respond to all of the other demands placed upon her.

For the well off, the explanation is harder to find. Oxford historian John McManners suggests:

> a certain harshness of mind, an unwillingness to become too attached to a pathetic bundle whose chances of survival were so limited, the desire to resume sexual relationships as soon as possible, the belief that loss of milk diluted the quality of the blood of the mother, a reliance on the therapeutic qualities of the country air to give the baby a good start or (very doubtfully) some unconscious reaction against an infant's "oral sadism." [1981, p. 11]

Many of the children sent into the countryside for care were foundlings—abandoned children. Employed unmarried women had few choices; the most expedient was often abandonment of the newborn child. Although religious and governmental programs had early been established to support these foundlings, these unfortunate children were often neglected and frequently died.

Only the poorest of rural women were interested in wet nursing, and the per-capita basis of payment was easily abused. For example, many of these children were fed on dirty and diluted animal milk that was dripped into their mouths from dirty rags. One report of an investigation of nurses' care of foundlings in a French province in the 1830s reads as follows:

> Many of these unsupervised nurses relegate their charges to some dark and unhealthy nook, cover them scarcely at all, leave them tormented by vermin, tossing in their own ordure and prey to all manner of skin diseases. It is to this lack of care that Monsiur le Prefet attributes the increase in the foundling mortality to 67 out of every 100. [Quoted in Shorter 1975, p. 186]

The numbers of such abandoned children were not small; in 1833, 164,319 French children were abandoned at birth (Fuchs 1984). Forty

FIGURE 3.1.
Proportion of Mothers Breast-Feeding Their First Infant

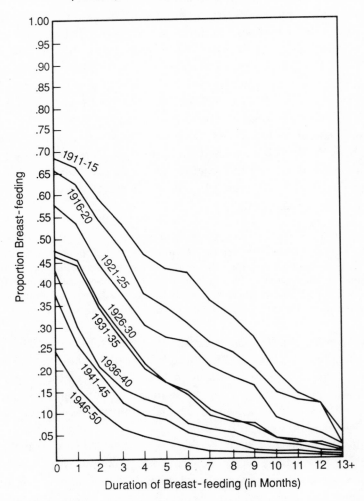

SOURCE: Reproduced by permission of the publishers, from G. Hendershot, "Trends in Breast Feeding," *Pediatrics* supp. to 74 (1984): 597, © 1984.

percent of illegitimate children were abandoned, and 30 percent of all births were illegitimate.

Early in this century, breast-feeding in the United States began a long-term decline, as measured by both the percentage of babies nursed and the duration of nursing (see figure 3.1). That long-term decline has now apparently been reversed and breast-feeding is again on the rise, predominantly among the most educated mothers (Smith 1985). Low incidence of breast-feeding is found among women with the following characteristics: youth, low income, little education, unemployed head of household, and single marital status (Russin et al. 1984).

Death Rates in Adequately Nourished Premodern Populations

If scarcity of food were an important contributor to infant and child-hood mortality, one would expect that the privileged classes or those populations with adequate access to food would have superior survival experiences. In fact, the infants of wealthy or noble families did not fare much better than did the poor. The Countess of Lincoln and Queen Anne had between them eighteen children by the end of the eighteenth century. All of them died. Louis XIV, the "Sun King," had six legitimate children, only one of whom reached adulthood. Studies of the ruling classes of Europe find infant mortality rates equaling those among the most deprived of populations. Prior to the nineteenth century, approximately 20 percent of all children born to these privileged families died in the first year of life, and 25 percent were dead before the age of five (Peller 1965).

Besides such privileged European classes, other populations were also protected from widespread hunger; yet they too experienced mortality rates equal to those observed in Europe. Livi-Bacci (1986) notes that early French Canadian settlers had a life expectancy of 35.5 years; Americans in the mid-nineteenth century had a life expectancy in the high thirties or low forties; and colonies in New Zealand and Australia had death rates similar to those of the homeland, in spite of the absence of crowding, poor sanitation, and "hidden hunger."

Wartime Deprivation in Modern Society

We have just seen that, by themselves, unlimited food supplies will have only a modest influence on health in premodern societies. But what happens to modern populations subjected to deprivation as a result of wartime shortages?

Denmark is a traditional source of fine hams and sausages. Prior to World War I the Danish population of pigs exceeded the human pop-ulation—5 million pigs compared with 3½ million people. At that time the grain with which to feed the animals was imported from the United States. Because of the wartime naval blockade, grain imports were severely curtailed, and the Danish government decided to slaughter the pigs and preserve the depleted grain supply for bread. Before the war Danes ate breads made from refined grains. During the war bread was made from unrefined rye, oats, and bran. This enforced national diet was associated with a remarkable fall in the death rate. Prior to the war it had been 12.5 per thousand. After the institution of the wartime diet, the death rate fell to 10.4 per thousand, the lowest registered in any European country at that time (Wrench 1972).

An even more impressive experience was observed in Britain during World War II. Again as a result of a German blockade, food supplies in wartime Britain were critically short. Food rationing was instituted, and both meat and butter or other fats were in scarce supply. In addition, the nation suffered intense bombing as well as a shortage of medical supplies and personnel. Still, after excluding deaths due to military action, mortality rates for the population declined. The report of the Chief Medical Officer of the Ministry of Health in 1946 reads in part:

> An outstanding feature has been the low mortality of children from disease. Despite the loss of 7000 lives at age under 15 as a direct result of military action and an increase in accidental deaths arising from war conditions the mean annual death rates during 1940–44 were below the rates for any previous year to 1939 at ages 1–5, 5–9 and 10–14. The year 1939 was remarkable in producing new low records for mortality at every age below 15 years, the fall being especially great at ages 1–10. It was not expected that better figures would be obtained during the war but new records for the second and third years of life were set up in 1942 and for the 1st, 2nd, 4th, and fifth years of age and at 5–9 years. The still-birth rate declined continuously throughout the war whilst successive low records for maternal mortality were established in 1940, 1942, 1943 and 1944. [Quoted in Barlow 1984, p. 49]

In addition to changes in mortality rates, wartime food shortages were also associated with changes in such painful conditions as gouty arthritis. Gout virtually disappeared in Europe during the two world wars when food shortages were common. On the other hand, gout has risen sharply in Japan in the period following World War II as protein intake has increased (Stanbury, Wyngarden, and Frederickson 1983).

In Holland and Germany during the war, there was a striking decrease in high blood pressure among those with chronic and severe disease. There was also a decline in the rate of complications such as angina pectoris and stroke (Brozek and Keys 1948).

I should not like to leave the impression that wartime food shortages were universally beneficial. Under conditions of severe famine, such as those that occurred in Holland during the harsh winter of 1944–45, an

52

increase in mortality at all ages occurred, but even here, where food intake was limited to an average of 800 calories per day, researchers believe that an epidemic of influenza may have been a major factor (Stein et al. 1975).

Animal Studies of Nutrition and Longevity

Animal studies of the rat as well as of a number of other species conducted over several decades have repeatedly demonstrated an apparent benefit from food deprivation. Under certain conditions animals' life-span can be significantly extended by food deprivation (McCay et al. 1939). This effect is produced only if the deprivation is relatively severe and if it is started very early in life. The effect appears to operate by extending the maturing process and cannot be produced if the deprivation is instituted after maturity had been reached.

In another experiment, rats that are permitted to choose freely from three qualitatively different diets in whatever amounts they like also show differences in life-span. Rats that ate the most also tended to choose the high-carbohydrate diet. These animals experienced death rates 62 percent higher than the average, while the animals that ate the least had death rates 38 percent less than the average (Ross and Bras 1975). While intriguing, the meaning of these observations for human health is not entirely clear, although they are consistent with the observation in human populations that those who eat less will live long and those who eat much will live short lives. As we shall see, however, differences in eating may be less important in humans than differences in activity levels.

A New Problem: Overnutrition

As modernization has progressed in the United States into the post-modern period, caloric intake has increased, mostly as a result of increased dietary fat. Concomitantly, obesity has also increased. Whereas periodic famines have been the nutritional problem of the nonmodernized world, overnutrition is the principal dietary problem of the postmodern world. I need not belabor the health significance of overnutrition; there is little dispute that obesity predisposes to and aggravates a number of diseases, including hypertension, heart disease, diabetes, and a number of cancers, particularly those of the rectum and female breast (Garrow 1979). In contrast, the evidence that malnutrition exists widely in the U.S. is weak. Although one does see occasional reports of "hidden hunger" in America, these are generally based on such biochemical measures as serum iron or vitamin concentrations, the clinical significance of which is unknown (Graham 1985); therefore, it would seem reasonable to conclude that there are far more deaths in the postmodern world from obesity than there are from diseases associated with undernutrition. Therefore the argument that improvements in health during the postmodern period are the result of continually improved nutrition is not plausible. I believe that in the United States, diet for the population as a whole was optimal in the early part of the twentieth century; as a nation, our health since that time has suffered rather than benefited from dietary change. Consider: the three largest sources of calories in the American diet today are white bread, doughnuts and cookies, and alcoholic beverages. These three together constitute 21 percent of all calories consumed. One-third of all carbohydrates come from white bread/crackers, soft drinks, doughnuts and cakes, and sugar (Block et al. 1985). At the beginning of the century, 70 percent of our protein came from vegetable sources; today 70 percent comes from animal sources. There is no reason to believe that eating large quantities of meat offers a dietary advantage. In fact, many studies show that a vegetarian diet is optimal for health; as an example, one recent report states that vegetarian diets prevent gallstones (Pixley et al. 1985).

No matter which measure of obesity is used—and in the various studies several have been—all show the same result: obesity is increasing among Americans.

International comparisons demonstrate marked differences in the prevalence of obesity among nations. In a study of seven different nations, more American men were obese—63 percent—than were men in any of the other national samples examined (Keys 1970). Subjects from the other countries—the Netherlands, Italy, Yugoslavia, Finland, Greece, and Japan—exhibited a decreasing frequency of obesity (in order listed), with only 2 percent of Japanese men being obese. It is no coincidence that Japanese men have the world's lowest mortality rates and that U.S. males rank nineteenth. The other countries fall between the United States and Japan with respect to mortality rates.

Clearly there are many differences other than dietary between the Japanese and the American lifestyle; however, the death rates from cardiovascular disease and from all other causes for Japanese living in the

United States is only about half that for white Americans (Frerichs, Chapman, and Maes 1984).

At the same time that obesity is increasing in the United States, other eating disorders—anorexia nervosa and bulimia—are also increasing. Both of these psychosomatic diseases affect young women who have greatly disturbed perceptions of themselves and fears of obesity. Women with anorexia reduce their food intake drastically; women with bulimia indulge in binge eating, often of "junk food," but then induce vomiting. Mortality rates from both conditions may be as high as 9 percent (Herzog 1985).

Is Obesity Solely the Result of Overeating?

Both medical professionals and the lay public often consider obesity to be predominantly the result of overeating; however, evidence on the point is far from clear. The content of body fat is the result of two factors—energy consumption and energy expenditure. Several studies show that obese people do not consume more calories than the nonobese. Differences in energy expenditures appear to be more important than caloric intake in explaining why some people are fat and others are not (Braitman, Adlin, and Stanton 1985; Epstein and Wing 1980; Thompson et al. 1982).

None of this is to deny the influence of a genetic factor in the etiology of obesity. Recent studies among adopted children show that obesity is much more likely in children whose biological parents are obese, whereas there is no correlation between obesity in the child and that of adoptive parents (Stunkard et al. 1986). Thus while it is clear that genetic factors predispose to obesity, it would be incorrect to conclude that no behavioral or cultural factors are involved in the development of obesity.

These observations lead me to speculate that the rising prevalence of obesity in the United States results from two factors: increasing consumption of calories as a result of a high-fat diet and decreasing energy expenditures as we utilize labor-saving devices both at home and at work. Nowadays we drive even short distances whereas we once walked. We put our clothes in a washing machine whereas we once used a washboard.

(How many American children have ever seen a washboard?)

In a study of an Eskimo community that has very recently become acculturated to "white civilization," it was found that in only ten years, there has been a significant increase in Eskimo body fat and a decrease in several measures of fitness as a result of change in diet and the increased use of snowmobiles and machine equipment (Rode and Shepard 1984). If these Eskimos follow the usual pattern of people undergoing modernization, they will undoubtedly experience an improvement in several measures of health. But is this because of or in spite of dietary change? Does anyone suggest that being fat and less fit contribute to health?

Summary

There is little scientific justification for the conclusion that improvements in food supply and quality are responsible for improvements in health. Historically, populations with abundant food supplies shared high death rates with their less fortunate contemporaries, whereas deprivation seems to benefit the health of modern populations deprived of this abundance during wartime, just as it does laboratory animal populations. Indeed, the evidence is that improvements in the health of the American people during this century have occurred in spite of rather than as a consequence of dietary change.

I cannot conclude this chapter without commenting on the frequent reports of hunger in the United States. I have no doubt that there are many who do indeed experience hunger. Yet I quarrel with the usual strategy adopted as a remedy—the provision of food—while the behavioral characteristics that often (but not always) are responsible for the existence of hunger—the absence of those social and educational skills necessary to provide adequate food—are ignored. Would it not be better, rather than increasing dependency and passivity by providing food (as with food stamps), to provide the skills of literacy and self-esteem so that individuals can provide for themselves? I do not mean to suggest that those who are needy be deprived of food supplements; but, this should be in addition to, rather than instead of, efforts to increase self-reliance.

4 Medical Care:

Its Influence on

Life Expectancy

"Nothing is more fatal to health than overcare of it."

—BENJAMIN FRANKLIN (cited in Robin, 1984, p. 119)

WHAT IS IT that we want from our doctors? I would suggest that we want, in approximately this order, four things. We want compassion, understanding, and a knowledgeable and sympathetic listener. Second, we want relief of the symptoms for which we seek medical attention. Third, we want information: What is wrong with us and what is likely to be the outcome? Are we going to get better or worse, and when? Last, we are interested in life prolongation. We want advice and treatment that, even in the absence of symptoms, is likely to enable us to avoid illness and prolong life. This chapter addresses only this last issue: how effective has medical intervention been in influencing the reduction of mortality? How effective is it today?

There is no doubt that therapy provides symptomatic relief and, occasionally, a significant extension of life for many individual medical and surgical conditions. The relief of symptoms and a demonstration of compassion are alone sufficient justification for the existence of the medical care system. However, both physicians and the public generally credit medical technology for more—for the extension of life expectancy that has occurred in the modern world within the past hundred or so years. One important presumption of those who urge the removal of economic barriers to medical care is that denial of such care may shorten the life-span.

Throughout this chapter I shall present evidence for my view that the medical care system has not materially contributed to the historical decline in death rates and even today may not be a significant factor in the explanation of modern life expectancy.

Most medical care is not primarily intended to be life saving. The vast majority of patients consult physicians because of the appearance of symptoms from which they seek relief, generally of pain or discomfort; physicians do not confront truly life-threatening emergencies all that often. Life prolongation is not the objective of most treatment; it is the quality of life for which most patients seek help, not the quantity of life.

Nevertheless, some therapy is beyond doubt life saving. Such therapies include surgical treatment of traumatic injuries, as in military combat or serious traffic accidents; treatment of other acute emergencies, such as bleeding or abdominal obstruction; and medical therapy of certain cardiac or other emergencies, such as diabetic coma. Yet in spite of these examples, there is reason to question whether the medical care system significantly contributes to the life-span of large populations. Although some medical treatment confers some benefit (in prolonging life), all medical and surgical therapy imposes some risk. Every surgical procedure that requires an anesthetic carries some small risk of an anesthetic death or some other complication. One consultant recently reported a series of fifteen cases of healthy women who had undergone a routine surgical procedure (such as hysterectomy) and who, within a day or two, suffered either permanent brain damage or death (Arieff 1986). Every time an antibiotic or any other medication is administered, there is some finite risk, no matter how small, of an adverse, even fatal reaction. Even diagnostic procedures—for example, coronary angiography, the x-ray visualization of the coronary arteries of the heart—carry some nontrivial risk.

Treatment complications may occur immediately and be easily recognized as such or may occur years later. Complications occurring after a very long interval are difficult to recognize. For example, only recently has it been recognized that surgery for gastric or duodenal ulcer may be followed decades later by cancer of the stomach (Viste et al. 1986).

In addition to various well-recognized reactions to therapy, more subtle psychological reactions may take an unrecognized toll in health. For example, when in a routine examination a patient is found to have high blood pressure and the physician initiates a course of therapy, the patient's anxiety regarding the newly discovered condition may have deleterious health consequences that are greater than the treatment benefits. These psychological consequences following the discovery and di-

58

agnosis of disease, or "labeling," have only recently become the subject of medical interest. Labeling patients as having high blood pressure has now been shown to result in an increase in work absence and a decline in the sense of psychological well-being (Macdonald et al. 1985). Interestingly, those who faithfully follow a course of therapy appear to suffer less from labeling than those who fail to pursue therapy, suggesting that those who see themselves as unable to alter the course of the disease suffer more than those who perceive themselves as able to control and influence the outcome of the condition.

Besides complications that result from largely unavoidable risks, there are also injuries and deaths that are the result of negligence. Although the frequency of these cannot be known with any certainty, the evidence is that the number is not small. For example, one study of the records of patients discharged from two large hospitals revealed that about 7 percent had experienced injuries during their hospital stay, and of these, approximately one-third were the result of negligence, mostly by physicians (Pocincki, Dogger, and Schwartz 1973).

The issue is not only whether some procedures and therapies are life prolonging; rather, the question is whether the aggregate impact of the millions of medical procedures and therapeutic decisions made daily have a net beneficial or negative effect on life expectancy.

Contrary to the common wisdom, the efficacy of most therapy has not been subjected to rigorous scientific validation; on the contrary, most medical therapy today is based on authority and tradition and has not been evaluated for efficacy in the sense of life prolongation. Until recently there simply has not been a great deal of interest in conducting studies directed to this point; generally physicians have been more concerned with comparing one treatment with another rather than with whether a treatment actually results in life prolongation.

Few studies have been designed to examine survival following treatment. Admittedly, such studies are extremely difficult to do. They require the selection of a population with defined disease characteristics—the "treatment group"—and an identical or comparison group—the "control group"—and finally, a group of clinicians who are "blind" to which patients are treated and which are control. One common means of achieving this "double-blinding" is through the use of drugs and identical-appearing placebo pills. The reason for the double-blind requirement in which neither the patient nor the physician knows which drug is being used is the recognized tendency for both physicians and patients to unconsciously attribute greater effects to the new than to the older means of therapy (hope springs eternal). Double-blind studies of surgical therapy are usually impossible—one cannot conceal from the patient or the doctor which patient is being treated with the experimental procedure.

Such studies are expensive, time-consuming, and difficult to interpret. Take, for example, the so-called Multiple Risk Factor Intervention Trial ("Mr. Fit"). This was an attempt to simultaneously treat several of the factors thought to adversely affect the progress of coronary artery disease, namely, cigarette smoking, hypertension, and serum cholesterol levels. The study design required the examination of 360,000 men aged thirty-five through fifty-seven from which a sample of 12,866 was selected. These men were then randomly assigned to two groups. One group would continue routine medical care from their private physicians. The second group of men were assigned to a therapeutic program in which an intensive effort would be made to reduce or abolish risks. For example, there were separate educational programs aimed at cigarette withdrawal, dietary change, and blood pressure control. All of these efforts were successful; that is, following the treatment period, the study group did manifest less smoking, less hypertension, and lower blood cholesterol levels than the men who were continuing under the care of their own physicians. However, when sufficient time had elapsed to compare mortality between the two groups, it was found that the intensively treated group had gained no advantage. Their mortality rates were, in fact, slightly higher than in the control group: 41.2 per thousand as compared to 40.4 per thousand, a difference that was not statistically significant. Although the reasons for this treatment failure were not obvious, the investigators speculated that the use of antihypertensive drugs may have produced sufficient harm to have overcome any benefit that may have been provided. That view has been challenged; one analyst concludes "the best explanation for the failure to detect a beneficial effect in Mr. Fit is that no benefit accrued" (Stallones 1983, p. 649).

This conclusion is consistent with two other large cardiovascular disease intervention trials. One took place in Finland and the other was conducted among a multinational population from countries throughout Europe (Salonen, Puska, and Mustaniemi 1979; World Health Organization and the European Collaborative Group 1983). Neither trial resulted in significant reduction in coronary disease among the participants. These results have led to the publication of an article questioning our ability to control heart disease entitled "Should We Not Forget About Mass Control of Coronary Risk Factors?" (Oliver 1983).

Even where effective and life-saving procedures or medications do exist, these are often administered to those persons with conditions for which there is no evidence of efficacy; for example, penicillin is effective

60

for certain conditions but is far more often prescribed for minor colds where it is not effective. Powerful forces—psychological, economic, and legal—act on both physicians and patients to administer some means of therapy whether effective or not. That is true of both surgical procedures (such as coronary artery bypass, hysterectomy, cesarean section) and medical procedures (such as the use of antibiotics and many hormones).

I shall examine the efficacy of the medical care system by using four different strategies. First I shall examine the influence of medical intervention on the historical decline in death rates observed in modernizing populations, particularly in the western world. How effective was medical therapy over the past two centuries during which the major improvements in mortality were achieved? Second, I shall examine the effectiveness of specific therapy for those diseases that are considered the major causes of death in the United States today, the cardiovascular diseases and cancer. A third strategy will be an examination of the marginal benefits of medical care. Is there a demonstrable relationship between the magnitude of medical resources available to a population and the level of health? Last, I present some observations of what has occurred after medical care has been introduced into traditional societies in order to test whether modern and postmodern medical technology could reduce morbidity or mortality. Since medical technology has evolved historically in parallel with other changes such as diet and sanitation, it is frquently difficult to isolate the influence of medical care alone. Therefore, these observations of the introduction and evaluation of ostensibly superior medical care into medically backward communities provides unique opportunities for quantifying benefits of medical care.

Did Medicine Contribute to the Historical Fall in Mortality?

There is good reason to conclude that, throughout most of history, medical care was more harmful than beneficial. Take the case of the treatment of a stroke that killed King Charles II of England. At eight o'clock on Monday morning of February 2, 1685, the king was being shaved in his bedroom. With a sudden cry he fell backward and had a violent convulsion. He became unconscious, rallied once or twice, and,

after a few days, died. Dr. Scarburgh, one of fourteen physicians called
to treat the stricken king, recorded the efforts to cure the patient:

> As the first step in treatment, the king was bled to the extent of a pint
> from a vein in his right arm. Next his shoulder was incised and the area
> "cupped" to suck out an additional 8 ounces of blood. After this the
> drugging began. An emetic and purgative were administered, and soon
> after a second purgative. This was followed by an enema containing an-
> timony, sacred bitters, rock salt, mallow leaves, violets, beet root, camomile
> flowers, fennel seed, linseed, cinammon, cardamon seed, saffron, cochineal,
> and aloes. The enema was repeated in two hours and a purgative given.
> The king's head was shaved and a blister was raised on his scalp. A sneezing
> powder of hellebore root was administered, and also a powder of cowslip
> flowers "to strengthen his brain." The cathartics were repeated at frequent
> intervals and interspersed with a soothing drink composed of barley water,
> licorice, and sweet almond. Likewise white wine, absinth, and anise were
> given, as also were extracts of thistle leaves, mint, rue, and angelica. . . .
> For external treatment, a plaster of Burgundy pitch and pigeon dung was
> applied to the king's feet. The bleeding and purging continued and the
> following medicaments were added: melon seeds, slippery elm, black cherry
> water, and extract of flowers of lime, lily of the valley, peony, lavender,
> and dissolved pearls. Still to come were gentian roots, nutmeg, quinine,
> and cloves.
>
> The king's condition did not improve, in fact, it grew worse, and in the
> emergency 40 drops of extract of human skull were administered to allay
> convulsions. A rallying dose of Raleigh's antidote was forced down the
> king's throat; this antidote contained an enormous number of herbs and
> animal extracts. Finally bezoar stone was given. Then, after an ill-fated
> night his serene majesty's strength seemed exhausted to such a degree that
> the whole assembly of physicians lost all hope and became despondent;
> still so as not to appear to fail in doing their duty in any detail, they brought
> into play the most active cordial. As a sort of grand summary to this
> pharmaceutical debauch a mixture of Raleigh's antidote, pearl julep, and
> ammonia was forced down the throat of the dying king. [Haggard 1929,
> pp. 334–35]

With the possible exception of surgical anaesthesia, little improvement in medical therapeutics occurred from King Charles's time until
the early twentieth century, and even then, progress was painfully slow.

There was no shortage of medical practitioners in nineteenth-century
America. Historical records demonstrate that the number of physicians
per 100,000 persons has not changed appreciably over the past 150 years.
However, these "physicians" were a motley group—herbalists, cultists
of various sorts, graduates of diploma mills, quacks, bone setters, midwives,
spiritualists, and manipulators. Whoever wished to do so could put out
a sign advertising themselves as "doctor" and sell their services for a fee,

the only constraint being the risk of being run out of town as a fake; until late in the nineteenth century there were no licensing requirements. Even the most prestigious of medical schools were, by today's standards, woefully inadequate. Training consisted of two years of lectures exclusively; there were no laboratories. When Charles Eliot became president of Harvard in 1870 he wrote, "The ignorance and general incompetency of the average graduate of American medical schools, at the time when he receives the degree which turns him loose upon the community, is something horrible to contemplate" (Starr 1982, p. 113).

Anyone could open a medical school, advertise for students, and confer degrees. When Mary Baker Eddy, the founder of the Christian Science Church, first realized her own therapeutic powers after being cured of a prolonged paralysis, she opened her own school.

In medical practices of the nineteenth century, there was little pretense of science. Doctors saw their role as that of the treatment of symptoms. They were more than anything empiricists—their concern was with that which was effective. They did not examine their patients; in the first decades of the century, they did not have stethoscopes or opthalmoscopes, and they had no laboratories. Even if they did have such instruments, they did not have sufficient knowledge of anatomy with which to exploit such tools. They had not witnessed an autopsy, much less conducted one. Such was the quality of medical care in the nineteenth century, the era during which U.S. life expectancy from birth increased by five years. It would seem unlikely that such an increase owed anything to the medical care available.

The Antibiotic Era

In the early twentieth century, a feverish research effort was undertaken to discover therapeutic agents specifically toxic to particular disease-producing organisms. The idea was to find agents that would kill organisms within the body but not harm the patient—that is, a "magic bullet." Paul Ehrlich's discovery in 1910 of salvarsan, a drug specific for syphilis, was followed decades later by the discovery of chemotherapeutic and antibiotic agents. Although salvarsan was effective against the syphilitic organism *treponema pallidum*, it was, as with many chemotherapeutic

FIGURE 4.1.

Mortality Rates, United States, Contrasted with GNP

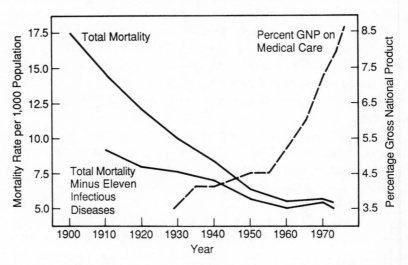

SOURCE: Reprinted, by permission of the publisher, from J. McKinlay and S. McKinlay, "The Questionable Contribution of Medical Measures to the Decline of Mortality in the Twentieth Century," *Milbank Memorial Fund Quarterly* 55 (1977): 413, Milbank Memorial Fund.

agents today, also toxic to the patient and thus of limited usefulness (Shryock 1960).

The introduction of antibiotics into clinical medicine in the late 1940s and early 1950s was indeed a moment of great historical significance. There can be little doubt that, when properly used, antibiotics can shorten the course of some infectious diseases; they often did so during the early days of the antibiotic era. Yet it is not at all clear that these agents have contributed to the overall fall in mortality from infectious disease. Why is that?

As noted earlier, death rates from the infectious diseases had already fallen to low levels by the time that antibiotics were introduced. As shown in figure 4.1, the decline in infectious disease mortality began long before the appearance of the first antibiotic, penicillin, and even long before the widespread use of the first chemotherapeutic agents, the sulfa drugs. By 1950, when effective antitubercular drugs first became widely available, the death rate from tuberculosis, the major infectious disease of young adults, had already fallen to a small fraction of what it had been in the nineteenth century. Still, percent of GNP spent on medical care has continued to rise. In 1985, the amount spent, 400 billion dollars, was greater than 12 percent of GNP.

A second reason for the failure of antibiotics to significantly influence infectious disease mortality rates results from their widespread overuse. Indeed, these once-useful agents have been so abused that they are now often ineffective.

Bacterial resistance has progressed to such a point that many infections which thirty years ago were easily controlled with antibiotics are no longer easily treatable (Finland 1979). For example, the gonococcus, cause of the commonest venereal disease, is often no longer sensitive to penicillin. Most recently pneumococcus, frequently associated with lobar pneumonia, has shown resistance to antibiotics.

Rather than declining in importance due to the availability of antibiotics, infections are becoming increasingly common among people who are hospitalized. Several major centers have reported an annual frequency of "blood poisoning" (bacteremia) of one per one hundred hospitalized patients, with fatality rates among those infected of 30 to 50 percent (Kreger et al. 1980). If similar incidence and fatality rates hold for the 30 million acute hospital admissions annually in the United States, as many as 300,000 episodes and 100,000 fatalities from hospital-acquired infections may occur in this country each year. The total number of less virulent hospital-acquired infections is many times higher; one recent survey of 6,449 hospitals found that hospital-acquired infections will occur among almost six of every one hundred admitted patients each year, producing a national total of as many as 4 million infections. Furthermore, the number appears to be growing (Haley 1985). Infections, then, rather than being diseases of the past, are still very much with us.

Part of the reason for the rising number of hospital-acquired infections is the increasing use of "invasive" procedures, such as the insertion of tubes into various organs, and the more frequent use of surgery. However, another reason is almost certainly the frequently unnecessary administration of antibiotics to hospitalized patients. For example, in one survey over 30 percent of patients were receiving antibiotics, yet only 38 percent of persons treated had evidence of infection. A panel of experts reviewing antibiotic use in a series of hospitals found more than half the uses unnecessary (Eickhoff 1986).

Many of the common infectious diseases that were associated with historically high mortality rates are no longer or never were susceptible to antibiotics. That is true for all viral illnesses, such as measles and polio, as well as the very common viral gastrointestinal and upper respiratory infections of children and adults. It is these childhood infectious diseases that produce such high death rates in the premodern world.

Many illnesses in ambulatory patients seen in postmodern practice are associated with viral infection—the common cold or flu (Moffet

1978). While there is no evidence that antibiotics are of any therapeutic benefit in these illnesses, patients are very frequently administered such drugs; if all that one has is a hammer, everything looks like a nail. According to infectious disease experts, studies indicate that enough antibiotics are manufactured and dispensed each year in the United States to treat two illnesses of average duration for every man, woman, and child. On the other hand, they estimate that illnesses which would significantly benefit from antibiotic medication occur about once every five to ten years (Kunin, Tupasi, and Craig 1973). Other studies show that even in hospitalized patients, about half of the antibiotics prescribed are not needed, or that the inappropriate agent is prescribed, or the dosage is incorrect. Forty-five percent of responses from 4,513 physicians to a survey questionnaire posing typical clinical cases devised by infectious disease experts were incorrect (Neu and Howrey 1975). Last, antibiotics may themselves produce complications. Some are simply annoying; skin rashes, for example, are usually transient. Others may be life threatening. There is clear evidence that the use of antibiotics predisposes to infection. This may occur through several mechanisms. By the inhibition of normally occurring bacteria in the body, other drug-resistant organisms are stimulated to proliferate. There is also evidence that antibiotics suppress the normal immune system; deleterious effects of antibiotics on the formation of antibodies and on the function of white blood cells have been observed (Eickhoff 1986; Hauser and Remington 1982). Indeed, some antibiotics may occasionally destroy bone marrow.

The fact is that infectious disease is still a major cause of death in the United States. In 1976 infections were considered to be the third most common cause of death, being shown on death certificates more often (123,000) than deaths from all accidents (100,000), or more frequently than deaths from diabetes, cirrhosis, suicide, and homicide combined (110,000) (Bennett 1978).

Thus the evidence is clear that medical therapy probably had little to do with the major decline in mortality from infectious disease. Although antibiotics were indeed "miracle drugs" for certain limited classes of infectious disease for a short period after their discovery, their widespread abuse both as a result of their common use in animal foods and their medical abuse has caused them to lose much of their effectiveness. While there are undoubtedly individual exceptions, for the population as a whole it appears unlikely that antibiotics contribute beneficially to our life expectancy.

The Role of Immunization

So far I have ignored the contribution of immunization to the decline of infectious disease. What role has the use of vaccines played in the decline?

By far the earliest immunization procedure to be widely used was the smallpox vaccine—"vaccination." While the development of smallpox vaccination is certainly one of the most glorious chapters in the history of medicine, medical historians are still debating just how much it contributed to the decline of smallpox mortality (Behbehani 1983). There are a number of reasons for this uncertainty, the most important of which is that the historical data are simply insufficient to resolve the issue. While there is no doubt that properly administered vaccination prevents smallpox, we do not know how often the vaccine was properly administered. Death certificates are not available, nor can we have much confidence in the accuracy of the incidence data that do exist, diagnoses being supplied by laypeople on British bills of mortality. Nor do we have any data on whether those who did die with smallpox had been properly vaccinated (Mercer 1985). Complicating the historical interpretation still further is the fact that death rates from smallpox and other infectious diseases were beginning to decline at about the same time that vaccination was being introduced in Europe. There is therefore reason to speculate that a decline in smallpox deaths may have occurred in parallel with the introduction of vaccination—not necessarily because of it. The reduced death rate from infectious disease led to speculation that smallpox vaccination prevented not only smallpox but typhoid and tuberculosis as well. There is no biological basis for such a conclusion; it undoubtedly arose from the fact that most infectious disease deaths were in decline at the beginning of the nineteenth century (Mercer 1985).

Efficacy of vaccination against smallpox is not perfect. The first attempts at immunization were not with the attenuated cowpox but with live, unattenuated smallpox virus. Was this technique successful? It seems unlikely; the hazard associated with the procedure must certainly have been high—that is, many or most of those treated in this manner would likely develop the disease with all of the classical risks associated with it. Furthermore, people vaccinated with the smallpox virus became a source of infection and occasionally produced outbreaks of smallpox and some mortality. Nevertheless, the decline in deaths from smallpox throughout the nineteenth and early twentieth centuries accounted for only a small percentage of the decline in death rates from infectious disease as a whole (less than 2 percent).

There is still another reason for reserving judgment regarding the contribution of vaccination to the decline in mortality. In chapter 2 I introduced the notion of a generalized resistance to disease and suggested that the level of resistance may be more important in controlling disease mortality than is a reduction in exposure to specific infectious agents. If this concept is valid, then eradication of an infectious agent would only open the door for other equally virulent organisms in the environment. Limited evidence of the existence of this generalized resistance can be inferred from the history of smallpox eradication in the Berlin parish of Dohrotheenstadt. When vaccination against smallpox became available in the early part of the nineteenth century, smallpox deaths, which occurred most commonly among children, fell precipitously. However, the overall death rate was relatively unaffected as deaths from gastrointestinal and other diseases subsequently rose. One cause of death was replaced by another, as would be expected if there had been no change in the immune defenses of the population (Imhof 1983).

It is unfortunate but nevertheless true that much of public health practice is instituted after the problem has already been solved. Although many vaccines are almost totally effective in preventing or at least greatly modifying disease, many were developed and introduced after the target disease had spontaneously declined. Deaths from whooping cough, measles, and diphtheria, as examples, were mostly under control by the end of World War II, when vaccines began to appear. This experience is shown graphically in figure 4.2. Nor has the introduction of these vaccines been without complication. Even today there is controversy regarding the safety of the whooping cough vaccine, such that it is not always clear that the benefits of using the vaccine outweigh the risks (Miller, Alderslade, and Ross 1982). During the late 1970s, when diphtheria vaccine fell into disuse in the United Kingdom because of attendant risks, the incidence of the disease rose dramatically; however, the death rate from the disease remained at its previous low level. Whether the benefits of the vaccine in preventing the disease outweigh the risks associated with its use is not the issue here; the point is that even without the use of vaccine, the death rate from the disease in a postmodern population is very small, and may not have been significantly reduced by the introduction of the vaccine.

I do not wish to be misunderstood here: whether or not immunizations influenced overall mortality rates is not the only or necessarily

FIGURE 4.2.
Introduction of Immunization and Fall in Disease Mortality

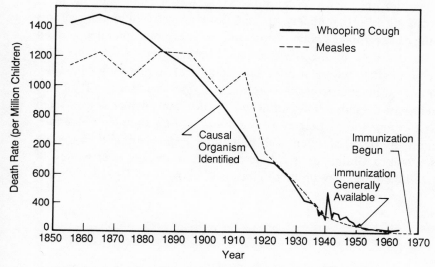

Whooping Cough and Measles: Death Rates of Children under 15,
England and Wales

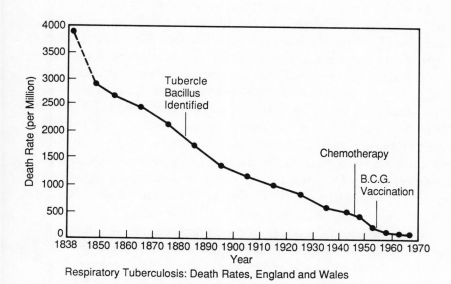

Respiratory Tuberculosis: Death Rates, England and Wales

SOURCE: Reprinted, by permission of the publisher, from T. McKeown, *The Modern Rise of Population* (New York: Academic Press, 1976), p. 93 and p. 96.

the most important consequence of their development and use. Childhood illness can be very frightening to both child and parents. Even the fear of these diseases can be burdensome. Those who lived through the polio era can attest to the anxiety that the disease produced among parents during each summer's polio season, and the enormous relief that greeted the discovery of an effective vaccine. The very recent discovery of a vaccine for the childhood diseases produced by the bacteria called he-mophilus influenza is another example of the importance of vaccine development. Hemophilus influenza is an organism that is associated with an estimated 30 percent of the diseases of children. For example, more than 10,000 children each year suffer from meningitis caused by this organism. Studies demonstrate the almost complete effectiveness of the vaccine in preventing these illnesses (Peltola et al. 1984).

The Recent Decline in Cardiovascular Disease Mortality

Over the past two decades cardiovascular mortality rates have de-clined throughout the western world, but more rapidly in the United States than elsewhere. An important category of cardiovascular diseases is that which affects the coronary arteries of the heart itself, so-called coronary artery disease (CAD). In the decade between 1968 and 1978, U.S. death rates attributed to this disease among those aged thirty to seventy-four years fell by 20.7 percent and have continued to fall (Stern 1979). If this decline were the result of medical intervention, it would indeed be a major medical triumph. Such an outcome might result from preventive efforts, such as in the treatment of hypertension, a known antecedent for CAD. If this were the case, it should be reflected in a decline in the incidence of CAD, that is, in the rate at which CAD appears in the population as well as in CAD death rates.

While statistics on deaths from any particular cause are easily avail-able, the ascertainment of disease incidence is often impossible. We keep careful tabs on who dies and of the causes of death, but we do not have a well-organized system of records for incidence of disease, except for those communicable diseases that physicians are required by law to report to health authorities. Therefore, accurate data on the incidence of CAD are not easily available. Furthermore, even where some data do exist, we cannot be certain that all cases come to the attention of a physician; some cases of CAD are known to be "silent," to occur without any pain. Nevertheless, the data that do exist support the notion that the incidence of CAD is declining in the United States, just as is the death rate from it. Evidence comes from a study of the employees of the Dupont Chemical Company. During the period 1957 through 1983, 6,286 episodes of myocardial infarction were reported as occurring among the company's male employees. In that same period, the annual age-adjusted rate of CAD fell from 3.19 per thousand to 2.29 per thousand, a decline of 28.2 percent. The investigators found that medical care made some contribution to improved survival, but the major source of the decline in mortality was a reduction in the incidence of the disease (Pell and Fayerweather 1985). They noted that their results are consistent with those of other investigators.

Might not the fact that the incidence of CAD has declined result from improved medical control of risk factors, such as high blood pressure? If changes in the risk factors were responsible for changes in death rates from CAD, the risk factors should rise and fall in some systematic fashion with the disease. The late Reuel Stallones, dean of the School of Public Health of the University of Texas, has examined the possible relationship of risk factors to CAD (Stallones 1980). He noted that mortality from CAD rose in the United States prior to 1960 or so, then leveled off and has since declined. He found no consistent relationship between the risk factors and CAD; none of the observed risk factors fluctuated in a manner that would explain a decline in the disease. The incidence of stroke, another disease even more strongly related to high blood pressure, has been declining since the 1930s when high blood pressure treatment was neither widely nor effectively practiced (Editorial 1983).

I have already described the "Mr. Fit" study, a very extensive effort to directly measure the efficacy of medical control of risk factors involved in CAD. That study and others like it have failed to show any benefit in reducing mortality, much less the nearly 20 percent reduction in CAD that has actually been observed.

If medical efforts at prevention have not been responsible for the decline in CAD deaths, could it be that better treatment of patients with heart attacks has improved the probability of survival? Two recent major thrusts of CAD treatment have been the development of coronary care units and coronary bypass surgery. The philosophy underlying the use of intensive care units stems from the observation that death in the early postinfarction period follows from the irritability of the cardiac muscle and the propensity to arrhythmia (an abnormal heart rhythm) that can

71

be quickly lethal. Therefore, therapy during the early postinfarction period has been directed toward maintaining the patient under close nursing and electronic supervision in a coronary care unit, so that appropriate treatment can be initiated immediately should an arrhythmia occur. Although there is logic to such a strategy, it has not been possible to demonstrate that it is effective. Comparison of death rates among those treated by conventional means and those treated in the most intensive fashion have failed to demonstrate any differences. Indeed, two cardiologists who have reviewed the entire literature have found no persuasive evidence that hospital-based treatment is superior to home-based treatment as measured by survival. They note that although the treatment of the abnormal heart rhythm is more effectively carried out in monitored patients while hospitalized, the frequency of this complication may be increased by the anxiety created by the hospital environment, particularly in the dehumanizing atmosphere of the coronary care unit (Eggertsen and Berg 1984). Persistent psychic costs of such treatment have also been observed to produce persistent neuroses among many of its survivors (Holland 1973).

Coronary bypass surgery has existed for only the past decade or so, at least as a routine means of surgical treatment of occlusive disease of the coronary arteries. Today it is one of the most commonly performed surgical procedures in the United States, yet its effectiveness in prolonging life, as compared with conventional medical therapy, has not been demonstrated conclusively (Braunwald 1983). Indeed, life extension was not the rationale for instituting the procedure in the first place; rather it was performed for the relief of intractable pain arising from narrowing of the coronary arteries, so-called angina pectoris. When the bypass operation was discovered to be effective for that purpose, the indications for performing it were quickly broadened from that of a therapeutic procedure to that of a (hopefully) preventive one. Asymptomatic men with coronary constriction are now being offered the procedure in spite of the fact that there is no convincing evidence of any possible benefit. Patients who have suffered a coronary occlusion are also being offered bypass operations with the hope of preventing a recurrence, although there is no sound evidence that the procedure is effective in preventing recurrences.

If medical efforts, either preventive or therapeutic, do not explain the decline in CAD deaths, then what does? Jeremy Stamler (1977) sees the decline in CAD deaths as the result of changes in lifestyle and, in particular, the increase in exercise among American males, the decrease in the use of cigarettes, and the decline in meat consumption. Stamler, a cardiologist at Northwestern University Medical School, also sees the more rapid decline in CAD deaths among the well educated as lending further support to the theory that changes in lifestyle are responsible for the decline rather than an improvement in CAD therapy. For example, he observes that the decline in CAD deaths among physicians has been significantly more rapid than for the population as a whole.

Efficacy of Cancer Treatment

Approximately 20 percent of American deaths are attributed to cancer. Therapy is based on a theory that assumes that the disease, at least at its outset, is localized, much as is an abscess or wound. Many physicians believe that the disease originates in a single cell, and that this cell, possibly as the result of damage to its genetic control system, undergoes rapid and disorganized growth. In recent years this genetic theory of cancer has become popular, and suspicion of industrial chemicals or naturally occurring carcinogens in food or air as the agents responsible for damage to the genetic material of the cell has strengthened. Once the cancer cell escapes its genetic control, its growth is thought to be relentless. Surgical therapy is based on the strategy of early detection of this aberrant cell or cells and removal of the growth before it has spread beyond its local origins. The theory is not new; in its basic form, it dates back to the nineteenth century.

The history of the surgical treatment of breast cancer is illustrative of the use of surgery as primary therapy for cancer. In 1894 William Halsted, a distinguished American surgeon (1852–1922), devised the modern treatment of breast cancer, the Halsted procedure. Not only is the breast removed (mastectomy), but the underlying tissues of the chest wall and the adjacent tissues are removed as well. The procedure is mutilating and often leaves patients psychological cripples. Nevertheless, it was rapidly and widely adopted and became the standard surgical treatment. More recently radiation therapy and chemotherapy have also been widely used in conjunction with surgery, but the mastectomy remains the mainstay of therapy for breast cancer. During the past few decades doubts have arisen regarding the wisdom of this radical and mutilating procedure. Modifications have been introduced that have limited surgery to the breast itself, and, even more recently, it has been proposed that only the cancer mass be removed from the breast, leaving the uninvolved breast tissue in place. Studies of this so-called lumpectomy show no increase in mortality as compared with women who have had the more extensive mastectomy. Among 1843 women with breast cancer, the overall survival rate for women who had not had total mastectomies was actually superior to that of women who had total mastectomies (Fisher et al. 1985). Two other randomized studies (in which patients were randomly allocated to lumpectomy or to mastectomy treatment) have confirmed this result (Sarrazin et al. 1986; Veronesi et al. 1981). Still, mastectomy remains the treatment most commonly prescribed not only for women with breast cancer, but is also sometimes advocated and used for women with lumpy or cystic breasts who might develop breast cancer. The evidence that this latter group is indeed at increased risk of cancer or that mastectomy will prevent such cancer remains controversial. Whatever the treatment, the fact remains that survival statistics for women with breast cancer have remained unchanged over the past eighty years (Wertheimer et al. 1986). That is, women today die of breast cancer at the same age as women in earlier decades.

The recognition that less surgery may often be better than more is not limited to female breast cancer. Evidence is now accumulating that the conventional amputation for cancer of the bone may not be superior to more limited procedures. Amputation of the cancerous extremity is particularly harsh treatment since many bone cancer patients are teenagers for whom amputation is socially disastrous (Consensus Conference 1985).

There is no debate regarding the observation that survival from first detection of cancer to the ultimate conclusion of the disease has gradually increased over the past three decades. But some dispute does arise from the interpretation of this observation. Improvement in survival has been widely attributed, both by physicians and the public, to improvements in therapy, yet some experts disagree. They believe that increased survival following diagnosis could well be the result of more intense medical surveillance, better diagnostic technology, and earlier detection rather than the result of more effective treatment (Boffey 1984). Such a result could occur if physicians made a more conscientious effort to search for occult or early cancers and if patients presented themselves more frequently for examination. Both events have occurred during recent decades. If this is the explanation for prolonged survival, then cancers would be discovered and treated at an earlier stage of their growth, the interval between diagnosis and treatment would increase, and there would be the illusion of longer survival.

There is indeed evidence that intense surveillance will uncover more cancer at earlier stages; but will this earlier discovery aid patients in extending their lives? It would be so only if available therapy were truly effective. A study of lung cancer was conducted among cigarette-smoking men. One-half of these men were assigned to a close-surveillance study in which their sputum was regularly examined for the presence of cancer cells, and they were given regular chest x-rays (Berlin 1984). Early results of this study were promising; as Dr. John Bailar, an epidemiologist at the Harvard School of Health, describes it:

> They found a series of interesting differences between the tested and control groups. The screened group had a lot more lung cancer. Everybody got excited. The lung cancers were at early stages and the patients had excellent survival rates. Everyone got really excited. It was all fine down until the bottom line: the numbers of men in the two groups who died of lung cancer were virtually identical. [Kolata 1985, p. 544]

Still another phenomenon could lead to an illusion of greater survival as a consequence of improvements in therapy. This results from what is known as "stage migration." As better diagnostic means become available, the wider extent of the disease is more accurately detected. Therefore, cases that with earlier, cruder diagnostic techniques appeared to be limited in spread, and therefore at an earlier stage of development, now are found to be more extensive and advanced. The longer survival of these "advanced" cases today, then, is only a result of greater facility in recognizing the advanced stage of the disease. One study at the Yale-New Haven Hospital has shown that this indeed was the explanation of what had appeared to be an improvement in the survival of patients with lung cancer (Feinstein, Sosin, and Wells 1985).

If, as a result of this more intensive detection effort, survival from diagnosis to death has been increased, might not surgical therapy have also prolonged lives? Which is it, earlier detection, better treatment, or both? If therapy were truly effective, then cancer patients would be expected to be dying at an older age than formerly. If, on the other hand, greater survival were the result of earlier detection of latent cancers, then the age at death of cancer patients would remain unchanged. The data on this point are quite clear; there has been no change in the age-adjusted cancer death rates throughout the fifty years during which such data have been available in the United States. As shown in figure 4.3, there has been a slight increase in overall cancer death rates, the increase explained mostly by lung cancer, which in turn is certainly the result of cigarette smoking (Bailar and Smith 1986).

What this means is that, at any given age, the risk of dying of cancer

FIGURE 4.3.
Mortality from All Malignant Neoplasms, 1950–1982

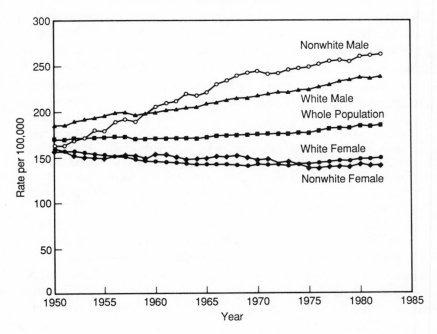

SOURCE: Reprinted, by permission of the publisher, from J. Bailar and E. Smith, "Progress Against Cancer?" *New England Journal of Medicine* 314 (1986): 1227.

is no different today than it was fifty years ago. True, the mortality rates of cancer at specific organ sites have changed—lung cancer, for example, has increased, stomach cancer has decreased—many, however, have remained unchanged. Other than for the role of cigarettes as a cause of lung cancer, the factors responsible for change in either direction or the frequency of cancer of other organs are largely unknown.

Many people will be surprised to find that there is really very little evidence whether cancer treatment prolongs life, shortens life, or has no effect at all. If that is the case, then why do patients undergo treatment? The answer is that desperate patients seek therapy and doctors provide it, with neither party demanding rigorous proof of effectiveness. Even the slightest chance of success appears to both patients and physicians to be preferable to doing nothing at all. As illustrated in the history of the treatment of breast cancer, most cancer therapy has been introduced into clinical practice and become established without thorough evaluation of effectiveness. The majority of cancer patients are both unlikely and unwilling to question the wisdom of therapy. Being desperate, they often seek even the most bizarre and patently unproven treatment.

In the absence of known effective therapy, a desire for even unproven therapy cannot be condemned, so long as patients or their families are not exploited in the process and the risks of therapy are not excessive. Still, the emotional and economic costs of prolonged hospital-based therapy, in the place of compassionate care in the home, needs justification.

I do not argue that cancer therapy is ineffective for all types of cancer; I do argue that the evidence of efficacy is limited and that cancer surgery, as with many other forms of medical treatment, has been far more radical and widely applied than necessary or useful.

In any case, the matter little affects the issue under examination here, the question of medical care and life expectancy. It is of limited importance because most cancer occurs among the elderly and therefore has little influence on life expectancy. It has been estimated that even if cancer were totally preventable or curable, the increase in U.S. life expectancy would be less than two years (1.39 years for white males and 2.05 years for white females, less for blacks [Dublin, Lotka, and Spiegelman 1949]). Since life expectancy has increased in the United States during this century by more than twenty years, cancer treatment could not have played, at the very most, more than a small role.

Obstetric Practices

Beyond any shadow of a doubt, there are many individual cases where obstetric surgery saves lives of mother, child, or both. While obstetric surgery undoubtedly contributed to the rapid decline in maternal mortality experienced over the past fifty years, there is evidence that it, as with so many other forms of medical and surgical therapy, is grossly abused today and therefore may no longer play an important role in the maintenance of a healthy population. We have an unfortunate tendency to overdo a good thing.

With American maternal mortality at the extremely low rate of less than one in ten thousand, a rate that continues to fall, is there any justification for cesarean sections to have increased at a rate of 300 percent over the past ten years? The procedure is by no means without risk to the mother; overall, the maternal mortality rate from cesarean section is probably three to five times higher than that of vaginal delivery—from one to two deaths per thousand operations (Danforth 1985). In 1983, 808,000, or about 18 percent of deliveries, were by surgical means in spite of the fact that authorities continue to decry so high a rate (Bottoms, Rosen, and Sokol 1980).

In studies of the effectiveness of surgical techniques for obstetric use conducted in several European countries, there was very little correlation between the frequency of obstetric surgery and perinatal mortality (Bergsjo, Schmidt, and Pusch 1983). The Netherlands, which has one of the lowest perinatal and maternal mortality rates in Europe, also has one of the lowest rates of operative delivery. At the Dublin National Maternity Hospital, the use of cesarean section in 1965 was equal to that in the United States, about 5 percent. In Dublin today it is still about 5 percent and the rate of perinatal mortality has dropped at a faster rate than in the United States (Danforth 1985). One American study demonstrates that children born in midwife-staffed birthing centers do as well or better than children born in a university hospital (Baruffi et al. 1984).

There appear no reasonable medical explanations for the obvious excess of obstetric surgery other than the convenience of the doctor, the patient, or to avoid charges of malpractice. While privately treated patients are significantly more likely to be delivered by cesarian section than are clinic patients, there is no significant difference in infant mortality rates among these two groups other than among the very small number of babies who weigh less than two pounds at birth (DeRegt et al. 1986).

Pediatric Care

Examination of the efficacy of pediatric treatment is of particular importance to our study since it is the fall in the death rates of infants and children that have been the most important element in explaining the increase in modern life expectancy. Death rates are characteristically greater among children than for any age group until advanced ages. Furthermore, the decline in children's deaths has been proportionately greater than for any other age group. To what extent has this been the result of improved medical care?

Undeniably, many childhood diseases are effectively treated and

FIGURE 4.4.
Death Rates for Children, Ages 1–14: 1900–1985

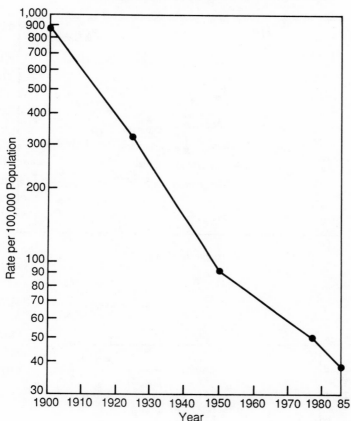

SOURCE: National Center for Health Statistics, Division of Vital Statistics.

lives are saved. Yet, for many reasons, I remain skeptical that an important part of the decline in children's deaths can be attributed to medical care. The major reason for skepticism is reflected in the data shown in figure 4.4, where death rates for U.S. children are shown for the years 1900 to 1985.

During the first half of this century, death rates for youngsters fell from almost 900 per 100,000 to less than 100 per 100,000. That represents a decline of almost 1,000 percent. That dramatic fall was mostly due to a decline in deaths resulting from infectious disease and occurred before effective therapy such as antibiotics became available.

Second, as will be described later in this chapter and as illustrated in the first portion of figure 4.5A, it is impossible to show any relationship

FIGURE 4.5.

Relation Between Infant Mortality and Doctor Population

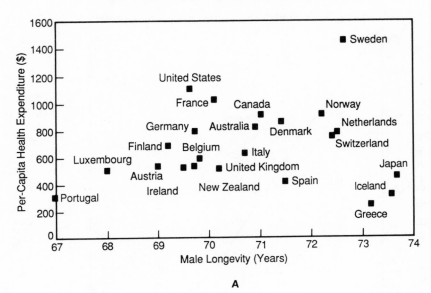

A

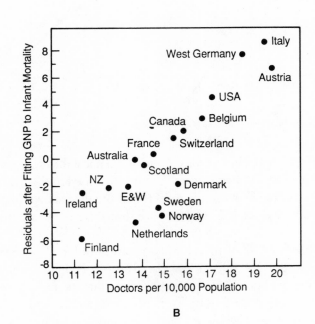

B

NOTE: Figure 4.5B reprinted, by permission of the publisher, from A. St. Leger, A. Cochrane, and F. Moore, "The Anomaly That Wouldn't Go Away," *Lancet* II (1978): 1153.

between expenditures for medical care and overall death rates. Indeed, as shown in figure 4.5B, infant mortality rates appear to show an inverse relationship with the number of doctors per capita in the country. That is, the more doctors available, the higher the death rate among children in that country. This result occurs after adjusting for the per-capita income of the country's population. While no explanation for this curious finding is available, the association is highly significant statistically (St. Leger, Cochrane, and Moore 1978).

Despite the lack of supporting evidence, the value of modern obstetric and pediatric care in the reduction of infant and perinatal mortality is widely and uncritically accepted. The 1976 report of the Committee on Perinatal Health, "Towards Improving Pregnancy Outcome," made specific recommendations for expanding maternal and perinatal medical care. Several ambitious studies were undertaken in order to test these recommendations. For example, the State Legislature of North Carolina provided $750,000 a year for five years to study the poorer counties of the state. The designated study areas were within two and a half hours driving distance of the medical centers of Duke University and the University of North Carolina, both of which became referral centers. Counties that were similar in ethnic and socioeconomic characteristics were chosen as control areas. Study and control areas had experienced similar neonatal mortality rates during the previous twenty years. Local practitioners in the study area were enthusiastic and cooperative. The study, now completed, reported that infant mortality did indeed fall in the study area when superior medical care was provided; however, infant mortality also fell to a slightly greater degree in the control area where no specific measures had been taken to improve pediatric or obstetric care (Siegel et al. 1985). This outcome was not an anomaly; the Robert Wood Johnson Foundation funded eight regional perinatal care centers. Mortality rates did not fall more in those centers than in control areas (McCormick, Shapiro, and Starfield 1985).

These findings suggest two conclusions: factors associated with lifestyle predominate in the determination of infant mortality rates and increasing the availability of expert medical care produces no detectable effect on infant survival.

Intervention Efforts

Several of the studies just cited are intervention studies—studies in which an aggressive effort is made to influence one particular disease (such as CAD) or some specifically vulnerable population (such as children). Other studies described in this section examine the health consequences following the provision of medical care to larger, less selected populations deprived of medical care because of economic barriers. Two such populations are the British lower social classes and the Navajo Indians of the American Southwest.

The view of medical care as a right, necessary to the preservation of life, was the principal motive behind the British adoption of the National Health Service (NHS) after World War II. It had long been observed that there was a strong socioeconomic gradient in mortality rates among the British social classes. This was assumed to be at least partly the result of differential access to medical care by members of different social classes. It was expected that with economic barriers to medical care removed, this gradient would disappear. Although utilization of medical services increased considerably following institution of the NHS after 1948, the differences in health among social classes remain as great now, forty years later, and actually appear to be widening (Marmot and McDowall 1986). The failure of Medicare and Medicaid to reduce the disadvantages in health outcomes among the elderly and the poor has also been observed in the United States (Benham and Benham 1975).

This failure of increased access to medical care to reduce differences in health among the social classes is consistent with the experience of those prepaid health plans that serve a wide spectrum of social classes; the differences in outcomes remain, even within the same medical facilities. For example, in studies of cancer patients seen and treated at identical clinics and hospitals in Boston, those of lower social class experienced consistently shorter survival. These differences were shown not to be the result of differences in tumor stage, age, or the specific kind of therapy (Lipworth, Abelin, and Connely 1970). This observation has been replicated in many communities, and with a great variety of cancer types; cancer consistently advances more rapidly in the poor than in the affluent and is less responsive to therapy. Differences in outcome are clearly not the result of differences in medical care (Savage et al. 1985).

82

Medical Care: Its Influence on Life Expectancy

Another ambitious and revealing intervention study was carried out in the late 1950s in a Navajo Indian population living on an isolated reservation in the southwestern part of the United States. The Indians were experiencing unusually high morbidity and mortality rates. In 1957 the Medical Department of the Cornell Medical School, together with the United States Public Health Service, undertook a six-year program in which modern medical care was introduced into the Many Farms reservation. The target population served numbered approximately two thousand. Previously the population had received only rudimentary medical care. Nutrition was adequate, and the water supply was considered to be of good quality at its source. Still, infant mortality rates were threefold higher than for the remainder of the United States. Tuberculosis was widespread.

The Cornell group provided a well-equipped medical facility, competent physicians, a "steady flow" of consultants, one Navajo teacher, and four Navajo auxiliary health workers. An air ambulance and radio-equipped vehicles for visiting nurses were available.

Surveillance was intense; over 90 percent of the population was seen at the central medical facility during the study, and two-thirds of the entire population were seen at least once each year.

During the study, there was a total of sixty-five deaths, fifty-two of which occurred among infants, who accounted for only 3.7 percent of the population. There was no reduction in the incidence of the pneumonia-diarrhea complex that was the most frequent cause of both illness and death among children. The investigators felt that there had been a "possible slight reduction in overall mortality" as a result of their effort, but mortality had been falling prior to the initiation of the study, and it was difficult to be certain whether improved medical care had provided any beneficial effect at all (McDermott, Deuschle, and Barnett 1972). There was, however, a definite reduction in the transmission of tubercle bacillus, as determined by the tuberculin skin test among young children when they entered school. There was also a marked reduction in the frequency of otitis media, or inner ear infections. Trachoma, a contagious eye disease, was unaffected by treatment, since the treated child was quickly reinfected upon return to the contaminated home environment.

Summary

Evidence reviewed strongly suggests that the availability of medical care in general has played little role in reducing death rates from their historically high levels to those found in modern societies. I do not mean to minimize the important contributions to health provided by modern and postmodern medicine or surgery in the treatment of certain diseases, but the effects of these therapeutics has contributed little to the overall decline in mortality rates. Others who have considered the issue have reached similar conclusions (McKeown 1976; McKinley and McKinley 1977). An important reason for this failure of medical care availability to affect mortality rates is that, while some remedies and procedures are clearly effective, physicians instinctively expand the indications for these remedies to many more persons than those for whom they are effective. I have elaborated on the example of antibiotics and cesarean sections, but to those could be added many other drugs, such as thyroid and other hormones, vitamins, and surgical procedures such as hysterectomy, prostatectomy, tonsillectomy, and, most recently, coronary bypass surgery. In each of these cases, the benefits to the few are overcome by the adverse effects that occur in the larger group for whom there is no benefit and where there exists a deleterious effect.

Unfortunately, that which is most noble about the medical profession, the ability to provide comfort and compassion, is rapidly being eroded in favor of increasingly sophisticated, mechanical, and dehumanized treatment of unproven benefit. Heroic means of treating the dying are consuming much of our medical resources while effective means of preventing illness and disease, which will be elaborated on in subsequent chapters, are being ignored.

5 The Rise and Decline of the Modern Family

Family life not only educates in general but its quality ultimately determines the individual's capacity to love. The institution of the family is decisive in determining not only if a person has the capacity to love another individual but in the larger sense whether he is capable of loving his fellow men collectively. The whole of society rests on this foundation for stability, understanding and social peace.

—MARTIN LUTHER KING, speech delivered at Abbott House, Westchester County, New York, October 1965

MOST PEOPLE have certain beliefs regarding the causes of our greatly enhanced modern life expectancy. Those beliefs are strongly influenced by the assumption that disease and/or health is largely determined by environmental and technical factors. Generally, most would cite some combination of improved nutrition, sanitation, and medical care to explain the fall in historically high death rates. Those assumptions form the basis for private and public health policies that are largely directed toward improvements in access to food, medical care, and the protection of the population against industrial chemicals or radioactivity.

In preceding chapters I have examined the evidence for these assumptions. Granting that some health benefits have been experienced as a result of improvements in the food and water supply, and that some specific medical therapies are efficacious, the evidence that these factors alone provide an explanation for the dramatic fall in death rates is inadequate. Furthermore, there is strong evidence that changes in personal behavior associated with improved sanitation and nutrition are as important as the quality of the air, food, and water.

85

In subsequent chapters we shall examine in greater detail just how changes in the behavior of modern populations do influence health and survival, but here we must start with an examination of the sources and determinants of this modern behavior, this lifestyle—the modern family. We shall also search for explanations for the recent decline in American health, particularly among members of the younger generations.

Cultural Patterns of Parenting

A child born into a premodern society has only a 50 percent chance of surviving to adulthood, while a child born into a postmodern family has better than a 95 percent chance of reaching adulthood. Therefore, if we are to understand the rise of modern health and life expectancy, we must focus our attention on the earliest period of life and on the changes in our attitudes toward childhood and in parenting behavior that may explain modern life expectancy. Furthermore, since there is a strong correlation between childhood death rates and those at all other ages, there is reason to believe that behavioral patterns established during childhood control health behavior throughout life.

Among various mammalian species, there is an enormous range in the competence of the newborn to fend for itself. Some are totally dependent at birth, while others are quite able to fend for themselves. None spends a longer period of dependency with a caregiver than the human infant. The relationship between child and family not only determines whether or not the child will survive, but also shapes the character, personality, attitudes, and values that will persist throughout life—the child's subsequent lifestyle. Our level of self-esteem, our trust and faith in others, our ability to control our impulses, to feel and express our feelings—all of these and more are shaped in the first years of life and strongly reflect the model of the caregiver and the relationship of the child to that caregiver. If the child cries, how does the mother respond? Does she smile, does she cuddle, does she care, or does she scold, threaten, or even worse, ignore? If parents are caring and respectful of their children, those children will be respectful not only of themselves but of others as well—they will be able to build effective support systems. If parents have been rigid, harsh, and authoritarian, the child will be harsh and authoritarian.

86

These parental patterns are transmitted at least partly through the style and form of language adopted by the mother in her treatment of the child. One example may be sufficient to clarify; consider two homes in which a child is playing noisily on the kitchen floor with pots and pans. One of these families is traditional and authoritarian in structure while the other is modern and individualistic. The telephone rings. In one home the mother says, "Shut up." In the other home the mother says, "Would you please keep quiet a moment, I want to talk on the phone." What do these two different experiences teach children? In one instance, the child is called upon to mindlessly obey. He or she is not called upon to consider the purpose of the request; there is no cognitive stimulation. In the other instance, the child is required to follow two or three ideas; he is asked to relate his behavior to a time dimension; he must think of his behavior in relation to its effect upon another person; his mind is stimulated by a more elaborate and complex command. The first mother is establishing a relationship based on fear. The second mother is establishing a relationship built on mutual respect. Failure to comply in either case is likely to be followed by characteristic means of forcing compliance. One mother will use physical force, for example, a slap, while the other will threaten to remove her love and esteem: "If you don't do that, Mama won't love you any more."

Through many such repeated experiences these two imaginary children will develop quite different personality patterns, one of which will be conformist and cognitively deprived, and inclined to the use of violence, whereas the other will be self-reliant and cognitively enriched (Hess and Shipman 1965). I know of no psychiatrist or psychologist who would disagree with these views. My thesis in this chapter is that parenting patterns associated with the modern nuclear family produce healthier children who are not only physically bigger and brighter, but are more resilient, more resourceful, and better survivors.

A History of Western Childhood

Throughout the traditional Christian world, the church held that the newborn child inherited the legacy of the fall from grace. Parental duty, therefore, required that the impulse-ridden child be subjected to the kind of discipline necessary to redirect the child's sinful instincts to more socially desirable goals. Discipline, particularly from the father, was harsh; "spare the rod and spoil the child."

This view of the basic unruliness of children and of the appropriate parental response is illustrated in the following quotation from a Pilgrim pastor, John Robinson:

> And surely there is in all children . . . a stubbornness, and stoutness of mind arising from natural pride, which must, in the first place, be broken and beaten down: that so the foundation of their education being laid in humility and tractableness, other virtues may, in their time, be built thereon. . . . For the beating and keeping down of this stubbornness, parents must provide carefully . . . that the children's wills and willfulness be restrained and repressed, and that, in time; lest sooner than they imagine, the tender sprigs grow to that stiffness, that they will rather break than bow. Children should not know, if it could be kept from them that they have a will of their own, but in their parents' keeping; neither should these words be heard from them, save by way of consent, "I will" or "I will not." [quoted in Demos 1972, p. 566]

It was accepted (and in some quarters, still is) that parents have every right to treat their children as property and as they alone see fit. Discipline was expressed physically in beatings and mutilation. Such practices were inflicted on kings and commoners equally; Frederick the Great and Henry the VI were said to have complained bitterly of being severely whipped as children (Radbill 1974). The term "whipping boy" is derived from the practice of using a surrogate to take one's beating. While Christianity specifically supported authoritarian training of children in order to produce conformity and obedience, this attitude toward children is almost universal under conditions of economic and social deprivation. The children of deprived and conformist families are seen primarily as serving the needs of the family, and the child's growth of self-awareness and individuality is inhibited for the same purpose.

The powerful social and political forces of the Enlightenment produced radical changes in the standards and goals of parenting behavior. Enlightenment philosophers encouraged rejection of passive dependence on traditional authority. If man is to survive in a disorderly and unpredictable world, they said, he must have his wits about him; he must be able to use reasoned judgment, a more flexible guide to a changing world than traditional authority. The model was Robinson Crusoe washed up and alone on a desert island.

Accordingly, child-rearing practices changed, slowly at first and primarily limited to the most highly educated classes. The child came to be seen as a *tabula rasa,* or blank sheet; it was the family's duty to provide gentle and affectionate guidance and those experiences conducive to the development of reason. There grew an enormous interest in the content of a proper education. This was the century in which John Locke's book on education was to outsell his now more highly regarded political treatises (Axtell 1968). In the eighteenth century, Jean Jacques Rousseau wrote an even more successful primer, *Emile,* to help fulfill this hunger for guidance on education (Rousseau 1979). Carlo Cipolla, professor of history at the University of California, quotes an eighteenth-century writer who observed, "Every week new writings on education appear . . . the rage this year is to write on education" (Cipolla 1975, p. 62).

The child, and childhood, gained a new respectability. The Enlightenment was the period for which the phrase "the discovery of childhood" was coined (Aries 1962). No longer was the child a "little adult" to be exploited economically and inducted into the workforce at the earliest possible age, sometimes as early as six; rather, children came to be seen as objects deserving of emotional investment rather than commercial exploitation. Bonds of affection replaced moral obligation as the cohesive force among family members.

The Rise of Romantic Love: The Modern Family

The modern view is that each individual is unique, and that those unique qualities should be cultivated. This view not only has consequences for the law but also produced a revolution in the relationships between the sexes. With individualism and affluence also came romantic love, which could not appear so long as individuals were considered as interchangeable.

> Young people growing up in twentieth-century North America take for granted certain assumptions about their future with the opposite sex, assumptions that are by no means shared by every other culture. These include that the two people who will share their lives will choose each other, freely and voluntarily, and that no one, neither family nor friends, church or state, can or should make that choice for them; that they will choose on the basis of love, rather than on the basis of social, family or financial considerations; that it very much matters which human being they choose and, in this connection, that the differences between one

human being and another are immensely important; that they can hope and expect to derive happiness from the relationship with the person of their choice and that the pursuit of happiness is entirely normal, indeed is a human birthright; and that the person they choose to share their life with and the person they hope and expect to find sexual fulfillment with are one and the same. Throughout most of human history, all of these views would have been regarded as extraordinary, even incredible. [Branden 1980, p. 15]

Considering the status of women in premodern society and the manner in which they are treated, it is hardly surprising that tender feelings between men and women were uncommon. Given the status of servant, with control over nothing, women could hardly be cherished and an object of love or affection. Not until the middle of the eighteenth century, McManners tells us, was it respectable in high society to be in love with one's wife, though it was not, of course, respectable to show it (McManners 1981, p. 454).

One might wish that there were some quantitative measure of the growth of affection, an "affection index." Such does not exist, but Edward Shorter suggests that the frequency with which women achieve sexual orgasm can be considered a measure of affection between couples. He quotes one survey, conducted in the United States in 1907, in which only one-fourth of women had experienced orgasm. By the time of the Kinsey report in the second half of the century, two-thirds of women claimed to reach orgasm at least a third of the time. Furthermore, far more women now say that they enjoy sex and do not feel exploited by the sex act. Only 5 percent of modern women said they would prefer sex less often, whereas in the 1920s two-thirds of women said that their husbands were too demanding (Shorter 1982, p. 253). We shall see later that this historical improvement in the relationship between sexes may, unfortunately, again be in decline and may well be an important factor accompanying the relative rise in morbidity in the United States.

Enlightened attitudes toward child-rearing did not occur uniformly throughout society; child-rearing practices followed economics. Not until the industrial system became increasingly productive in the early twentieth century and the populace sufficiently affluent could most families afford to have mother stay at home to care for her child. Resources are required to maintain children in a state of dependency until adulthood, resources that are not available in a premodern society. According to the U.S. census of 1870, one in eight children aged ten to fifteen was gainfully employed. By 1900, less than a century ago, one child in six was employed, and in southern mills of that time, one-third of the workers were children, many less than ten years old (Lesser 1985). As late as 1920, there were still one million American children aged fifteen and less who were fully employed.

Parenting Elsewhere in the Premodern World

The description of traditional parenting I have just presented is drawn from western European and North American experience. While the evidence regarding parenting in nonwestern societies is limited, that which does exist supports the view that the authoritarian behavior of premodern parents can be generalized and that economic conditions of scarcity lead to neglect and even harsh treatment of children. For example, in Sub-Saharan Africa, the parent's objective is "to produce an obedient and respectful toddler whose compliance with familial authority will be automatic" (LeVine 1981, p. 43). In South America, an observer writes:

> During the period when the baby is investigating the outer world it is almost continually in tears. Not only is it frightened by contact with strangers, but its mother leaves it more and more alone as she goes about her work. Formerly she had left the baby for hours; now she leaves him alone for a whole day. The result, as seen in doll-play observations, is that children are hungry for attention, extremely violent, and quarrelsome. [Henry 1944, p. 16]

Turkish parents "tend to treat their young so as to provide for the comfort of the parent rather than for the ego of either the parent or the child" (Olson 1981, p. 99). These observers attribute this general indifference to children to an overall lack of solidarity within the household, repressed hostility between husbands and wives, and the reluctance to share food in times of scarcity.

Swaddling, or the use of restrictive clothing for the infant, has been used throughout the world in a great variety of cultural settings—among ancient Romans and Egyptians, among the Japanese, and among the Navajo and Hopi Indians (Lipton 1965). Evidence exists that the main purpose of swaddling was to reduce the requirements for caregiving. Mothers throughout history and in many cultural settings have found that restricting the newborn's movement produces a sedative effect on the child. As I shall suggest in chapter 6, this parenting behavior is likely to contribute to learned helplessness and a high degree of vulnerability to stressors throughout the remainder of life.

In contrast with the restriction, confinement, and conformity imposed on infants by premodern mothers, modern mothers encourage their child's exploratory behavior. They greet with joy and encourage each new demonstration of developing abilities and continually stimulate the child's interest with toys, games, and their own voice and attention. Mothers are able to do this because they have fewer young children to attend to; have fewer responsibilities for wood or food gathering, water hauling, animals to care for, vegetable plots to care for, clothes washing to do by hand, and so forth. More important, however, is the affection of the mother for her child, her interest in raising a creative and self-reliant person.

My thesis is that such modern parenting behavior has had a major and generally unrecognized influence on the health and development of children, who are bigger, smarter, and more competent as children and adults.

How does this happen?

Maternal–Child Relationships

It is recounted in medieval histories that Frederick II, Emperor of Germany in the thirteenth century, became convinced that his native tongue would be the natural and universal language of all children if they were not exposed to other languages. To test this thesis, he ordered that a group of children be removed from their parents immediately after birth. He further ordered that they be cared for by nurses who were instructed to remain silent so that the infants would not hear the spoken human voice. The tyrant's expectation was that the children would spontaneously speak his native tongue. Instead, these children sickened and died (Salimbene 1949, p. 366).

More modern observations on human infants are entirely consistent with such an outcome. Infants develop poorly, and even die, if given food and warmth but are otherwise denied intimate contact with caregivers (Spitz 1945).

In one study, infants who were orphaned and placed in an institution at a very early age were separated into two groups. One group remained in the institution, the other group of children was placed in foster homes. At the end of the first year, the children placed in foster homes did better in every case, both mentally and physically, than did the control group. The institutionalized children were then, at the age of one, also placed in foster homes. Their performance and behavior improved but even at the age of five there were still deficits in comparison with the children who had been placed in foster homes at an earlier age. The psychic trauma of the first year of neglect was never overcome (Provence and Lipton 1962).

Throughout the literature of maternal deprivation, the importance of the first years of life is seen as paramount in establishing a normal and healthy personality. People who have been deprived of one parent during childhood have a greatly increased risk of many individual diseases, as well as of suicide and alcoholism (Chen and Cobb 1960).

Many questions related to defective or interrupted maternal bonding are yet to be answered. For example, are there periods of infancy in which the child is more sensitive to neglect than others? In what ways might the length of separation influence the child's development? Do the characteristics of the substitute caregiver influence the outcome, and if so, which characteristics? For example, how important is the intelligence of the adoptive mother in providing for a newborn? In the study just cited, the foster-home children displayed superior behavior and performance, but was that the result of the home environment, more intelligent caregivers, or simply the nurturing of a caring person? Some of these questions are addressed in the following study in which retarded institutionalized children were individually placed in the care of retarded hospitalized women.

Twenty-six one-year-old institutionalized children whose biological mothers had an average IQ of seventy and who were unable to care for their children were chosen for study. The children were significantly retarded. Half of the children were randomly selected and placed in a hospital ward of mentally retarded adults, but in a one-to-one relationship with an individual woman who adopted a motherly role. The other thirteen children were left in routine institutional care. Three years later, those children remaining in the original ward were found to have deteriorated and were now severely retarded, having lost an average of twenty-six IQ points. On the contrary, the children cared for by the retarded women were found to have gained twenty-nine points in their IQ. Thirty years later those who had been cared for by foster mothers were found to be self-supporting, and most had completed the twelfth grade. A few had completed one year of college. In contrast, the children who had remained on the original ward had completed at most the third grade and were institutionalized. A number were dead (Skeels and Dye 1966). This example illustrates the debilitating effect of neglect during childhood, and of the benefit to intellectual development of affectionate care even by retarded mothers. The example is indeed extreme, but other studies, to be cited, indicate that even very brief periods of isolation, particularly during early infancy, may leave the child's health significantly impaired.

Until recently, it was believed that the newborn could neither see nor hear very well. We now know that this is clearly not the case. Messages actually pass, in both directions, between mother and child beginning immediately after birth and, some people think, from before birth. In fact, it has been demonstrated that newborn infants can distinguish their mother's voice from others and will respond to poems their mothers read out loud before birth, but not to poems previously unheard (Kolata 1984).

Until recently, little scientific attention was directed to the importance of breast-feeding, or of the accompanying cuddling, warmth and touch of the mother's skin as determinants of the mother-child relationship or of the health of the child. The recognition of the importance of early mother-child "bonding," as it is now called, came in the midst of cultural and medical practices that tended to separate mothers from their newborn infants. As artificial milk preparations became available, it was fashionable for mothers to use these "formulas." They are, after all, considerably more convenient; the mother's presence is no longer required throughout the day. The mother is free to work or pursue social commitments if the baby can be nourished artificially.

In addition to the appearance of milk substitutes, a second innovation in birthing and newborn practices served to focus attention on the nature and significance of the maternal-newborn relationship. That was the increasing use of hospitals for delivery and early prenatal care. In the early part of this century, most Americans were born at home. Today home delivery is uncommon; birthing has become "medicalized."

Hospital delivery implies more than a change in location. Until recently, when trends have again changed, hospitalization also implied isolation of the mother from her child; usual practices required separation of the mother from her child for the first eight to twelve hours, in order to allow her to "rest."

These two postmodern phenomena, bottle feeding and hospital delivery, drew attention to the possible importance of early mother-child contact. How important is it? How much should there be? When should it start? How important are the first hours of life? Does breast-feeding have any importance to the newborn other than nutritional? Will the child thrive equally well on artificial formulas? The evidence of early attachment between mother and child, first derived from experimental studies on primates, has now been replicated in humans as well. We now know that human infants, as with other animals, derive enormous benefits other than nutrition from breast-feeding and its associated cuddling and nurturing.

Knowledge of the importance of the first hours and days to the normal development of the child and to the mother's commitment to the child's nurturing came late in medical history. Only in 1972 was it first reported that mothers who had extra contact with their children during the first hours after birth seemed to behave differently. They demonstrated significantly more soothing, fondling, and eye contact with their children even when examined one month after hospital discharge. At two years, mothers with extra child contact after birth spoke to their children with fewer commands, more questions, and more words per proposition (Klaus 1982).

In another study, 301 new mothers were randomly assigned to different postpartum nursing schedules. In the twenty-one-month follow-up period, only one instance of parenting disturbance required hospitalization among 134 infants whose mother had been roomed with her baby following delivery. Of the 143 mothers who had received routine visits from their child during the postnatal period, nine children were hospitalized for causes related to parenting (failure to thrive, abuse, neglect, or abandonment) (O'Conner 1977). These studies, demonstrating a longlasting and beneficial effect from increased mother-child contact during the very earliest hours of life, were important in setting policy for hospital obstetric and pediatric practices, but they also demonstrate the extreme sensitivity of the infant to the care given in the first hours of life.

These human experiences have their counterpart among farm animals. For example, separation of goats from their newborn kids for only an hour during the early postnatal period permanently affected maternal behavior in an undesirable manner. Workers at the Cornell animal behavior farm also discovered that if mother lambs are prevented from licking their newborn after birth, many of the lambs will be unable to stand on their legs and will subsequently die (Hersher, Moore, and Richmond 1958). "Gentling" of young animals will enhance their immune response when they are experimentally exposed to vaccination later in life. In one experiment, this enhanced immune response was noted in every animal tested (Solomon, Levine, and Kraft 1968).

These studies make abundantly clear the possible catastrophic effects on the health of the child that may follow abandonment and neglect. Earlier I discussed the prevailing attitudes toward young children found in premodern and impoverished societies, attitudes that often lead to abandonment and neglect. Almost certainly, these parenting practices are a major factor explaining the high infant morbidity and mortality rates found in those societies.

The Decline in Family Size

Premodern families who view their children as economic assets will optimize those assets by creating large families. Modern families who view their children as objects of love and affection, but with certain economic and emotional costs as well as benefits, will limit family size. Given these value systems, it is not surprising that family size is strongly associated with childhood health—that is, small sibships are healthier than large sibships. These same differences in parental values and in children's health occur among social classes as well, but to a lesser degree than among premodern and modern societies.

The young children of the large family are subject to more infections, more accidents, and a higher overall mortality rate than are children of small families. Children of large families show slower development of physiological functions. Their performance on intelligence tests and at school is inferior and juvenile delinquency rates are higher (Wray 1971). The interactions between family size and social class are complex. Figure 5.1 shows infant death rates for children of various social classes and family size. Social classes I and II are professionals, managers, and farmers. Social class III, shown in the middle panel, are clerical, sales workers, and foremen, while social classes IV and V are semiskilled workers, laborers, and domestic workers. Mortality rates are on the average lowest for children of social classes I and II, and highest among children of classes IV and V. Of equal importance is the consistent increase of mortality among larger families, regardless of social class; the larger the family, the greater the mortality rate. The single child of the lowest-class family has about the same chance of surviving the first year of life as do the children of large (five or more) families of professionals and managers

FIGURE 5.1.

Variations with Parity in Neonatal Mortality by Social Class

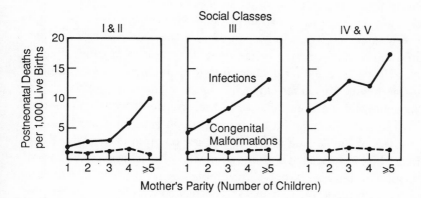

NOTE: Reprinted, by permission of the National Academy of Sciences, from J. Wray, "Population Pressures on Families: Family Size and Child Spacing," in *Rapid Population Growth*, ed. National Academy of Sciences, p. 411. Baltimore: Johns Hopkins Press, 1971.

(Wray 1971). It appears, then, that both small sibship size and high social class operate in the same direction.

A number of factors contribute to the small family's superior health experience. Unlike mothers of large families, mothers of smaller families delay childbearing until they are older, beyond the younger years when childbearing is more hazardous to mother and child. Still another reason is that the interval between births is greater, providing the child with a longer period of nurturing (Wray 1971). At the beginning of the nineteenth century, the average American woman bore six children. A third of all women had more than seven children. The average number of children born to women born between 1920 and 1924 was 2.7. In 1985 the average completed family had 1.85 children (Bureau of the Census 1975, p. 53). This smaller family size as a factor contributing to a reduction in infant mortality has undoubtedly played an important role in reducing infant mortality rates over the past century. The continuing decline in family size is thought to account for approximately 27 percent of the fall in infant mortality rates observed in the United States during the decade of 1955 to 1965 (Morris 1975).

Some consider that the decline in family size explains a major part of the fall in modern mortality rates (Reves 1985). That hypothesis is consistent with the observation that most premodern families, regardless of social class, have large families and that high mortality rates occurred equally among rich and poor alike (Shorter 1975, app. 1). Children of the wealthiest families died with the same frequency as those of the poor.

It was only when upper-class families began to cherish their children and limit family size that mortality rates first began to fall. When modern parenting practices spread to other social classes, those classes also experienced a decrease in infant and childhood mortality. In 1880, high income women, who generally married at a later age and spaced their children more widely, had only half the children of low income women (Degler 1980). This earlier decline in fertility among the more affluent is consistent with the earlier emancipation of women and greater use of contraception by the upper classes in the nineteenth century (Shorter 1973). The same observation has been made in England (Stone 1977).

Causes of the decline in family size are obscure; each of the characteristics that is associated with modernization has been proposed as an explanation for reduced fertility. The problem is a familiar one; all factors associated with modernization are also correlated with fertility decline— the two almost always occur together. The sense of self-efficacy, orientation toward time, social mobility (Kasarda and Billy 1985), and openness toward new experiences have all been suggested as factors that contribute to declining fertility (Fawcett and Bornstein 1973).

One commonly held view is that falling mortality rates themselves provide a feedback mechanism—that is, when parents become convinced that their children will survive and that it is no longer necessary to rear twice as many children as one wishes to have reach adulthood, reproductive behavior is altered so as to produce fewer children. Furthermore, there are economic barriers to large families that increase as modernization progresses. A longer period of dependency and a costly education create strong economic disincentives to the formation of large families (Birdsall 1983).

Another element that appears with modernization is a decline in the expectation that children will be the main source of support for people in their old age. Studies in Taiwan and the Philippines demonstrate that as education increases, expected dependency on children for support during old age also declines (DeVos 1985).

The means by which parents are able to limit fertility in a pretechnical age has been a matter of interest to generations of scholars, but there is little question that some means of control are available to even primitive populations. Delaying marriage is a common means of controlling fertility. Anthropological accounts of primitive societies reveal that abortion, infanticide, and postpartum abstinence are practiced and age-old means of fertility control (Hawthorn 1970). Although widely used, deliberate infanticide is not the only process that selects against unwanted children. Almost certainly, neglect is far more often used as a means of eliminating children than is the purposeful killing of infants. Those children who are most vulnerable to such neglect and death are those of high birth order, those who are misshapen, or those who are of the unwanted sex (Scrimshaw 1978).

Earlier Physical Maturation

It is commonly observed that children seem to be taller than they used to be, and recorded data reaching back to the eighteenth century document the point—children are much taller than they used to be. The data show that wherever modernization occurs, the size of children, both in height and weight, increases, and where modernization does not appear, children remain small. Of course, adults are also larger, but not to the same extent as are children.

Studies of the increased growth rate of children in modernized societies are quite extensive and consistent. Records are available, for example, for British, Japanese, and Swedish schoolchildren; Harvard freshmen; and Dutch military recruits (Tanner 1968). Boys of the upper social class are the tallest, whereas boys of the working class are consistently the smallest. An urban-rural difference also exists, with the advantage to the urban populations. Finally, family size is still another factor that influences children's size—the larger the family, the smaller the children are likely to be.

In general, physical size is associated with survival at all ages; that is, both low birth weight as well as short stature are associated with increased mortality rates. Birth weight below 2500 grams (about five and a half pounds) is far more common among children of low socioeconomic status. Yet when low-birth-weight children are born to middle-class families, they are indistinguishable from other children by the time that they start school. Indeed, the best indicator of whether a newborn is at high risk, because of low birth weight for example, is the socioeconomic status of the mother. Thus it appears that the deficits that do appear in such high-risk children are not determined by the low birth weight per se but by whether the child and family are able to compensate for the initial additional risk factor during the first few years of life (Kaye 1983). Fortunately, the frequency of low-birth-weight infants has been declining

TABLE 5.1

Age-Adjusted Mortality in Ten Years from Coronary Heart
Disease, Other Causes, and All Causes by Height

Height (cm)	No	10 year mortality percent (and relative risk*)		
		CHD	Other causes	All causes
≤ −168	2,290	5.8 (1.61)	6.5 (1.15)	12.2 (1.36)
−175	6,672	3.9 (1.14)	5.4 (1.02)	9.3 (1.08)
−183	6,433	3.5 (1.10)	5.1 (1.03)	8.6 (1.06)
>183	2,132	3.3 (1.00)	4.9 (1.00)	8.2 (1.00)
Total	17,527	4.0	5.4	9.4

* Adjusted for age and grade. 168 cm = 5 ft. 6 ins.; 183 cm = 6 ft.
NOTE: Reprinted, by permission of the publisher, from M. Marmot, M. Shipley,
and G. Rose, "Inequalities in Death—Specific Explanations of a General Pattern?" *Lancet* I (1984): 1005.

steadily over the past several years (Kessel et al. 1984).

Final adult height is also related to the risk of disease and death.
Since physical height is determined early in life, this phenomenon provides important evidence that health is determined by factors operating
early in life. Table 5.1 shows data collected from among 17,527 British
civil servants whose medical histories were followed for ten years to determine, among other things, the relationship between height and death
rates. Death rates were higher for the shorter men from coronary heart
disease and all causes of death. Men six feet tall (183 centimeters) had
one-third less mortality than did men who were less than five feet six
inches (168 centimeters). These rates were the result of confounding
height with social class only to a small extent. Although occupational
class was also strongly related to risk of death, the differences in height
among the occupational classes were small (Marmot 1984). An even
stronger influence of body height on mortality has been found in a Nor-
wegian study (Waaler 1984).

Deprivation Dwarfism

How can the increased growth and ultimate size of modern children
be explained? One popular explanation is improved nutrition. Although
that may indeed be part of the explanation, it does not alone explain all

of the modern improvement in stature. After all, children of this generation are taller than those of the last; were our parents undernourished? Were the children of the ruling families of Europe who were until recently also small also undernourished? Another possible explanation is related to better nurturing of the modern child. Children raised in an affectionate environment grow more rapidly and reach greater size as adults. On the other hand, there is ample evidence that emotional deprivation can have a deleterious effect on growth. As so often happens in biology and medicine, we gain insights into phenomena from their abnormal or excessive operation. In its extreme form, the effects of emotional deprivation on growth are known as deprivation dwarfism.

A remarkable natural experiment demonstrating the influence of nurturing on growth occurred shortly after World War II. Elsie Widdowson, a British nutritionist, noted that children in two orphanages in occupied Germany showed very different growth patterns even though they were both fed the same basic rations. She also noted that the matron in charge of the orphanage called Vogelnest, where growth was superior, was kindly and admired by the children, whereas children at the orphanage called Bienenhaus, who were doing poorly, were in the charge of a matron, Fraülein Schwarz, who was described as a strict disciplinarian. A group of children at Bienenhaus who were favored by the matron appeared to grow somewhat better than the others, but not as well as the children at Vogelnest. It so happened that the kindly matron at Vogelnest left for other employment. It was decided to switch the strict matron, Fraülein Schwarz, from Bienenhaus to Vogelnest, where the children had previously done so well under the care of the kindly matron. At the same time, the rations at both orphanages were supplemented with bread, jam, and orange juice. Subsequently, growth of children at Vogelnest, which had been superior, began to fall behind, in spite of the increased rations, whereas the children at Bienenhaus, which now had a new matron, accelerated. Changes in weight, which exactly paralleled height, are shown in figure 5.2.

Subsequent observations confirm the influence of the caregiver's affection on children's growth. Stunted and deprived children placed in a hospital setting and warmly cared for will show a growth spurt. The neuroendocrine effect is mediated through changes in the secretion of growth hormone (Martin 1973).

Phenomena similar to deprivation dwarfism are widely recognized in animal husbandry and laboratory animals. Farmers know that gentle handling of animals can have profound effects on growth. The same is true of experimental animals, including the familiar laboratory rat. Many

FIGURE 5.2.
Growth of Children at Two German Orphanages

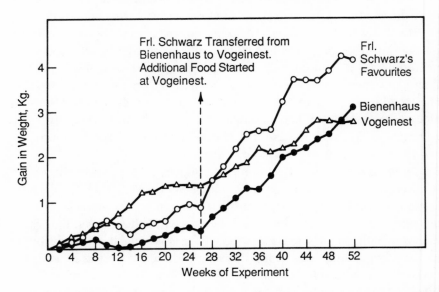

NOTE: Reprinted, by permission of the publisher, from E. Widdowson, "Mental Contentment and Physical Growth," *Lancet* 1 (1951): 1317.

an experiment has been misinterpreted because this factor was ignored and the effects of handling confused with that of the treatment (Bernstein and Elrick 1947; Ruegamer, Bernstein, and Benjamin 1954; Weininger, McClelland, and Arima 1954).

Family Cohesiveness

The smaller and more affectionate modern family has been a powerful factor contributing to improved health of individuals and to the historical fall in mortality rates. The recent increase in morbidity, particularly among children, may also be explained by changes in the postmodern family, changes in the direction of increasing family instability and decreasing family commitment and responsibility.

Until recent decades, the nuclear family with the father as breadwinner and the mother as keeper of house and children was almost ex-

FIGURE 5.3.
Divorce in the United States, 1925–1981

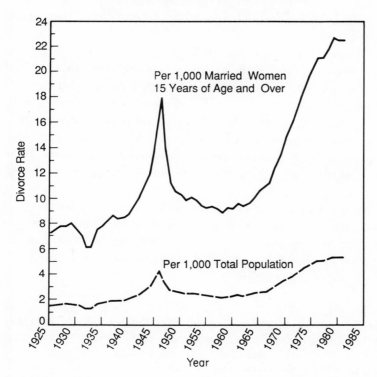

NOTE: Reprinted, by permission of the publisher, from *Monthly Vital Statistics Report* 32 (1983): 1.

clusively the norm. During my own childhood, divorce was considered scandalous; it was not spoken of. That has clearly changed, as shown in figure 5.3, which provides data on the rate of divorce in the United States over the period from 1925 to 1981. Following the war and the transient high divorce rate associated with the return of soldiers to their homes, the rate again fell to pre-war low levels. Since the postwar period, there has been a steady increase in divorce, rising from less than 10 to more than 20 percent of all marriages in 1980. For the youngest age groups, the risk of divorce from a first marriage now approaches 50 percent. Although divorce rates appear to have leveled off during the past few years, they are still higher than those of any other country, 5.2 per thousand population (Kitson, Babri, and Roach 1985).

The effect of this rising divorce rate on the number of one-parent families is predictable enough; from 1970 to 1984 the percentage of children living with two parents fell from 87.1 to 74.3, whereas the percentage of children in one-parent families rose from 12.9 to 25.7; in other words, the number of one-parent families has doubled since 1978. Fifteen million children live in homes without their fathers (Hanson and Sporokowski 1986).

Of all single-parent families, the largest category are those headed by divorced mothers (36.8 percent), the second largest by never-married mothers (24.4 percent). The number of children living with fathers alone has more than doubled since 1970. The decrease in two-parent families over these fifteen years conceals the large number of children of two-parent families who are living with one parent who is not their natural parent, inevitably larger now than earlier (Hanson and Sporokowski 1986). The often-hostile relationships that exist between stepparents and stepchildren are only too well known.

The stress of divorce and the influence of the conflict that precedes separation take a large toll on the health of children. Studies show that children from divorced families as a group perform less well than children of two-parent families on a wide variety of academic, social, and health measures (Guidubaldi et al. 1986).

> One-parent children, on the whole, show lower achievement in school than their two-parent peers. . . . Among all two-parent children, 30 percent were ranked as high achievers, compared to only 1 percent of one-parent children. At the other end of the scale, the situation is reversed. Only 2 percent of two-parent children were low achievers—while fully 40 percent of the one-parent children fell in that category.
>
> There are more clinic visits among one-parent students. And their absence rate runs far higher than for students with two parents, with one-parent children losing about eight days more over the course of the year.
>
> One-parent students are consistently more likely to be late, truant, and subject to disciplinary action by every criterion we examined, and at both the elementary and secondary levels. . . . one-parent children are more than twice as likely to give up on school altogether. [Kettering Foundation report, 1980 quoted in Moynihan, 1986, pp. 92–93]

Increasingly, children are being subjected to a second divorce. Statistics from the 1980 census indicate that a child born in 1983 will have a 40 percent chance of experiencing a parent's second divorce by the time he or she is eighteen. The children of these twice-divorced parents are often seriously disturbed (Wallerstein and Kelly 1980).

The impact of divorce and family instability on the health of children is not yet well accepted or recognized, yet a wealth of circumstantial evidence substantiates permanent harm to children psychologically, educationally, and economically. For example:

1. Children of single-parent families will, as a group, achieve less education than those of two-parent families. We shall see later that education itself strongly influences health.

2. Children of single-parent families will have experienced the pain and anxiety of separation and loss of a parent. We shall see in chapter 6 that loss of a parent, particularly at an early age, may leave deep psychological scars that will adversely and permanently influence the child's health. This effect will be very much modified by, for example, the nature of the loss (death or divorce), by the age of the child, the nurturing and caring qualities of the remaining parent, visitation rights, and so on.

3. Single-parent families are less affluent than two-parent families. In addition, then, to the pain and suffering associated with divorce, the children of divorce will as a whole also confront the stress of reduced economic advantages. The divorce system operates to reward the former husband and penalize the former wife and her dependent children; they are in general 73 percent poorer than they were during the marriage (Weitzman 1985).

4. Observations of health among various ethnic groups strongly suggest that members of those cultures where family cohesiveness is high also have improved health. For example, mortality rates among Jews, Japanese, and Chinese are traditionally lower than among members of other ethnic groups (Frerichs, Chapman, and Maes 1984).

Some sociologists deny that increasing family instability can be shown to have deleterious effects on the child. If this is true, some other explanation will have to be found for the overwhelming evidence that subjective and objective well-being of our children is in decline. In the twenty years from 1960 to 1980, high-school seniors showed a steady decline in Scholastic Aptitude Test scores. In the same period, delinquency rates rose by 130.8 percent and suicide rates rose by 139.5 percent (Uhlenberg and Eggebeen 1986). While the direction of causation among these phenomena is difficult to establish, the weight of evidence reviewed in this chapter supports the view that the weakening of family bonds is unhealthy for the child. Are these psychological consequences of divorce, separation, or "modern marriage" on children likely to persist into adulthood? In an extensive review of the subject, two psychologists from the University of Texas found that the literature as a whole suggests permanent damage to these children. Their conclusion: "The increase in the proportion of adults who are children of divorce in the next few decades will lead, in the absence of countervailing influences, to a steady and non-trivial decline in the overall level of well-being of the American adult population" (Glenn and Kramer 1985, p. 911).

Parents of conventional two-parent families cannot remain smug about their children being protected from the damaging consequences of divorce—there is reason to believe that with the increasing prevalence and visibility of divorce, anxiety about parental loss also affects children of stable families. One ten-year-old New York child told of the effect the movie *Kramer vs. Kramer* (about a couple undergoing divorce) had on her: "My parents had a fight the other day, and my mother walked out of the house. I thought to myself 'This is it!' and I cried and cried. But she had just gone next door to the neighbors'." In the same study, a fifth-grader said, "We're one of those families that arn't divorced," adding after a pause, "at least, not yet" (Winn 1983, p. 136).

Teenage Pregnancy and Illegitimate Births

A second ominous phenomenon of American family life that also may do much to explain faltering infant morbidity and mortality rates is the increasing frequency of teenage pregnancies, a large number of which are illegitimate.

Teenage pregnancy rates among nations are strongly associated (negatively) with economic development—the higher the level of economic development, the lower the teenage birth rate. In this sense, the recent experience of the United States is highly anomalous. American rates resemble those of still modernizing countries such as Hungary and Romania and are far higher than those of countries at equivalent levels of development (see figure 5.4). As shown in the figure, the U.S. rates are increasing while those of other developed countries are decreasing. These observations regarding U.S. teenage fertility are influenced only to a small extent by the black population, whose rates of teenage pregnancy exceed those for whites. However, white rates also very much exceed those for other developed countries. Why is this? Differences in teenage sexual activity do not explain the differences in rates of pregnancy; in fact, Swedish rates of teenage sexual activity are greater than for the United States. Differences in teenage sex education and in the use of birth control are the important explanatory variables (Jones et al. 1985).

FIGURE 5.4.

Teenage Pregnancy Rate per Thousand Women Aged 15–19, by Country, 1980–1981

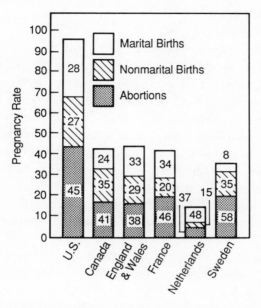

NOTE: Reprinted, by permission of the publisher, from E. Jones et al., "Teenage Pregnancy in Developed Countries: Determinants and Policy Implications," *Family Planning Perspectives* 17 (1985): 56.

Although the rate of illegitimacy fell throughout the first part of the twentieth century (Shorter 1982), since 1940 the numbers of illegitimate births have grown almost explosively, particularly among teenagers. White teenager pregnancy occurring out of wedlock increased from 8 percent in 1940 to 20 percent in 1970 and by 50 percent again during the 1970s (O'Connell 1980). The problem is even greater among young black women—86 percent of all black teenage mothers are single compared to a third of white teenage mothers. In 1980 there were 134,000 illegitimate black and 131,000 illegitimate white children born in the United States. To me this is not a moral problem; it is a health problem. Fetal and infant death rates among illegitimate children are twice those of legitimate rates.

Child Abuse

Deliberate infanticide is now probably rare in modern societies.*
Child neglect and abuse are tragically common, but the magnitude of
the problem cannot be adequately estimated. For one thing, the definition
of "abuse" lacks precision; what may be abuse to one parent may be
appropriate disciplinary measures to another. Still another problem is
discovering the crime. Child abuse occurs in the privacy of the family;
even those parents who are the worst child abusers are aware of societal
disapproval. Abuse comes to light only when physical evidence is flagrant
and the child is brought for medical treatment, or when a teacher or
neighbor brings injuries to the attention of the police. For this reason,
the prevalence of abuse is likely to be underestimated—we see only the
tip of the iceberg.

Severe psychological abuse is probably more common than physical
abuse. Pediatricians have long recognized children who with no apparent
disease fail to thrive, the "failure-to-thrive" syndrome. It is not known
just how commonly this syndrome occurs. In its extreme form, such
children may reach medical attention, particularly when there is
also physical abuse. More moderate cases undoubtedly escape medical
attention.

At the greater extreme of abuse are the too frequent instances of
flagrant brutality, the so-called "battered child" syndrome. The following
is a typical case history:

> A female child aged twenty months was admitted to the hospital with
> the classic syndrome. There were numerous bruises of different ages on
> all parts of her body. The child was dwarfed, being below the third percentile
> in length and weight. Her skull circumference was below the mean. She
> had a severe iron deficiency anemia. Radiological survey showed two recent
> fractures of the skull, probably of different dates. There were two fractured
> ribs, probably suffered three weeks before the time of the radiograph.
> On admission, the child showed notable "frozen watchfulness." She
> did not raise her head or move her hands in any useful way. She was
> entirely silent, neither crying nor cooing. The only exception to this be-
> havior was when she was approached by a male adult: she would fixate

* Infanticide does exist in covert form; many deaths among hospitalized children with congenital
malformations are the result of deliberate neglect by medical professionals (Duff and Campbell
1973; Weir 1984).

him and, as he picked her up, she would utter a brief piercing scream.

The mother, who was 21, had been harshly reared in another country. She had conceived out of wedlock, and had been deserted by her fiancé when she became pregnant. The mother was found to be suffering from pulmonary tuberculosis and to be pregnant by her second spouse. She was an inadequate weak woman who refused to visit the child in hospital. [Ounsted, Oppenheimer, and Lindsay 1974, p. 448]

This clinical example illustrates many of the risk factors for child abuse; the mother was unmarried, a teenager at the time of conception, and of lower social class. A single parent is more than twelve times more likely to abuse a young child than is a parent of a two-parent family. Living with a stepparent does not improve the child's situation—a child living with a natural parent and a stepparent is forty times more likely to be abused than is a child living with two natural parents. A mother who is less than nineteen years old is at least seven times more likely to be abusive of her child than an older mother (Daly and Wilson 1985). Although there has been controversy regarding the role of social class as a determinant of child abuse, evidence is now emerging that children of working-class families are at greater risk of abuse than children of professional families (Pelton 1978).

Whatever the causes, child abuse is now common in the United States. One expert estimates that somewhere between one in one hundred and one in ten children are seriously abused: "Ten percent of children live through extremes of wretchedness" (Oliver 1978). In a national survey, 3.8 percent of all children aged three to seventeen were victims of "severe or abusive violence" (Straus, Gelles, and Steinmetz 1980). While the National Study of the Incidence and Severity of Child Abuse found 77,000 cases of child abuse per year reported to U.S. hospitals, household surveys demonstrate numbers ranging from 1 to 4 million cases per year (Hampton and Newberger 1985). Children bear physical and emotional scars of these brutal experiences throughout their lives. Abused children have been shown to have higher rates of drug and alcohol abuse, criminal behavior, psychiatric disturbances, and juvenile delinquency (Gelles 1985). Clearly, here is a health problem crying for resources. While illegitimacy is generally viewed as a moral and/or social problem, it is as much or more a health problem, one that is growing to epidemic proportions. While billions are spent to remove probably harmless chemicals or radionuclides from the environment or in expensive, heroic, but often inhumane efforts to save the dying elderly, little is done to mitigate this growing tragedy that exists among us—a hidden holocaust.

Summary

The search for causes of disease and death tends to focus on conditions surrounding the onset of disease. Childhood conditions or experiences that may predispose to disease and be predictive of survival following disease onset are rarely investigated. In this chapter we have examined the crucial role of the relationship between caregiver and child in determining the developing personality and subsequent behavioral patterns. We have seen that personal efficacy and mutual trust are far more likely to develop in children whose parents care and nurture and who perceive their children not as economic investments but as cherished members of the family. In subsequent chapters we shall see that these behavioral patterns play an important role in determining health.

What have we learned that may shed light on the troubling evidence of declining health of the U.S. population? Why are we falling behind other postmodern countries, and, specifically, what might this have to do with child-rearing patterns? Just as the growth of the affectionate nuclear family was associated with improvements in health, deteriorating family relationships of the past several decades may well be associated with a relative decline in health, particularly among children and teenagers. As the modern nuclear family has come unglued, crime, suicide, and drug use have soared, just as have divorce and teenage pregnancy while scholastic achievement has declined. These associations and causal relationships have yet to be widely appreciated.

6 Stress, Resilience, and the Hopelessness–Helplessness Syndrome

> Just a little acid bath for the linings to round off the day ... the usual day in New York—the whole now-normal thing keeps shooting adrenalin into the body, breaking down the body's defenses and winding up with the work-a-daddy human animal stroked out at the breakfast table with his head apoplexed like a cauliflower out of his $6.95 semispread Pima-cotton shirt, and nosed over into a plate of NO-Kloresto egg substitute, signing off with the black thrombosis, cancer, kidney, liver, or stomach failure, and the adrenals ooze to a halt, the size of eggplants in July.
>
> —TOM WOLFE, 1968

THIS QUOTATION reflects two widely prevalent views of stress: one is that stress is harmful to health; the other is that our postmodern society is a highly stressful one. How much truth is there in these assertions? In this chapter we shall review the literature on stress, disease, and death. I conclude, with Wolfe, that there is incontrovertible evidence that stress can kill. The other assertion, that ours is a highly stressful society, is one that I shall challenge. On the contrary, I believe that one of the important reasons for the lower mortality rates in modern society is that we have largely learned how to manage and control stress, both on a personal and on a societal basis.

What Is Stress?

The difficulty in assessing the importance of stress to health is that there is no agreement on a definition of stress; nor do we have any adequate measure of levels of stress that exist in people. Although the term has been in widespread medical use since its introduction some thirty years ago, its meaning is still confused. Hans Selye (1983), the pioneer investigator of the physiology of stress, refers to stress as "a nonspecific response of the body to any demand." In common usage, the word is sometimes used to refer to the external source of stress, at other times to the physiological and psychological response. For example, in the Wolfe quotation, both elements appear; the external source of stress ("overcrowding," "noises,") and the pathological response ("head apoplexed," "adrenals oozing to a halt"). Which do we mean when we say "stress," the external source, the internal response, or both? And when we say that modern society is more stressful than life in premodern society, which do we mean, that the external sources of stress are greater than in premodern society, or that we are more vulnerable than our traditional ancestors?

Some writers have suggested that this confusion be resolved by referring to the environmental source as the "stressor" and the response as the "stress," or "strain." I prefer to use "distress" to describe the physiological and psychological response.

Stress Versus Challenge

Still another difficulty with the concept and understanding of the relationship of stressors to health is that we have such a one-dimensional view—we consider only those stressors that are undesirable, excluding those experiences that are desirable or challenging. Clearly, events or conditions that for some are stressors are, for others, challenging. We all have in some degree the desire to participate in struggle, to be challenged. This drive may express itself passively in games, by witnessing theatrical drama or sports, events in entrepreneurial activity, or, in its most violent form, in war. Why else do we seek pleasure in riding roller coasters except to experience the exposure to danger with the expectation of overcoming a challenge? In the same way, the New York environment described by Wolfe as stressful also has for many an enormous attraction, challenging millions of people who claim that they could not happily live elsewhere. They find the noise, the bustle exhilarating. Others are revolted. The difference between stressor and challenge is at least partly a matter of the individual's competence, experience, and coping skills. If people see new conditions as within their ability to cope,* they view them as challenge. If people believe these conditions are likely to exceed their coping skills, then these conditions will be perceived as frightening or distressing.

Studies of many of the world's cultures reveals that members of modern and achievement-oriented cultures are stress-seeking, not stress-avoiding.

> Outstanding creative achievement involves a step into the unknown, getting away from the obvious and the safe. It involves being different, testing known limits, attempting difficult jobs, making honest mistakes, and responding to challenge. All of these behaviors are part of the definition of stress-seeking. [Torrance 1968, pp. 195–96]

Life in a society of scarcity, whether it be in eighteenth-century London, an African village, or in the shantytown ghetto of a modern city, debilitates psychological defenses. Furthermore, these defenses are often crippled from the very beginning of childhood by a culture that denies the individual a sense of autonomy and psychological strength. The traditional child is taught that bad outcomes are the result of forces beyond control, that life must be lived in the present, since, in an incalculable world, individual effort counts for naught. Such a belief system is not irrational in a culture of scarcity; on the contrary, in a society where there are inadequate resources with which to defend against stressors, a useful psychological defense is to view circumstances as uncontrollable and oneself as helpless—the very attitudes found in premodern cultures. The psychological price paid for this sense of impotence and helplessness is apathy and depression. In a society marked by scarcity,

---

* Our psychological strategies for managing and moderating stressors, whether internal or external, are referred to as coping skills, and I shall have more to say about these later; suffice it to say here that there are successful means of coping that contribute to and protect psychological health—for example, confiding in others and seeking information—and unhealthy means—for example, drug abuse and violence—which shall be described in chapter 8. The great value of social support systems ("valuable others") is discussed in chapter 7, while the cognitive skills necessary to coping are considered in chapter 9.

where hopelessness and threats are both present in abundance, disease and death will flourish.

To sum up, whether altered conditions are viewed as threatening or challenging and, whether the consequences contribute to personal growth or to apathy and despair is the result of the interaction of two factors: the magnitude and quality of the external stressor and the capacity of the individual to cope. Distress, then, is that which "occurs when there are demands on the person which tax or exceed his adaptive resources" (Lazarus 1976, p. 47). Demands may be external, as in many of the examples to be cited later in this chapter, or may arise from conflicting internal demands, as when personal values clash—for example, a soldier's loyalty to his comrades and his self-protective instincts.

As with the response to most other noxious agents, people differ greatly in their vulnerability to stressors, but here again, we have only the most primitive means of assessing the coping skills of particular individuals. Great differences in coping skills do exist, and childhood experiences and education are important factors in explaining these differences. The common view that distress in human populations increases with modernization is almost certainly wrong; modern society provides a number of defenses against stress, most of all by endowing the individual with adequate coping skills, but also through the provision of increased security protection against emotional, economic, or physical disaster.

Learned Helplessness

Our coping skills are for the most part learned. We can be taught to be vulnerable—to be helpless—just as we can be taught to be resourceful and resilient. In the 1930s, Curt Richter, a psychologist at the Johns Hopkins School of Medicine, made some experimental observations that provide the foundation for the current clinical interest in hopelessness. He noted that when wild rats had been held tightly in the hand and persistently squeezed prior to being placed in a water tank, they displayed dramatically shortened survival times. Normally animals placed in these jars would swim until exhausted, usually in sixty hours. However, when pretreated by being tightly and unremittingly held, the animals swam poorly and drowned within a matter of minutes or at most a few hours.

Yet if the animals were intermittently released during this pretreatment period, they were able to survive in the water for near-normal periods of time.

Richter's interpretation of these observations was that the persistent and unrelenting grasping of the animals had created in them a sense of hopelessness and apathy. The animals had, in effect, been taught that there is no escape from external threats, no matter how much they should struggle. Therefore, when they were placed in the water jars, they quickly lapsed into a state of helplessness and died quickly. When the pretreatment had included an occasional release of pressure, the animals behaved as if they believed that struggle would eventually have a successful outcome. Richter compared this behavior with that seen in premodern people who believe that they have been hexed in voodoo rituals and who often die as a result; when confronted with insuperable forces, they become apathetic and lose the will to live.

The experimental psychologist Martin Seligman (1975) has done some remarkable laboratory investigations with animals under conditions designed to simulate and study helplessness in humans. His classical experiment involved training dogs to avoid electric shock by placing them in a box constructed in such a way that they could escape the shock by jumping over a barrier. Since the shock was preceded by a sound, normal dogs quickly learned to avoid the shock by jumping over the barrier. Some of the dogs, however, had first been subjected to shock training in a hammock from which there was no escape or by means of other control. Dogs pretreated in this manner behaved in an unexpected way. Seligman describes the outcome in the normal and in the pretreated dogs in the following words:

> When placed in a shuttle box, an experimentally naive dog, at the onset of the the first shock, runs frantically about until it accidentally scrambles over the barrier and escapes the shock. On the next trial, the dog, running frantically, crosses the barrier more quickly than at the preceding trial; within a few trials it becomes very efficient at escaping, and soon learns to avoid the shock altogether. After about fifty trials, the dog becomes nonchalant and stands in front of the barrier; at the onset of the signal for shock, it leaps gracefully across the barrier and never becomes shocked again.
>
> A dog that has been given inescapable shock showed a strikingly different pattern. This dog's first reactions to shock in the shuttle box were very much the same as that of the naive dog: it ran around frantically for about thirty seconds. But then it stopped moving. To our surprise, it lay down and quietly whined. After one minute of this, we turned the shock off; the dog had failed to cross the barrier and had not escaped the shock. On the

next trial, the dog did it again; at first it struggled a bit, and then, after a few seconds, it seemed to give up and to accept the shock passively. On all succeeding trials, the dog failed to escape. This is the paradigmatic learned-helplessness finding. [1975, p. 22]

This experiment has been replicated under a great variety of conditions and with a variety of animal species, including human volunteers.

Some clinicians have described similar behavior in their patients who have apparently succumbed to a state of apathy and helplessness. In fact, all physicians know that the will to live is crucial in overcoming serious illness or in recovering from surgery. The opposite is also true: patients who are pessimistic about outcomes will often not survive.

The sense of helplessness often appears in vulnerable individuals as a consequence of serious loss. Psychiatrist Arthur Schmale (1972) referred to this as the helplessness-hopelessness syndrome, which he defines as follows:

> Helplessness is a feeling of being deprived, let down or left out which is perceived as coming from a change in a relationship about which the individual feels powerless to do anything. The gratification which was lost is something without which the individual feels he cannot go on.
> Hopelessness is defined as a feeling of frustration, despair or futility perceived as coming from a loss of satisfaction for which the individual himself assumes complete and final responsibility and nothing more can be done that will undo the failure. [p. 23]*

According to Schmale's definition, both of these concepts appear to represent a mental state that arises as a result of a discrete event, particularly a loss (of job, friend, relative, property, pet, and so on). Feelings of helplessness may appear not only as a response to stress or threatened loss, but may constitute the pervasive or learned response to the common tribulations and frustrations of everyday living. Children of authoritarian families are taught this response pattern. The parenting strategy adopted by such families is "do what I tell you to do, and don't ask why." A child's failure to comply is met with punishment instead of with explanation. Such children never learn how to cope effectively or how to control stressors; they learn passive acquiescence, and with that comes helplessness and resignation: "It is the will of God." This explains, in part, why natural disasters take such a high toll in premodern countries.

Can the sense of hopelessness be fatal? Almost certainly it can.

---

* The distinction between these two concepts, in my mind, lacks precision. Similarly, the distinction between these concepts and those of "meaninglessness," "powerlessness," and "alienation" are not clear (Travis 1986), nor is it clear how all of these are related to clinical depression.

Stress, Resilience, and the Hopelessness–Helplessness Syndrome

When massive threats to the integrity of the individual appear inescapable, death can follow, and often quickly. "Voodoo death" is apparently an example of this. Here individuals, so thoroughly convinced by their religious beliefs that their situation is hopeless, become resigned to death and in fact may die. For more than one hundred years firsthand reports have been published by scientifically trained people detailing "voodoo" deaths among individuals who believe themselves "hexed" and doomed to die. According to one account:

> the man who discovers that he's being hexed by an enemy is indeed a pitiable sight. He stands aghast with his eyes staring at the treacherous pointer. His cheeks blanch, his eyes become glassy. He attempts to shriek but usually the sound chokes in his throat. Unless help is forthcoming in the form of a counter-charm and administered by the hands of a medicine man, death occurs in a short period of time. [Huxley 1959, p. 18]

How many deaths in modern society result from possibly less dramatic but equally overwhelming stressful events? We do not know, but we do know that if the stressor is sufficiently severe, even the strongest can be overcome. Even with young highly trained military men, subjection to extreme stressors can produce hopelessness and rapid deterioration, as the following account of death among prisoners of war by J. E. Nardini, a U.S. Navy psychiatrist who was himself a prisoner of the Japanese in the Philippines, attests.

> . . . shortage, wearisome sameness, and deficiency of food; much physical misery and disease; squalid living conditions; fear and despair; horrible monotony almost completely unrelieved by pleasurable interludes; inadequate clothing and cleansing facilities; temperature extremes; and physical abuse. . . . Hungry men were constantly reminded of their own nearness to death by observing the steady relentless march to death of their comrades. The death rate in the main prisoner camp at Cabanatuan, P.I. was between 40 to 60 per day in a population of 6,000 to 9,000, or roughly 1 percent per day during the months of June, July and August, 1941. Hungry men were often reduced to attitudes and actions incompatible with their own previously accepted levels of behavior and self-respect. Men quibbled over portions of food, were suspicious of those who were in more favored positions than themselves, participated in unethical barter, took advantage of less clever or enterprising fellow prisoners, stole, rummaged in garbage, and even curried favor with their detested captors. [Nardini 1952, p. 24]

Under such deplorable conditions, men experienced frequent bouts of apathy, depression, and death.

117

Occasionally an individual would develop a depressive reaction in which he would lose interest in himself and his future, which was reflected in quiet or sullen withdrawal from the group, filth of body and clothes, trading of food for cigarettes, slowing of work rate to a level that invariably invited physical abuse from the Japanese and an expressed attitude of not giving a damn or what's the use. If this attitude was not met with firm resistance by companions, camp leaders, or medical personnel, death inevitably resulted. [Nardini 1952, p. 245]

Similar findings have now been reported among former American military prisoners of the North Koreans and the Vietnamese (Strassman 1956; Ursano 1981).

In the next section I shall examine data showing that characteristics that predispose to a state of hopelessness-helplessness may be acquired in infancy (learned helplessness) and, as a result of exposure to stressors later in life, may predispose to psychological decompensation. I shall also consider why others, even under severe conditions, persevere and survive. These are persons who as children were encouraged to accept challenges and who, with the experience of mastering those challenges, developed the confidence and the successful coping strategies necessary to survival.

Childhood Experiences That Weaken Psychological Defenses

We now turn from the influence of parenting style on the child's future coping skills to another important factor influencing those skills— the child's experience of psychological trauma, particularly that resulting from loss of a parent.

A phenomenon well known to toxicologists is the increased sensitivity of very young animals to harmful agents. Human infants exhibit that same increased vulnerability to psychological stressors. Some children will, of course, be much more vulnerable than others; what characteristics determine the resilience and strength of the child's ability to cope? In chapter 5 I described how premodern parenting practices produce children who will be, like their parents, conformist and authoritarian. These experiences in turn lead to a personality that, lacking the experiences of being subjected to challenge and coping successfully, is marked by learned helplessness.

Discrete traumatic experiences as well as incompetent parenting can also weaken children's psychological defenses, leaving them vulnerable to stessors in adult life. British psychiatrist John Bowlby has focused attention on a specific source of trauma—the loss of the mother or caregiver during the early developmental years of life when the child is most vulnerable to separation and loss. Most psychologists agree that the greatest stressor of all is the loss of an important other person, either through death or other cause. Because of the child's helplessness and extreme dependency, the loss of a parent creates permanent psychological scars.

Whether loss of a parent due to death or divorce produces greater psychological damage to a child is uncertain. It is curious, however, that as the probability of parental death has fallen historically in the United States, the likelihood of the loss of a parent due to divorce has moved in the opposite direction, resulting in a roughly constant risk of parental loss. For example, in 1900 the likelihood that one parent would die before the child reached age fifteen was 24 percent, whereas the likelihood of divorce among parents was negligible. By 1976, the probability of the death of a parent had fallen to 5 percent, the probability of loss of a parent due to divorce had reached 36 percent (Uhlenberg 1985).

What is the evidence that parental loss leads to later health consequences? Figure 6.1 presents data collected at the University of Pittsburgh. The investigators were interested in the influence of childhood parental loss on subsequent development of certain diseases and other causes of death. Each of the horizontal lines in the figure shows an estimate of the frequency of parental loss derived from a survey of all existing literature. Parental loss was defined as that resulting from death of a parent, separation of the parents, or divorce.

The high prevalence of parental loss among people manifesting certain disease conditions, as shown in the figure, is striking. Note, for example, the behavioral conditions of suicide, delinquency, accidents, and psychosis, all of which are increased among those who have experienced parental loss. The investigators estimate that for those who have lost both parents—orphans—the risk of suicide is seven times greater than for those raised in an intact family. In another study confirming this observation, the author concludes that among all of the sequelae attributed to early childhood loss, the evidence with respect to suicidal behavior is among the strongest (Adam 1982).

More astonishing is the increase in the rate of just thinking about suicide among those who had experienced such loss. For example, in one study, almost half of the college students interviewed who had been separated from a parent during childhood had had serious thoughts of

119

FIGURE 6.1.
Parental Deprivation and Disease

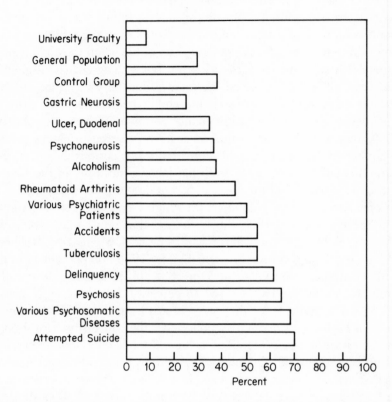

NOTE: Reprinted, by permission of the publisher, from E. Chen and S. Cobb, "Family Structure in Relation to Health and Disease," *Journal of Chronic Diseases* 12 (1960): 546.

suicide, whereas only 10 percent of students from intact families had had such thoughts (Adam 1973). In addition to suicidal thinking, several of these students had participated in unusually hazardous sports, suggesting a disregard for personal safety.

Two scientists from the Johns Hopkins Medical School have studied the health of 1,337 physicians, members of medical school classes from 1948 to 1964 (Thomas and Duszynski 1974). All of these former students had completed a questionnaire while in school concerning their attitudes toward their family as well as family size, age of parents, and marital status. A score representing closeness to parents was constructed and then compared with the subsequent health history of the young physicians. Closeness to parents and father's age at the time of the subject's birth were found to be powerful predictors of suicide, mental illness, and tumors; fathers of those who committed suicide were substantially older at

120

TABLE 6.1

*Association of Performance on a Mental Health Evaluation Scale
with Subsequent Physical Health*

	Best Score (10–12)		Intermediate Score (13–15) no. & % of men		Worst Score (16–23)	
Excellent health or minor problems (154 men)	57	97%	67	86%	30	62%
Chronically ill, disabled, or dead (31 men)	2	3%	11	14%	18	38%

NOTE: Reprinted, by permission of the publisher, from G. Vaillant, "Natural History of Male Psychologic Health: Effects of Mental Health on Physical Health," *New England Journal of Medicine* 301 (1979):1251.

the birth of their children than other fathers. For example, of the twenty male medical students who later developed malignant tumors, there had been significantly less closeness to parents than in the study group as a whole.

Other evidence regarding consequences of parental loss or deprivation comes from a study of 188 men begun in 1942 through 1944, during their sophomore year at Harvard. These men were selected on the basis of their excellent physical and mental health. In 1964 mental health status was evaluated through both questionnaires and personal interviews. Information regarding early childhood experiences, marital status, job performance and satisfaction, and use of drugs, including alcohol and tobacco, were obtained, and ranked on a scale of 10 (worst) to 23 (best). Complete physical examinations were performed and evaluated by an internist in 1975, eight years after the mental health status was determined. Results of the survey are shown in table 6.1.

Of the men who had been in excellent mental health in 1967 (fifty-seven men), 97 percent were in excellent physical health eight years later, whereas of those who had been in the worst mental health in 1967 (thirty men), only 62 percent were in excellent health in 1975. Only 3 percent of those who had been in excellent mental health at the earlier examination were dead or disabled (two men), whereas 38 percent of those with worst mental health scores were now dead or disabled (eighteen men).

These results are of particular importance because the influence of education, socioeconomic status, and access to medical care have all been removed. Even cigarette smoking and alcohol use had relatively little effect compared to that of mental health or childhood experiences (which were highly correlated with each other). By fifty-three years of age, eleven of the thirteen men with the highest childhood ratings were still in excellent physical health, and only one fit the category of chronically ill or dead. Only one of the ten men with the lowest childhood ratings was judged to be in excellent health, and seven were chronically ill or dead (Vaillant 1979).

A growing body of medical thinking now suggests that early life experiences play a powerful role in the ultimate appearance of cancer. One of the earlier proponents of this view, psychologist Lawrence LeShan, found in the history of many of his cancer patients a pattern he described as follows:

> In the emotional life of these persons damage is done to the ability of the child to relate to others, resulting in marked feelings of isolation, a sense that intense and meaningful relationships bring pain and rejection, and a sense of deep hopelessness and despair. Later, a strong relationship is formed in which the individual invests a great deal of energy. For a time, he enjoys a sense of acceptance by others and a meaningful life, although the feelings of loneliness never completely disappear. Finally, with the loss of the central relationship, whether the death of a spouse, forced job retirement, or children leaving home, comes a sense of utter despair and a conviction that life holds nothing more for him. [LeShan 1966, p. 781]

Death in the Premodern Family

How do these observations of the health consequences of parental loss help us to understand high mortality rates in premodern populations? It is difficult for us to grasp just how omnipresent death and dying are to those who live in premodern societies. Just as half of the newborns fail to survive to age ten, adults by no means are assured of the proverbial three score and ten, nor can they be assured that their spouse will survive with them. McManners found that in eighteenth-century France, a marriage rarely lasted for more than twenty years before one of the partners died. At Crulai, 51.5 percent of marital unions lasted less than fifteen years and 37 percent less than ten; at Azereix, by the age of forty-five half of the men had been widowed. In a particularly unhealthy village in Basse-Auvergne, no less than 43 percent of the first marriages were broken within ten years by the death of one of the partners (later in this chapter I shall review the evidence that death of a marriage partner increases mortality and that this effect is greater among young widows and widowers than among elderly people). Few children knew their grandparents, and to live long meant loneliness among a generation of strangers (McManners 1981). Their loves and friendships were doomed to be more fragile, less assured, than those we cherish today. Just how deeply those frequent losses were felt, or whether they were felt as deeply as those of today, we cannot know with any certainty, yet I would agree with McManners that "it would be presumptuous to say their grief was easier to bear."

As we shall see, the risk of separation from a parent during childhood, whether permanent or intermittent, is again on the rise in American society, not as a result of mortality but as a result of divorce and/or desertion.

Other Acute Stressors During Childhood

Acute episodes of stress other than those resulting from death can also scar children, no matter how well they have been nurtured and loved. One illustrative episode occurred in June 1976, when three young kidnappers commandeered a school bus filled with twenty-six youngsters on their way to school in Chowchilla, a small town in California. They were driven about at gunpoint for eleven hours and then were buried alive in a truck trailer ("the hole"). Two of the kidnapped boys eventually dug their way out of the bus and released the children. Four years later a San Francisco psychiatrist, Lenore Terr, examined the children. She found that every child exhibited posttraumatic symptoms, including pessimism about the future, belief in omens, shame, fear, nightmares, and dreams of death. The severity of these symptoms varied, however, depending on the child's preexisting personality, family pathology, and community bonding. We do not know how these symptoms will influence the future coping abilities of these children, but reason and plausibility would suggest that these psychic wounds will impose a high price to health. Almost identical observations have been made on a much larger group of children who were survivors of a natural disaster in which a West Virginia dam gave way, destroying towns and killing 126 people (Newman 1976).

Studies Related to Loss of Spouse

Although children may be those most sensitive to separation and loss, severe psychic trauma such as the death of a spouse can also be life threatening to adults. Young widows and widowers have the greatest increase in mortality—for those under age forty-five at the time of bereavement, mortality rates are seven times greater than for married people of the same age. Widows and widowers both have been reported to experience an increased mortality during the period of mourning, but this effect clearly seems to be greater among men than among women. The excess of deaths is found to be predominantly due to suicide, accidents, and infectious diseases among males and from cirrhosis of the liver in females. Sudden death, as from cardiac arrest, is particularly common (Institute of Medicine 1984).

In addition to the increased mortality in this grieving population, researchers have also investigated the characteristics of individuals most susceptible to extreme grief and even death. Clearly, not all surviving spouses die quickly. Who are those who are likely to suffer the most? John Bowlby has found that all of the following characteristics appear to increase risks of decompensation among the surviving spouse: (1) The death occurred suddenly and without warning; (2) The surviving spouse demonstrated a delayed response to the death. He or she appeared, at least at first, to be unaffected by the death; (3) The survivor complains of nightmares associated with the death; (4) The survivor is noted to be quarrelsome with family members and others; (5) The survivor makes an attempt to escape the scene; (6) There is a history of an unsettled childhood; and (7) The survivor has been brought up to "bottle up" feelings.

Of all of these, Bowlby finds, the most influential factor in predicting the outcome of mourning appears to be the personality of the bereaved, "with special relationship to his capacities for making love relationships and for responding to stressful situations" (Bowlby 1958, p. 172).

Loss of a Child

Of all deaths, the loss of a child is probably the most intense stressor to the modern family. Casualty rates among families who lose a child are appallingly high; divorce, alcoholism, and the development of illness are common. Bowlby (1958) cites one study of forty families who had suffered the loss of a child. In thirty of these families, one or both parents were found to be suffering from psychiatric or psychosomatic symptoms or were drinking heavily. In twenty-five of these families, there were problems with the surviving children. Although no studies of mortality have been conducted, the increase in morbidity justifies the tentative conclusion that mortality is also increased.

Happiness and Modernization

If it is true, as I have asserted, that people living in modern society are under less stress than those in premodern societies, not more, should they not be happier? Can that be, given the widespread notion that people living in modern societies have an enormous burden of stress?

There is a romantic notion that life in premodern communities is serene and that people living in such communities are, somehow, happier. Nothing could be further from the truth. For the great majority of persons, life in preindustrial society is not only precarious, but is also often associated with a personality type lacking in joy, fearful, susceptible to depression and anxiety, pain, and sorrow. No observation in social anthropology has been replicated more often than this. For example, sociologist Daniel Lerner states:

> a very powerful finding of our study is that Middle Easterners who are modernizing consider themselves happier than do those who remain within traditional lifeways. This is in striking contrast with the impressions conveyed by some observers, often from highly modern settings themselves, who feel that the undermining of traditional ways by new desires must be a net loss. Among such observers, the passing of cherished images of passive peasantry, noble nomads, brave Bedouin evokes regrets. But these regrets are not felt by the modernizing peasants, nomads, Bedouin them-

125

selves, or felt less disapprovingly than by the moderns who study them and love the familiar way they used to be. [1958, p. 74]

Here, in a personal account, are the recollections of a British farm worker reminiscing about changes in agricultural practices imposed by modernization of agriculture and the ways in which new technology has influenced his sense of well-being and his relationship with his employer:

> I'm definitely happier than I was years ago and I'm sure most farm workers are. We had depressing jobs which lasted so long. Sugar beeting was very depressing. You'd start it in September and it would go on until January. It made life seem worthless. Now you just sit on the harvester! The farmers have changed for the better too. I work for an exceptionally good boss, although he's a Tory. I pull his leg about the Tories and he pulls mine about the Labour. You wouldn't have got this before the war. He's an altered man, particularly in these last ten years. It used to be, "Get here" or "Get there"—that is how farmers spoke to their workmen. [Blythe 1969, p. 96]

Results of a national survey conducted by the U.S. Department of Health and Human Services confirm the existence of a high level of perceived happiness. When asked about happiness in 1980, 47 percent of people said that they were very happy, 45 percent said that they were pretty happy. Only 7 percent said that they were not too happy (Eisenstadt 1982). When asked how often they felt loved and wanted, 71.6 percent of women and 66.7 percent of men answered "very often" and only about 2 percent of both sexes answered that they never felt loved and wanted. Thirty similar studies have been conducted in many countries with similar results. In all thirty studies wealthier people were happier than poorer people (Easterlin 1974).

Although these data strongly support the concept of an increased sense of psychological well-being with modernization and greater economic security, they are not adequate to address the question of whether that sense of well-being has continued to improve during the postmodern period. One can only offer opinions. Mine is that recent decades have not witnessed an improvement in happiness, well-being, or whatever term is chosen, but that family disruption and the decline in the sense of trust and commitment, both toward others as well as toward the institutions of society, have damaged that sense of well-being.

Summary

The response to psychological stressors resembles the physiological response to all other environmental or dietary agents such as sunshine, alcohol, or vitamins; in low doses these may be beneficial whereas high doses may be harmful. In the susceptible individual, repeated stressful events may lead, either immediately or many years later, to psychological/ physiological decompensation, disease, and death.

Perhaps the most common stressor in human experience that leads to death is the death of a loved one for whom there is a strong attachment, whether that person be parent, spouse, or child. Separation, such as what a child of divorced parents experiences, in our society may be the psychological equivalent of parental death. Many other life events, such as those associated with natural disasters, have been shown to predispose to physical and psychiatric distress. In chapter 2 I alluded to a likely mechanism—the impairment of the body's immune system through psychoimmune depression. There is extensive evidence that the immune system plays a powerful role in protecting us against not only infectious disease but also against many of the so-called modern or chronic diseases. Other mechanisms, not yet well understood, may also operate to depress resistance to disease. For example, it has been found that the repair of DNA, the genetic material in the nucleus of cells, is defective in people subjected to psychological stress (Kiecolt-Glaser et al. 1985). Since these repair systems are an important factor in protecting cells against assault from carcinogenic materials, repair defects might well explain some of the increased vulnerability of depressed people to cancer.

Individuals differ greatly in their ability to avoid and mitigate stressors. These differences in psychological reserves, the ability to cope, are largely determined during the earliest childhood years when children acquire "life skills." Such skills include both the confidence and self-esteem necessary to foresee and avoid stressors (see chapters 5 and 9). Children reared in authoritarian families, typical of premodern societies, will have limited, fragile psychological reserves and will easily decompensate, the result described as the hopelessness-helplessness syndrome. Other "moderators" that can mitigate the effects of stress will be discussed in later chapters. One of these is the existence of social support networks (Sarason 1985). Another, apparently, is physical fitness (Roth and Holmes 1985).

In addition to the increased ability of modern populations to withstand exposure to stressors, a modern productive society also reduces the levels of stressors to which the individual is exposed. An affluent society is able to provide both engineering safeguards against natural disasters (through flood control, fire-fighting equipment, sanitation, and so forth) and economic security against personal disaster (illness, unemployment, and so on).

In many ways our view of stress, reflected in the epigraph, is simplistic. While we focus on the pathological aspects of stress, we ignore the likely benefits of the human need for challenge. We overly emphasize the role of a hostile environment in producing disease. Just as we presume that the smallest amount of radioactivity in the environment is harmful, we assume that the smallest amount of stress is harmful, ignoring the stimulating benefits to human development of environmental challenge. Certainly excessive stressors can overwhelm the defenses of the most robust, as demonstrated throughout this chapter. Rather than concern ourselves solely with the harmful effects of stressors, we should also concern ourselves with the need to strengthen the coping skills of the weak so that they too can benefit from the challenges that we all need for healthy development.

7 Social Networks as Health Support Systems

The experience of separateness arouses anxiety; it is, indeed, the source of all anxiety. Being separate means being cut off, without any capacity to use my human powers. Hence, to be separate means to be helpless, unable to grasp the world—things and people—actively; it means that the world can invade me without my ability to react. Thus separateness is the source of intense anxiety. . . . The deepest need of man, then, is the need to overcome his separateness, to leave the prison of his aloneness. The absolute failure to achieve this aim means insanity.

—ERICH FROMM, 1956

HUMAN BEINGS ARE, above all, social animals. Most people are very well aware that human companionship can have a marvelous effect on those who are ill. That is, after all, one reason why most of us feel it is important to visit friends and relatives who are hospitalized; we know that such visits speed recovery. To be involuntarily isolated from others is the most feared of punishments. For schoolchildren, the harshest punishment is to be removed from their peers and told to stand in the corner. For the prisoner, solitary confinement is the most dreaded of punishments.

In the last chapter we examined the evidence that stressful life experiences can increase the likelihood of disease and death. With severe stress such at that experienced in concentration camps or in natural disasters, even the most well-balanced individuals will suffer. However, there are great differences in individuals' ability to resist the effects of less severe stressors. Why? What factors protect some and leave others vulnerable? What factors mitigate or otherwise modify the individual's response to stress? Elsewhere in this book, some of these factors, such as education and social class, are examined; in this chapter we shall examine social networks as a modifying factor and, in particular, the likelihood that differences in the existence and intensity of social support systems may explain some of the differences in mortality that exist between modern and premodern societies and among the social classes.

By social networks I mean all of those relationships that exist with others. The individual might be considered to be at the center of a vast network. Nearby, and bound to the individual with strong linkages, are close family members and intimate friends. In larger concentric circles are neighbors, occasional friends or acquaintances, perhaps coworkers. There may also be in this network agencies, churches, and fraternal organizations to which the individual feels comfortable in turning for advice or assistance.

If social support systems contribute to health, then it might be predicted that isolation and loneliness are associated with poor health outcomes. We know that loneliness can be not only damaging to health but even fatal. Indeed, to deprive an individual of all sensory inputs ("sensory deprivation") can very quickly produce symptoms resembling acute depression. These include decreased appetite and weight loss, restlessness, anxiety, and sleep disturbances (Heron 1961).

We shall begin with an examination of what is traditionally the most important and enduring support system, the family, and the mechanisms through which it provides such support. We shall then consider other networks, such as the church, friends, doctors, and pets, and the evidence that these contribute to health. Next, we shall examine the deleterious effects of loneliness caused by the absence or deprivation of important social support systems. Then we shall return to our persistent problem: why do people living in modern societies experience better health and lower death rates than those living in premodern societies? To what extent can those differences be attributed to improvements in human relationships among family members, spouses, and friends?

Family Closeness and Adult Health

In our individualistic society, it is often assumed that the individual is the appropriate unit of analysis in understanding the response to stressors. Yet family characteristics may be the more important unit in predicting a person's response to stressors. In other words, rather than ask how John Doe will respond to catastrophe, disease, or misfortune, one can and should ask how strong is the Doe family? There are six mechanisms through which families operate to shore up defenses and assist members in coping:

1. The family as a collector and disseminator of information about the world: Adequate and accurate information, after all, is crucial to getting on in the world and avoiding the frustrations and aggravation of not knowing how the system operates, or not knowing the points of entry (jobs, schools, health care systems, and so forth). The younger generation provides information in a reverse direction—it alerts the older generation to new social trends.

2. The family as a feedback guidance system: For the individual, the family functions as a "sounding board." At dinnertime, family members exchange information about the day's events. Reactions of other family members permit individuals to test opinions against those of a friendly and sympathetic "encounter group."

3. The family as a source of ideology: To a large extent, values and attitudes are acquired during the earliest developmental years of life. But these values will often conflict (for example, family interests may conflict with loyalty to community, friends, or others). When such conflicts in values occur, we need to compare our judgment on these matters with others who share those values. We need a "reference and control group." The family provides such a function.

4. The family as a source of practical service and concrete aid: To whom do we turn for such functions as baby-sitting, loans, the exchange of shopping chores, the celebration of marriage, births, and so forth? Friends, yes, but most of all, family. Consider the loneliness of those who must shoulder these hopes, joys, and frustrations alone (Sussman and Burchinal 1962).

5. The family as a haven for rest and recuperation: When things get tough, what better therapy than a permissive environment with few demands and supportive relatives?

131

6. The family as a source and validator of identity: During periods of crisis, as doubts arise and confidence flags, families offer reassurance and bolster the individual in his resolution. This is particularly important during periods of loss, desertion, or other crises (Caplan 1976).

How important is this family support system to health? Studies of family response to the Depression and the stresses of World War II show that family integration, family adaptability, and marital adjustment were the strongest predictors of family adjustment to crisis (Drabek and Key 1984). That people who are married have mortality rates lower than people of equal age who are single, widowed, and fully half of those experienced by people who are divorced has been well established (MacMahon and Pugh 1970). The protective effect of marriage is not limited to death. For example, a study of 10,000 Israeli men found that when middle-aged men were subject to anxiety, the existence of a loving and supportive wife was sufficient to reduce the risk of angina pectoris by 50 percent (Medalie and Goldbourt 1976). While these observations can be interpreted in a number of ways, taken as a whole they support the notion that marital relationships do provide an important source of psychological support, possibly more so for men than women (Darcy and Siddique 1985) and that loss of such a relationship increases the risk of disease and death.

Just as families can be a source of support and a mitigating factor for stressors and disease, they can also create tensions that exacerbate disease, a fact often ignored by our medical care system. Take, for example, the case of three young diabetic girls, all seen in the same clinic. These girls were much alike, members of apparently stable, pleasant, and cooperative families. Yet each had frequent recurrent loss of diabetic control, requiring hospitalization. Usual psychiatric counseling, aimed at shielding the girls from family stress, was a complete failure. The desperate physicians decided to take a new tack; they began treating the three families rather than only the diabetic member. In their research, they found that each of these girls had become enmeshed, in a variety of ways, in family conflict. Parents would implicitly demand that the child ally herself with one of them, mediate, or in some way become a party to the family feud. This pattern is found commonly among families of other children with medical problems, particularly asthmatics and girls with anorexia nervosa. The families of these children were characterized by their inability to contain conflicts to any two members; such conflicts inevitably involved all of the family members, including children (Minuchin, Rosman, and Baker 1978).

Friendship

Families are not the only source of social support; friends can also provide many of the same functions. The spectrum of friendships and the many functions that they fulfill may be even more varied than those within the family. Psychologist Judith Viorst (1986) offers the following useful taxonomy:

1. Convenience friends. These might be office mates or neighbors with whom we exchange pleasantries; we may occasionally ask them for help, such as sharing a car pool. We engage in pleasant chitchat but do not share intimate feelings. We keep a pleasant face with such convenience friends. They are, nevertheless, important to us.

2. Special-interest friends. These are friends with whom we may share some particular interest or activity; tennis partners are an example. We do things together but, as with convenience friends, we do not share feelings together.

3. Historical friends. These are people with whom we may have been close at some period of our lives, but for one reason or another, our paths have now diverged. We may exchange Christmas cards, an occasional telephone call, or a nostalgic reunion. I maintain a friendship with a woman who was, almost fifty years ago, my English teacher. The relationship is an important one to both of us. Through it, both of us maintain links to a past that might otherwise be lost.

4. Cross-generational friends. Friendships between members of different generations can be close and even intimate, but they are usually marked by an inequality—the senior member gives advice, the junior member is on the receiving end.

5. Close friends. These are by their nature the most significant of friends, those whom we see and talk with most frequently, whose advice and confidence are most meaningful to us. Casual observation would suggest that in our society, if not in most, intimacy among friends is more common among women than among men.

How do friends contribute to our health? First, friends can provide all of the functions families provide. In some cases, friends may indeed be closer confidants than family members. Those persons who are able to build such close friendships are buffered against the effects of stressful life events. For example, women who have been raped and who have been able to vent their feelings to a confidant recover much more readily

TABLE 7.1
*Percentage of Women Experiencing Depressive
Illness by Whether They Had a Severe Event
and by Intimacy Index*

	Intimacy Index		
	High	Medium	Low
Severe Event or			
Major Difficulty	10	26	41
No Severe Event or			
Major Difficulty	1	3	4

NOTE: Reprinted with permission, from Brown, G. and Harris, T. *Social Origins of Depression*, p. 77. New York: The Free Press, 1978.

than those who have been unable to do so (Burgess and Holmstrom 1974). Close friendships are likely to protect against an array of stressful life events.

Recognizing the role of stressful events in the precipitation of acute psychiatric illness, psychiatrists studying the antecedents of depression among working-class women in London were interested in studying whether the existence of intimate friendships might protect against the effects of such events. On the basis of their interviews, they identified women who were clinically depressed and compared them with others who appeared to be in good mental health. They then inquired about the women's recent history of severe life events or major life difficulties. They also inquired about the existence of friends, that is, confidants with whom the women could share their feelings—not only about the number of such friendships, but about their closeness and intimacy as well as the frequency of such contacts. The scale used ranked women as high, medium, or low with respect to the number and intensity of such contacts. The data were analyzed to see whether such closeness might mitigate the effect of a severe stressful event. The results are shown in table 7.1 which depicts the now well-recognized association between severe life events and the onset of depression. Those women who had experienced severely stressful events were far more likely to suffer from depression; however, among these women the risk of psychiatric illness was four times less among those with a high level of close relationships than among those with a low level of such relationships. The protective effect of confidants or social relationships explains, at least in part, the increased vulnerability of working-class women to psychiatric illness—such women have fewer confidants than middle-class women (Brown 1978).

A few studies have estimated the impact of the social network as a

134

FIGURE 7.1.
Mortality Rates and Social Network Index

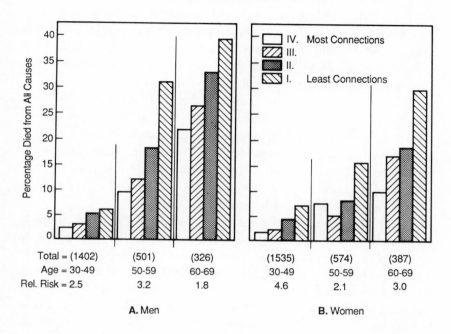

NOTE: Reprinted, by permission of the publisher, from L. Berkman and S. Syme, "Social Networks, Host Resistance, and Mortality: A Nine-Year Follow-up Study of Alameda County Residents," *American Journal of Epidemiology* 109 (1979):190.

whole, including the effect of friendship, church attendance, and so forth. One such study was carried out among residents of Alameda County, California, located on San Francisco Bay (Berkman 1979). About seven thousand people were interviewed regarding contacts with friends and relatives, church membership, and marital status, among others. Nine years later, mortality that had occurred in the interval was ascertained.

The authors then constructed a Social Network Index for each person studied. This index was adjusted for all of the person's social contacts, including friends as well as formal groups. The index was constructed to reflect not only the number of relationships but their intensity as well. Among all age and sex groups mortality was greatest for those with the fewest such memberships (or networks), highest among those with the fewest relationships (the loners) (see figure 7.1).

This index was correlated with socioeconomic status, cigarette smoking, and other health practices, but remained significant even when the effects of these other variables were removed. Social isolation, as measured by a low index, was associated with increased mortality from ischemic heart disease, cancer, cardiovascular diseases, and all other diagnoses, including suicide and accidental death. Since there existed the possibility that people were lonely and without social networks *because* they were sick, the authors examined separately the influence of social networks on mortality among people with the same degree of disability at the time of interview. The beneficial effects of social networks persisted even when disability was accounted for.

Could the increased loneliness and absence of social networks been the result of disease and illness, rather than its cause? A second community-based study shed light on this question, since here a medical examination of all participants identified disease. Results of this study, conducted in Tecumseh, Michigan, were identical to those of the Alameda study—social isolation predisposed to disease and increased mortality (House, Robbins, and Metzner 1982).

The tantalizing question that arises from these studies is, how do these social networks operate to reduce mortality? Why do people who are socially active appear to be more resistant to disease and death? Do healthy people—that is, those who have a high sense of trust in others, who feel comfortable with themselves as well as with others—seek out and encourage social relationships, or does the existence of such relationships contribute to better health? In other words, in which direction does causation flow—from health to friendships and other social relationships, or from friendship to health? We are not likely to find a precise and satisfactory answer to these questions, but the most plausible conclusion is that both occur. As one investigator has concluded, "there also remains the possibility that engagement in these relationships and activities is both cause and consequence of a more general psychologic sense of 'coherence' and 'will to live'" (House, Robbins, and Metzner 1982, p. 140).

A key question is whether the social support system protects health by buffering the individual during periods of stress, the so-called buffering theory, or whether it operates to protect health even in the absence of stress? As so often is the case, both effects seem to occur. According to a recent and thorough review of the literature on social support systems, there are as many studies supporting one hypothesis as the other (Cohen and Wils 1985).

Church Membership

According to studies of the health of people belonging to an organization—almost any kind of organization—"joiners" show remarkably better health than "nonjoiners." There is no difficulty in demonstrating this advantage; the difficulty lies in understanding whether this advantage is a consequence of self-selection* or one of the benefits of membership.

The Church of Seventh Day Adventists (SDA) is a conservative religious denomination with about 600,000 members in North America. About half of their members are vegetarians. A high proportion are college graduates and professionals. Virtually all abstain from tobacco and alcohol. Many will not consume caffeine-containing foods, sweets, or other refined foods. When compared with other Americans, SDA members as a group have very low death rates, particularly for younger members whose death rates are about half of what might be expected (Phillips et al. 1980).

Are the benefits of SDA membership the result of specific health behavior, or is it simply that the church consists of members who, because of social class differences, share with all upper-class Americans the health benefits associated with higher social class (see chapter 8)?

A study conducted at the Loma Linda School of Medicine in southern California was specifically directed to test this question. In this study, SDA members were compared with a selected population carefully matched as to education and marital status. The interesting finding was that even with this careful matching, SDA death rates were still found to be low, although not as low as when the wider comparison was made. For example, in the comparison of SDA members having some college education with non-SDA members of an equal educational level, overall death rates were 25 percent lower for the church members. This effect was greater for males than for females. The church members had some advantage in almost all specific causes of death, including those unrelated to cigarette smoking, as well as those known to be related to cigarettes (Phillips et al. 1980).

These findings suggest that the low death rates of SDA members cannot be explained merely by differences in lifestyle, such as abstention from cigarettes and alcohol. Indeed, a study of mortality in Maryland

* By "self-selection" I refer to the fact that people who spontaneously engage in any activity, whether to join an organization, to smoke cigarettes, or any other behavior, may well have different characteristics from those who do not choose to do so. Studies of participants and nonparticipants always must attempt to sort out causation under these circumstances of "self-selection."

among any church goers found the entire group to benefit as much as did members of the Church of Latter-Day Saints (Comstock and Partridge 1972).

Is the protective effect of church membership a result of religious practices that might influence lifestyle and thus secondarily benefit health, or is improved health the result of the support provided by the social network? Both factors may be operating, but I am inclined toward the latter explanation. For one thing, membership in other organizations, such as the military services, is also associated with a reduction in mortality. For example, mortality rates of servicemen are significantly below that of the U.S. population generally. For all personnel ages seventeen and over, the death rate is only 57 percent of that of nonmilitary people of the same age (Metropolitan Life 1982). The advantage of military personnel increases with age, so that for people over fifty, the military mortality rate is only 38 percent of that for the population as a whole. Certainly, there are rather obvious reasons for this superb health record, including a rigid selection process and careful medical monitoring. Those factors alone, however, are insufficient to explain the remarkable health advantage associated with military service. For one thing, the advantage persists for many years after discharge from the service. One study shows that although there is some slight decline in the health advantage of veterans over nonveterans, nevertheless the effect is still significant after twenty-three years (Seltzer and Jablon 1977). An additional insight comes from the observation that this advantage is not equally distributed among all ranks, but is greater among officers than noncommissioned officers, and that former privates have no significant advantage over nonveterans. An analysis was carried out to determine if the effect were nothing more than the health benefits long known to be associated with education. Education level was found to explain some of the advantage, but it did not totally explain it.

Doctors as Social Supports

Do physicians provide significant emotional support to their patients? Are there health benefits other than those that are inherent in the use of drugs and surgery? Could kindliness, sympathy, and compassion play a role in therapy and recovery that is quite separate from the medicine and surgery?

There have been a few isolated attempts to evaluate the effectiveness of careful patient counseling on the outcome of disease, accident, or surgery. The bottom line of these studies is that careful explanation to patients together with sympathy and understanding has a consistently beneficial influence, as measured by speed of convalescence, amount of pain medication required, or number of postoperative complications (Caplan 1981).

We also know that information inadequately communicated can be frightening to patients who may be too intimidated by the physician or too frightened of the possible answer to ask for clarification. The physician's mere hesitation while listening to a patient's heart or the request for a consultation may terrify a patient. It is known that suggestion can have a powerful effect on the outcome of disease. We also know that a powerful personality, whether a faith healer, witch doctor, or Harley Street surgeon, can provide the difference between life and death through the force of personality alone.

There is a long history documenting the therapeutic value of the laying on of hands. The history of Franz Anton Mesmer (1733–1815) is a remarkable example. Toward the end of the eighteenth century, this Austrian physician created a sensation in both Vienna and Paris by his use of suggestion and by merely touching his patients (Zweig 1962). Mesmer explained these dramatic effects by suggesting that physical forces flowed from his body into those of the patient. He was widely ridiculed by his medical colleagues for this, but many years later his biographer, Stefan Zweig, wrote:

> Why should not the proximity of the human body, which can restore the brilliance of a faded pearl, exert upon a neighboring body, by means of an aura or radiation, an influence which stimulates or tranquilizes the other's nerves? Surely there may be attraction and revulsion, sympathy and antipathy, between individual and individual. Who shall venture, in this sphere, to utter an absolute yes or an absolute no? It may well be that someday, with more delicate apparatus than we now possess, a physicist will be able to demonstrate that there is something substantial in the forces which we at present incline to regard as purely spiritual and immaterial. [Zweig 1962, p. 100]

James Lynch, psychologist working at the University of Maryland School of Medicine, has written a remarkably perceptive book in which he recounts observations of comatose patients (1977). The electrocar-

139

diograms (EKGs) of these patients were monitored constantly. When a compassionate nurse or doctor stopped at the bedside to comfort and reassure patients, their EKGs showed a slower heart rate in response to the soothing voice or the comforting hand. One wonders whether all of the space-age gadgetry of the postmodern hospital substitutes for the benefits of Dr. Mesmer's hands.

Human–Animal Attachment

In chapter 5, I noted that human contacts can have a powerful effect on both laboratory and farm animals in their growth, milk production, and behavior. But what of the opposite: can pets influence human health? Although the almost-human relationship many people have with their pets is generally recognized (but sometimes ridiculed), there has been little systematic study of the importance of this relationship to the health of the human partner. Given the strength of the attachment, one would expect that not only mood but general health will be influenced by the relationship with an affectionate, trusting, and nonjudgmental pet.

One such study was carried out at the University of Maryland. It was found that of ninety-two patients discharged from the hospital following treatment for heart attack, the great majority of those who had pets to which they returned following their hospitalization survived (fifty of fifty-three); of those without pets at home, a considerably smaller proportion survived (twenty-eight of thirty-nine) (Friedman et al. 1980).

While investigations of human-pet interactions on health outcomes are few, recent symposia have been devoted to the beneficial influence of pets to mental health, especially among the elderly (Bustad 1980; Fogle 1981). In one study of patients in a nursing home who were failing to respond to conventional therapy, pet dogs were offered to fifty elderly patients. Of the forty-seven who accepted the pets, remarkable improvements were noted. One man who had not spoken for many years began to speak after acquiring the dog (Corson et al. 1980).

140

Loneliness and Social Isolation

Although fictional literature often explores themes of loneliness, there has been relatively little medical research interest in the subject, at least until very recently. As so often happens, scientists avoid studying phenomena that are difficult to specify and to quantify. What, after all, is loneliness? Quite clearly, it is different from being alone. Many people benefit from at least temporary periods of quiet and reflection. They like themselves and can enjoy periods of reflection and contemplation. Others, in the midst of crowds, may be intensely lonely. It is these latter feelings of anguish or isolation that are now being found to be associated with untoward health consequences.

According to one definition, loneliness is the psychological state that results from discrepancies between one's desired and one's actual relationships (Peplau and Perlman 1982). If this is true, then loneliness cannot be ascertained by quantitative measures of the number of relationships, but rather lies in the satisfaction that those relationships bring. A growing body of evidence attests that loneliness is strongly associated with a number of negative emotional states, including anxiety, hostility, and depression (Jones, Carpenter, and Quintana 1985).

Is loneliness a medical problem? People living in poverty and isolation in Massachusetts have recently been found to have an increased risk of cancer. C. David Jenkins, a psychologist at the Boston University School of Medicine, studied the occurrence of cancer mortality in thirty-nine mental health districts in Massachusetts (Jenkins 1983). Poverty and family disruption were found to be frequently associated with cancer, but interestingly, only among men. The sex difference was unexplained. Are women more resistant to loneliness than men? Do lonely men more easily resort to alcohol or cigarettes, or were undetected social support systems available to the women studied?

Catastrophic Destruction of Social Networks

One might well expect that if social support systems mitigate the effects of disaster, then harm associated with disasters might be compounded if the support systems themselves are also destroyed. Such appears to be the case. In chapter 6, I referred to the Buffalo Creek disaster in West Virginia where 125 people were killed and whole townships swept away by the flood resulting from the failure of a dam. Professor Kai Erikson, a sociologist at Yale University, studied the surviving population and concluded that the widespread and intense apathy and demoralization were not solely the result of personal tragedy and loss, but also resulted from the loss of social support systems. He says of the survivors: "They had never realized the extent to which they relied on the rest of the community to reflect a sense of security and well-being, or how much they depended on others to supply them with a point of reference" (1976, p. 303). In short, many of these people suffered from a sense of isolation and loneliness. Many found that the community had been stronger than the sum of its parts.

Although social networks can be seriously damaged by natural disaster, they can be remarkably resistant and useful even under conditions of extreme social disintegration, such as those found in Nazi concentration camps. Bruno Bettelheim, a psychologist who was himself a survivor of concentration camps, gives the following example of how these networks operate to save lives:

> Yet in reality, even while seemingly standing passively at attention, prisoners, to survive, had to engage in protective behavior. Those endless roll calls were physically and morally so destructive that one could survive them only by responding with determination to their destructive impact, through action when this was possible and, when it was not, then at least in one's mind—and this was true for everything else that made up the prisoners' lives. Like the many thousands of others who experienced it and survived, I remember vividly a bitter-cold winter night at Buchenwald when the prisoners were threatened with having to stand at attention for the entire night as punishment because some prisoners had tried to escape. Roll call was taken with the prisoners standing ten rows deep. Those in the front row were doubly exposed—to the ice-cold wind and to the mistreatment of the guards—while those in the other rows were somewhat protected from both. Soon the prisoners, with the connivance of indifferent prisoner foremen, or under the direction of responsible foremen, took turns standing in the front row, so that this extra hardship was shared by all but the extremely weak and old who were exempted. [1979, p. 292]

Trust–Distrust in Modern and Premodern Societies

What is the nature of relationships that prevail under conditions of scarcity and fear, the commonest of human conditions prior to modernization?

One human characteristic that distinguishes the modern from the premodern personality is the quality of trust. Traditional individuals view all of those who are not members of their extended kinship with distrust and suspicion, not as members of a coherent community with whom they share common interests. The guiding morality is, implicitly, self-interest. Personal security comes first. The welfare of the extended family is primary, and the interests of the larger community count for little. That is why corruption so dominates traditional society; all members of such a society understand and expect that each individual will act in accordance with his or her personal or family interest.

There is evidence that conflict and distrust marked early colonial life in America as well. The men and women of those early communities went to court again and again to do battle over land titles, property losses, wayward cattle, not to mention slander, witchcraft, and assault and battery. "Particular testimonies given in such cases often suggest a deep strain of bitterness" (Demos 1972, p. 563).

The fear and distrust of neighbors remains today or at least did until very recently in rural European villages. Sociologist Laurence Wylie has studied French village life for the past twenty-five years. Some years ago he moved his family to a small community in the Vaucluse region of France. The following is his description of their arrival:

> When we arrived in Peyrane it seemed as though everyone was trying to warn us against the danger of getting involved with everyone else. Our first and most natural contacts were with our landlord Martron, with the Provins family next door and with the Arenes across the narrow street. Martron warned us to stay away from both families. "I'm not saying why, you understand, but it's a friendly warning. Take it as you will." He added with a suggestive wink, "And I am sure that you will enjoy trading more with Reynard than with Arene who is . . . well you will see for yourself."
>
> The Provins family was less discreet in talking against Martron. They detailed their griefs against him and warned us never to trust him under any circumstances. When we talked with the Arenes we found that they agreed with Martron that the Provins were shady characters and agreed with the Provins that Martron was not to be trusted.

As we came to know other families we found that relationships were frequently no better. [Wylie 1957, p. 194]

This was France in 1950. Consider what relationships must have been like one or two hundred years ago, when scarcity and the threat of catastrophe and unemployment made families considerably more distrustful and suspicious of neighbors.

The quality of relationships that one adopts with others is largely determined by the pattern of relationships within the family during the earliest years of life. If those relationships are marked by fear, as they are in the authoritarian and traditional family, then that will be the quality of the relationship the child will adopt with others during his or her adult years. We have already noted the largely commercial nature of the marital relationship in premodern society. It was hardly a relationship that encouraged confidence and communication. While there was a romantic element among the knights of the Round Table, the romance was not between husbands and wives. Given that in premodern society, women were not treated as equals, as confidants with whom to share intimacies, but rather as servants (some would say slaves), then clearly those living in the twentieth century have a great advantage over their predecessors in terms of social support systems. It would be interesting to assess whether those living in more traditional male-dominated societies experience the same degree of increased mortality following the death of a spouse seen in modern America. I doubt it.

Many people perceive Americans as alienated and lonely; yet the data do not support such a conclusion. Although there are many who are lonely and neglected, the majority of Americans claim to have rich networks of friends and relatives. The National Health Survey found that, when asked about numbers of close friends, those "that you feel at ease with, can talk to about private matters, and can call on for help," the median number people claimed was four. Only 3 percent of respondents said that they have no such friends (Eisenstadt and Schoenborn 1982). When asked how frequently they see these close friends, the reply supports the closeness of the relationship. Half of the respondents see close friends or relatives at least five times a month, and 30 percent see these friends or relatives ten or more times per month.

Social Networks and Health

The studies described in this chapter provide clear evidence of a close relationship between the number and strength of an individual's social relationships with others and his or her health and longevity. While each of the studies reviewed may be open to alternative interpretation, as a whole they offer irrefutable evidence of a powerful association between social networks and health. As summarized by a scientific panel convened by the U.S. government, social supports not only reduce mortality as a whole but can be shown to:

1. Reduce the number of complications of pregnancy for women with high life stress.

2. Help prevent posthospital psychological reactions in children who have had a tonsillectomy.

3. Aid recovery from surgery.

4. Aid recovery from illnesses, such as congestive heart failure, tuberculosis, and myocardial infarction.

5. Reduce the need for steroid therapy in adult asthmatics during periods of life stress.

6. Protect against clinical depression in the face of adverse events.

7. Reduce psychological distress and physiological symptomatology following job loss and bereavement.

8. Protect against the development of emotional problems that can be associated with aging.

9. Reduce the physiological symptomatology in those working in highly stressful environments.

10. Help keep patients in needed medical treatment and promote adherence to needed medical regimens. [Hamburg and Killea, 1979]

As so often occurs with complex biological systems, the nature and direction of causation is not clear; is a person's ability to form friendships and close personal relationships independent of other personal qualities, or do resilient individuals with a more developed sense of self-esteem more easily form meaningful relationships with others? In which direction does causation move? Some evidence suggests that people who have little social support are those who are conformist and have a low sense of self-esteem (Sarason et al. 1985). There is also evidence that those who possess high levels of social skills themselves are more likely to possess strong social networks (Sarason et al. 1985). Intuitively, one would

145

expect that those who are physically attractive and socially engaging would attract more numerous and more meaningful relationships. Still, while a certain amount of charm is helpful, other characteristics may well be important, such as intelligence, loyalty, empathy, and so forth.

How do we acquire those characteristics that attract others? Psychoanalytically trained researchers such as Bowlby and Erikson believe that the relationship formed with the caregiver during the first year of life becomes the model for all subsequent human relationships. If that early experience has been marked by warmth, a high level of caring, and mutual respect, then that child will also become trustful, warm, and caring in his or her relationships with others.

Modern people, existing in a modern social system and as a result of modern parenting behavior, appear better able to form and maintain such relationships. Herein lies an important element in understanding one source of modern health and life expectancy. They are more trusting and more likely to regard the motives of others as altruistic rather than selfish. They have a greater sense of empathy. They have matured in an environment that is economically secure. They have been nurtured by a caring family and have been educated in a manner that endows them with a high sense of self-esteem.

This description is, of course, idealized; not every member of a modern society will experience such an environment or display such attributes. This leads me to consider still again the implications of observations on social support systems and health for our faltering U.S. health gains. Given that the health of people who have wide social support networks benefits, then what can be done for those who lack such advantages?

Apparent Epidemic of Homelessness

Possibly the most vulnerable group in our society, those who are truly abandoned, are the homeless. Among these, those who are homeless as well as mentally ill are at highest risk. These are the "bag ladies" and the shabby and faceless men who shuffle the streets, crouch in entrances, sleep on warm air grates, and scrounge through garbage cans. Who are these people? How many are there? Estimates of the number of homeless

Americans vary widely; there are no fewer than a quarter million while there may be as many as 2 to 3 million, roughly 1 percent of the American population. They are clearly a heterogeneous population. Some of these are the classic hoboes, men who have chosen this way of life and who would resist any alternative or offer of assistance; they are in the minority. Many are mentally ill. In 1984 the Task Force on the Homeless Mentally Ill of the American Psychiatric Association estimated that 25 to 50 percent of homeless Americans have serious and chronic forms of mental illness (Lamb 1984).

How and why did this apparent epidemic of homelessness happen? The explanation is not without controversy. Some say that the origin of the problem is economic—that homelessness results primarily from the shortage of low-priced housing. Others say that it is primarily a mental health problem. Between 1955 and 1984, the number of residents of public mental hospitals declined from 559,000 to fewer than 130,000 (Frazier 1985). The intent of this effort was to return the institutionalized mentally ill to local care in community mental health centers. Whether or not this strategy was well founded is not important; the local care facilities were never constructed. As a result, hundreds of thousands of people landed on the streets.

Increasingly, whole families are among the homeless. The situation for these children is particularly desperate. One scientist found that 40 percent of these children had been battered. They were extremely depressed and anxious. "I think we are raising a population of kids who don't stand a prayer" (Bassuk, quoted in Holdren, 1986, p. 570).

Elsewhere I review the evidence that the mentally ill experience increased mortality rates from a wide variety of causes. Here I review the evidence that loneliness increases and social support systems decrease death rates. Although we do not have data on the homeless mentally ill, one can be quite certain that their mortality rates are very high; addressing this serious health problem should be a national priority.

Our interest is more than in reducing death rates. We do not yet know with any certainty just how much can be done to rehabilitate the homeless mentally ill. Nor do we know the best means by which to do this. Clearly, we will not know until we devote adequate resources to conduct the studies necessary to answer these questions.

Salvaging bag ladies, derelicts, and alcoholics may be far less dramatic or glamorous than the implantation of artificial organs, but almost certainly the results will be less costly. Our interest is by no means limited to financial ones; our primary concern should be to bring the greatest good health to the most people, regardless of their origins or social class. Our

147

medical care and public health systems, directed as they are to the exploitation of technology, the use of hospitals and the medical establishment, and to the chemical sanitization of the environment, often ignore the needs of the homeless, the elderly, the derelict, the abandoned, and the battered. These populations are as much in need of health care as are those with overt disease. The medical care system cannot do everything, but it can use its limited resources to their greatest effectiveness. More often than not, the most effective use of those resources will be preventive rather than in the treatment of disease.

8   Mortality Gradients
Among Social Classes

> The very idea of "social class" is inconsistent with
> the American ideal of a society composed of free
> and equal individuals, individuals living in a society
> where they have identical opportunities to realize
> their inborn potentialities. The acceptance of this
> "American dream" is easy and popular. To suggest
> that it may be more myth than reality stimulates
> antagonistic feelings.
>
> —AUGUST HOLLINGSHEAD
> AND FREDRICK REDLICH, 1958

ALTHOUGH health differences among national populations may be
much larger than those that exist among the social classes of a single
nation, these latter are nevertheless significant in magnitude and provide
us with an additional insight into the determinants of health.

To a large extent, members of the various social classes exist in the
same environment, they are served by the same medical care system,
they breathe the same air and drink the same water, have access to the
same food supply, are served by the same educational system, and have
access to the same information sources. They differ primarily in the
consumption of these goods. They also differ in other ways that may be
important to health: in their attitudes, values, and behavior; in the ways
in which they think of themselves and relate to others; in the degree to
which they are willing to postpone present gratifications for future gain;
in the ways in which they marry, reproduce, and bring up their children.

In many ways, these social class differences resemble those that
distinguish people living in premodern and modern societies, but to a
lesser degree. Working-class families often are authoritarian, resistant to

149

change, and likely to prefer present gratification to future rewards. Members of the working class are more likely to support extremist and intolerant political groups; they are less likely to support civil liberties (Lipset 1960). How are these personal characteristics instilled? In chapter 5, I noted how the treatment of the child of the working-class family differs from that of the more individualistic and caring middle-class or professional family. The working-class mother is more likely to resort to physical punishment, and her child is likely to receive little affection or intellectual stimulation.

While these characterizations will often not apply in the case of individual families, these patterns have been generally validated by a number of psychologists and sociologists (Bradburn and Noll 1969; Kohn 1969; Lefcourt 1976). Members of middle and professional classes, on the other hand, are more likely to be oriented to the future, to change, to scientific rather than authoritarian cosmologies, to independence and personal responsibility. Attitudes toward children are likely to be affectionate, yet they are likely to set strict guidelines for their children, and to establish high expectations.

Whether measured by mortality, morbidity, or self-perceived health, there are differences in health outcomes among the social classes. Are these health differences the result of economic or external factors (for example, access to medical care and better nutrition), or are they the result of differences in behavior?

In this chapter we shall first review the data with respect to health differences among the social classes. We shall then examine the social class distribution and health consequences of a number of behavioral and lifestyle patterns, which appear to contribute to differences in health. These patterns include: (1) mental illness, (2) cigarette smoking, (3) alcohol use, (4) obesity, (5) exercise, (6) marital and sexual practices, and (7) accidents. Finally, we shall examine the extent to which differential access to medical care may explain social class differences in health.

Social Class Gradients in Mortality

There is no consensus regarding the definition of social classes, their number or their historical origins. Furthermore, the concept of social class implies that the individual classes are distinct from each other. It

TABLE 8.1

Mortality by Social Class, England and Wales,
for Four Historical Periods, Men Aged 20–64

	Social Class					
Period	I	II	III	IV	V	V/I
1930–32	90	94	97	102	111	1.23
1949–53	98	86	101	94	118	1.20
1959–63	76	81	100	103	143	1.90
1970–72	77	87	103	114	137	1.80

NOTE: Reprinted with permission from Black, D., Morris, J., Smith, C., and Townsend, P. *Inequalities in Health: The Black Report*, p. 67. New York: Penguin Books, 1982.

would seem more likely that on the basis of any specific characteristic, such as income, there is a smooth transition from very high to very low. Still, most people recognize the existence of social classes and can identify their own social class (Centers 1949). It is a constant feature of modern society; even in so-called "classless" societies, the persistence of social classes is generally recognized.

A number of personal characteristics have been used for the purpose of identifying the social class of the individual or family: education, social status, income, residential neighborhood, and occupation, among others. These indices tend to be highly correlated, so that knowledge of any one is usually a good index of other characteristics. There are, of course, exceptions. A gang-land leader may be wealthy and live in the finest house in town, but be poorly educated and generally be held in contempt. On the other hand, the son of the leading family in town, a true blueblood and a graduate of Harvard Law School, may have become an alcoholic and be eking out a living as a manual laborer. Still, these are exceptions. Most commonly, occupation is used as a marker of social class or, as it is often called, socioeconomic status (Susser 1985).

Measures of health among social classes have historically not been collected in the United States, possibly because, as noted in the epigraph, we prefer to ignore the existence of social classes. The British, on the other hand, have identified social class on death certificates since the last century. Table 8.1 is taken from British data (Wilson 1966). Class I is the highest social class (professionals and managers) and Class V is the lowest (laborers and the unemployed). The table (and table 8.2) sets overall death rates equal to one hundred and then compares the rate for each social class with that for all classes. The last column is the most important. The numbers there can be read as a percentage. For example, in 1970 to 1972, members of Class V experienced an 80 percent higher

151

TABLE 8.2
*Mortality Trends (Standardized Mortality Ratios), Males, Aged 20–64,
by Social Class, 1921–23, 1930–32, 1949–53*

		Social Class					
Cause	Period	I	II	III	IV	V	V/I
Cancer	1921–23	80	92	99	97	123	1.54
	1930–32	83	92	99	102	115	1.39
	1949–53	94	86	104	95	113	1.20
Tuberculosis	1921–23	49	81	95	97	137	2.80
	1930–32	61	70	100	104	125	2.05
	1949–53	58	63	102	95	143	2.47
Pneumonia	1921–23	85	84	90	97	150	1.76
	1930–32	71	80	91	109	139	1.96
	1949–53	53	64	92	105	150	2.83
Bronchitis	1921–23	26	55	94	121	177	2.68
	1930–32	31	57	91	124	156	5.03
	1949–53	34	53	98	101	171	5.03
Heart Disease	1921–23	106	109	90	92	115	1.08
	1930–32	237	147	96	57	67	0.28
	1949–53	147	110	105	79	89	0.61
Stroke	1970–71	75	80	97	110	150	2.00
Accident	1921–23	76	69	93	127	119	1.57
	1930–32	95	74	102	116	96	1.01
	1949–52	137	64	96	120	119	0.87

NOTE: W. Wilson; stroke data from R. Acheson.

mortality from all causes of death than did persons in Class I (Morris 1979). Although data comparable to that shown in the table is not available for 1980, recent differences in social class mortality appear to be widening, not decreasing (Marmot and McDowall 1986).

As shown in the table, differences in death rates are not dichotomous, separating the poor from the rich—there is a graded response, that is, a stepwise progression that marks each rise in social class. Just as the skilled tradesman has an advantage over the laborer, so too does the professional have an advantage over the middle-class manager—at least with respect to length of life. The magnitude of social class differences noted in the table are not unique; such differences are universal and have been observed repeatedly in all nations, including the United States (Guralnick 1964; Kitagawa and Hauser 1973), and several European countries (Black et al. 1982).

While table 8.1 shows death rates for all causes of death, table 8.2 depicts mortality rates by social class for individual disease categories. Interestingly, the gradient among the social classes for deaths resulting from infectious disease has not narrowed appreciably. The advantage experienced by the upper classes for tuberculosis was as great from 1949 to 1953 as it was in 1921 from 1923. Death rates for pneumonia and bronchitis actually show a greater discrepancy among social classes in the later period than they do in the earlier, the rates for bronchitis reaching a fivefold difference.

Although at one time heart disease was more common in higher social classes than in lower, it now is higher among lower-class members, as are most diseases. In 1970 to 1972, the ratios of deaths from heart disease from highest to lowest class were, 88, 91, 110, 108, and 111, respectively (Morris 1979). Stroke is also more common in lower social classes than in higher classes. The increased risk of mortality from cardiovascular disease is paralleled by an increased frequency of hypertension in the lowest social class (Fouriaud et al. 1984; Syme et al. 1974). The usual stereotype of heart disease and high blood pressure as more common among harassed businessmen no longer has a basis in fact. If hypertension and heart disease are the result of stress, as many believe, these figures would suggest that managers experience less stress than do their employees.

Differences in accident experience explain the largest part of the differences in life expectancy among the social classes. In New Zealand, for example, accidents account for 39 percent of the "excess deaths" among the lowest class, followed by neoplasms (18 percent) and cardiovascular diseases (16 percent). Because death from an accident typically occurs earlier in life than that from other causes, the number of years lost per accidental death is greater than from deaths from other causes; deaths due to accident, therefore, have a large influence on life expectancy, and account for approximately 60 percent of the difference in life expectancy experienced by the highest and the lowest social classes.

Historical Trends in Health Among Social Classes

As discussed in chapter 1, prior to modernization there do not appear to have been social class differences in health. It is also true that, with the advent of modernization, the most privileged classes were the ones to first experience a decline in death rates. Although the class advantage persists to this day, during this century the absolute fall in death rates

TABLE 8.3

Shifts in the Occupational Structure of the United States
Percent in Grouped Occupations, 1900–1978

	Percent				
	1900	1950	1960	1970	1981
Professional, technical, and kindred workers	4.2	8.6	11.4	14.2	16.4
Managers, officials, and proprietors (except farm)	5.9	8.8	8.5	10.5	11.5
Clerical and kindred workers	3.0	12.3	14.9	17.4	18.5
Sales workers	4.5	7.0	7.4	6.2	6.4
Craftsmen, foremen, and kindred workers	10.6	14.2	14.3	12.6	12.6
Operatives and kindred workers	12.8	20.3	19.9	16.4	10.5
Laborers (except farm and mine)	12.4	6.5	5.5	4.7	4.6
Service workers (except private household)	3.6	7.8	8.9	10.4	13.4
Private household workers	5.4	2.6	2.8	1.4	1.0
Farmers and farm managers	19.8	7.5	3.9	4.0	2.7
Farm laborers and foremen	17.8	4.4	2.4	1.2	1.3
Total	100.0	100.0	100.0	100.0	100.0

SOURCE: M. Susser, W. Watson, and K. Hopper. *Sociology in Medicine*, table 5.1, p. 199. New York: Oxford University Press, third ed., 1985.

has been more rapid among the lower social classes than among the upper classes. This is not surprising since lower-class death rates were the highest to start with and had much farther to fall. For example, sociologists Evelyn Kitagawa and Philip Hauser (1973) have examined data for the city of Chicago during the years 1930 to 1960, when life expectancy from birth for males increased by 4.4 years (from 63.0 to 67.4 years) for the upper class but by 8.8 years (from 51.2 to 60.0 years) for the lowest class. Although still lagging behind whites, life expectancy is increasing more rapidly for nonwhites than for whites. Between 1960 and 1984, life expectancy at birth for the nonwhite population rose by 6.5 years, 40 percent more than for the white population (National Center for Health Statistics 1985).

Although the relative health advantage of upper social classes over the lower ones remains quite constant, a much larger percentage of us are now in the middle and upper classes than was true of our parents' generation; the earlier social class "pyramid" has evolved into a "diamond," with the majority of people in the middle class. As shown in table 8.3, laborers and domestics have declined as a percentage of the population, whereas members of the professional class have more than tripled and members of the managerial class have almost doubled in this

154

century. Upward movement among the black and other nonwhite races has been even more rapid during the past decades. Their membership in the professional class has almost tripled in the last twenty years alone.

Social Class Differences in Morbidity

We have been focusing on social class gradients in mortality, but there are equally great and parallel discrepancies in nonfatal illness and disability among the social classes. In the United States and the United Kingdom, members of the lowest social class lose the greatest number of days per year because of acute illness and/or chronic invalidism. This observation is consistent for all age groups, including children, and for both sexes (Morris 1979). The data for the United States are shown in figure 8.1. These data were obtained by the National Health Survey from household interviews and are shown by education, income, and for certain occupations. Income has the greater effect on disability, but education follows the same gradient. The four occupational groups show small differences in disability, with white-collar workers showing the least.

Mortality Among Children of Different Social Classes

Does poverty and lack of education predispose to ill health, or is it the other way around—that is, do those with ill health become impoverished? The answer is undoubtedly complex, but some insights can be gained from examining the health of children. Poor health among children is less likely to influence family income than is poor health among adults. Again, the best data on this point come from the United Kingdom and are shown in table 8.4. Generally, death rates among children of the various social classes parallel those of their parents. Deaths (from all causes) among boys of the lowest social class are more than twice those of boys of the highest social class. Thus among children, as among people of all ages, social class appears to be most strongly associated with deaths

FIGURE 8.1.
Disability by Socioeconomic Level

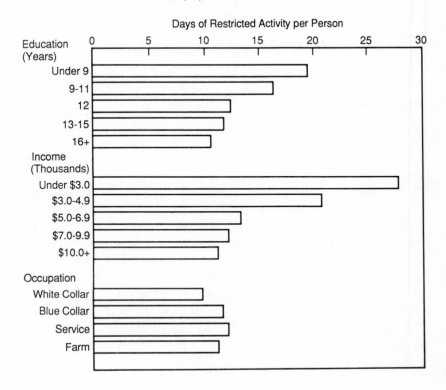

SOURCE: Courtesy of *Statistical Bulletin*, Metropolitan Life Insurance Company.

due to accidents, poisoning, and violence. Interestingly, social class even influences death rates of the unborn; fetal losses are greater in the lower classes and lowest in the highest class in both the United Kingdom (Baird 1947) and the United States (Shapiro 1968). Studies of social class and childhood mortality rates conducted in the United States provide results similar to those obtained in the United Kingdom (Mare 1982; Wicklund, Moss, and Frost 1984).

Health differences among children of the various social classes are not limited to mortality rates. Dr. Barbara Starfield of the Johns Hopkins School of Hygiene and Public Health puts it this way:

> Poor children are more likely to become ill, more likely to suffer adverse consequences from illness, and more likely to die than other children. For example, low birthweight, cytomegalic inclusion disease (the most common congenital infection), iron deficiency anemia (the most common hema-

TABLE 8.4

Class Differences in Mortality, England and Wales (1970–72),
for Children Aged 1 to 14

Cause of Death	Standardized Mortality Ratios by Occupational Class						
	I	II	IIIn	IIIm	IV	V	V/I*
Boys							
All causes	74	79	95	98	112	162	2.19
Neoplasms	99	103	125	98	96	135	1.36
Respiratory	101	66	101	105	108	136	1.35
Congenital anomalies	76	100	91	104	123	114	1.50
Accidents, poisonings,							
and violence	44	67	76	92	114	208	4.76
Girls							
All causes	89	84	93	93	120	156	1.75
Neoplasms	104	107	124	98	102	117	1.13
Respiratory	87	83	79	96	135	150	1.72
Congenital anomalies	63	66	105	94	123	101	0.99
Accidents, poisonings,							
and violence	63	66	72	84	120	214	3.40

* Indicates the ratio of mortality among those in class V as compared with those in class I. Occupational classes are: I = Professional; II = Managerial; IIIn = Skilled Nonmanual; IIIm = Skilled Manual; IV = Partly Skilled; V = Unskilled.
NOTE: Reprinted, by permission of the publisher, from R. D. Mare, "Socioeconomic Effects on Child Mortality in the United States," *American Journal of Public Health* 72 (1982):540.

tological disorder), lead poisoning, hearing disorders, functionally poor hearing, and psychosocial and psychosomatic conditions are all more common among poor children. Poor children are 75 percent more likely to be admitted to a hospital in a given year. Average lengths of hospitalization are twice as great for poor children and their average total hospital days are four times that experienced by children in the highest social class. A much greater proportion of poor children are unable to attend regular school because of a chronic condition than is the case for more affluent peers. They have thirty percent more days of activity restriction and forty percent more days lost from school due to acute illness. . . . Severity of illness such as asthma is greater among poor children and they have poorer survival from at least some life threatening conditions (such as leukemia). [1982, pp. 532–33]

Does this occur solely because of indigence? I think not. For one thing, the health differences between upper- and middle-class children are as great as those of the middle and lower class—there is a smooth gradient from lowest class to highest. While it is plausible to conclude that economic barriers to medical care could account for some of the illness and disease among children of poor families, one cannot conclude that the equally large differences between middle- and upper-class children

157

results from inferior medical care for the former. Nor do middle-class American children suffer from malnutrition. Clearly something more complex than the effects of indigence is operating here, something that affects children as well as parents.

In addition, if this social class gradient of illness and mortality were the result of economic differences among social classes, one would anticipate that the effects would be limited to infectious diseases as a result of crowding, differences in food quality and quantity, and other environmental factors associated with social class. The truth, however, is that *all* causes of death are influenced by social class—an observation that suggests a more generalized phenomenon. A more likely explanation is that social class membership reflects cultural or psychosocial differences in lifestyle, particularly those related to the family, reproduction, and parenting behavior, differences that were examined in chapter 5.

Mental Illness and Social Class

Unlike most other diseases, which can be characterized and defined by specific organ pathology, most of the so-called mental illnesses are defined on the basis of behavioral abnormality. (I exclude here those very rare psychoses that do have specific etiology and pathology, such as the psychosis associated with syphilis.) Some deny that mental illness can be considered a disease, according to our definition of disease; is mental illness a disease, a disability, or is it abnormal behavior? It may include all of these (Wing 1978). What we do know is that most mental illness, while influenced by genetic factors as well as by uncontrollable life events, nevertheless has a behavioral component that has its roots in early childhood (Watt and Lubensky 1976).

Our interest here is not so much in the origins or causes of mental illness; rather the question is whether there is a social class difference in mental illness and whether that difference may help us to explain differences in health and mortality among the social classes. This question is important since I believe that "mental health" and "physical health" is an artificial distinction. There is *one* health. If this is so, one would expect that those with poor mental health to exhibit poor physical health.

Beyond any reasonable doubt, mental illness of all varieties is as-

158

TABLE 8.5

Class Status and the Rate of Different Types
of Psychoses per 100,000 of Population
(Age and Sex Adjusted)

	Class			
Type of Disorder	I–II	III	IV	V
Affective psychoses	40	41	68	105
Psychoses due to alcoholism and drug addiction	15	29	32	116
Organic psychoses	9	24	46	254
Schizophrenic psychoses	111	168	300	895
Senile psychoses	21	32	60	175

NOTE: Reprinted by permission of the publishers from Hollingshead, A., and Redlich, F., *Social Class and Mental Illness: A Community Study*, p. 223. New York: John Wiley & Sons, Inc., 1958.

sociated with increased death rates. Social class gradient is also strongly associated with mental illnesses. Possibly the earliest examination of the influence of social class on the frequency of mental illness was carried out in New Haven, Connecticut, in the 1950s by August Hollingshead, a social scientist, and Fredrich Redlich, a psychiatrist (Hollingshead and Redlich 1958). They found that all diagnostic categories of mental illness were most prevalent in the lowest class and were least prevalent in the highest. That observation has now been replicated under many conditions and in many communities; forty-four different studies of social class and mental illness conducted by different investigators in different populations with a variety of methodologies all conclude that a strong association exists (Dohrenwend and Dohrenwend 1969). Table 8.5 depicts data collected from British mental hospitals, arranged by social class and diagnostic category. In each diagnostic category (with the exception of behavioral disorders), there is a clear gradient from highest to lowest social class, with the greatest incidence in the lowest class.

Early studies demonstrated an increased risk of mortality among the hospitalized mentally ill. Often those studied were in large state institutions. There was therefore justifiable suspicion as to the meaning of these results. For this reason, a study of mortality among all psychiatric patients, both hospitalized and outpatient, private and public patients, is of particular importance (Babigian and Odoroff 1969). This study took advantage of a county register in New York State that identified all psychiatric patients from all available sources of treatment and permitted researchers to compare death rates with all other persons living in the county. The researchers found what others had found, an increase in mental illness in the lowest income groups, and a significant increase in mortality among those under psychiatric care. An approximately twofold increase in mortality rates appeared among all age groups in the patient population, and in both sexes. For example, a person twenty years old at the time of the study would have had a life expectancy of 50.2 years. A psychiatric patient of the same age would have had a life expectancy of 41.8 years. While death rates from all causes of death increased by at least twofold, neoplasms in females increased by 50 percent and in males, 20 percent. The increase in mortality rates was also rather uniform for all treatment categories, both inpatient and outpatient, and was unaffected by the patient's socioeconomic status. That is to say, in comparison with other members of their own social class, those with mental illness will have death rates approximately three times greater than those members of their social class without mental illness.

The frequency of mental illness in American communities is astonishingly high. Studies consistently find that 17 to 23 percent of the American population has at least one psychiatric disorder at any one time. Over the course of life, 30 percent of Americans will have an episode of significant mental illness (Freedman 1984; Robins et al. 1984).

Social Class, Stress, and Mental Illness

To what can these social class variations in mental illness be attributed? In chapter 6 I discussed the contribution of stress to psychopathology. Could the frequency of mental illness, greatest among the lowest social class and least frequent among the most affluent, reflect a differential exposure to stress? To clarify, do the poor have more mental illness because they are exposed to more stress? Or, as an additional hypothesis, does the different frequency of mental illness among social classes reflect a differential ability to cope with stressful life events?

Investigators studied this question in a community sample selected in New Haven, Connecticut (Myers, Lindenthal, and Pepper 1974). A sample of 720 adults was interviewed on two occasions with an interval of two years between interviews. Social class was estimated in the usual way—through the use of an index composed of educational and occupational status. Psychopathology was estimated through a symptom questionnaire (Do you have trouble getting to sleep; how often? How often do you feel fidgety and nervous?). Respondents were also asked to indicate whether any of the following significant life events had occurred recently:

Failed in school	Demoted in job
Problems in school	Laid off
Moved to worse neighborhood	Business failed
Widowed	Trouble with boss
Divorced	Out of work
Separated	Financial status
Trouble with in-laws	Foreclosure of mortgage
Serious physical illness	Been in court
Serious physical injury	In jail
Death of a loved one	Arrested
Stillbirth	Lawsuit
Frequent minor illness	Loss of driver's license
Mental illness	Major catastrophe in neighborhood
Death of a pet	

These investigators found, as have all others, that mental illness is more common in the lower social classes. They also found that stressful life events are more common among the poor than the rich and concluded that this increased exposure to stressors would account for the excess of mental illness among the poor.

This study, then, appears to provide a clear-cut answer—poor people have more mental illness because they are exposed to more stress. Unfortunately, the study fails to provide an answer to why undesirable life events are more common among the poor. While a few of these events, such as "major catastrophe in the neighborhood," might well be beyond an individual's control, most are events to which the individual's behavior undoubtedly contributed.

Smoking and Social Class

The detrimental influence of cigarette smoking on the development of lung cancer and other diseases has been so thoroughly demonstrated as to require no supporting evidence here. Is there a social class difference in smoking behavior? Table 8.6 shows that when occupational categories are ranked by percentage of members who are college educated, there is a strong inverse relationship with current cigarette smoking, particularly

TABLE 8.6

Male Controls by Specific Occupations, Ranked by Education and Smoking Habits

	No.	College Educated %	Never-Smokers %	Cigar/ Pipe Smokers %	Current Cigarette %	Current Cigarette 21+/day %	Current Cigarette 21+ mg Tar %	Ex-Smokers[b] %
Physicians and dentists	61	100	46	16	11	7	0	70
Lawyers and judges	63	97	29	11	17	8	2	71
Engineers	56	95	30	9	21	1	4	65
Teachers— college	37	92	27	24	19	11	5	61
Religious workers	26	89	46	19	4	0	0	89
Business executives	66	86	32	11	17	6	3	71
Accountants	68	78	28	7	26	5	6	59
Managers— salaried	255	61	25	8	25	2	4	62
Police— detective	34	50	12	9	38	24	12	52
Sales workers	165	46	27	8	27	6	5	58
Managers— self-employed	71	45	24	27	21	1	4	57
Managers— retail and wholesale	191	39	22	10	22	8	3	68
Clerical workers	93	32	27	7	29	15	6	57
Printers	38	18	32	13	24	8	3	57
Metal workers	50	14	26	4	30	14	12	57
Machinists	31	13	26	3	52	29	10	27
Farmers	52	12	35	10	40	10	19	28
Carpenters	48	8	19	2	48	21	21	40
Taxi, truck and bus drivers	109	6	17	12	46	26	6[a]	36
Painters	38	5	18	5	42	24	16	45

NOTE: Reprinted, by permission of the publisher, from L. S. Covey and E. Wynder, "Smoking Habits and Occupational Status," *Journal of Occupational Medicine* 23 (1981):541, © by Am. Occupational Medical Association.

[a] All six were truck drivers.

[b] Based on ever-cigarette smokers.

when tar content is considered. Because of the very strong association of education with social class, one can reasonably conclude that cigarette smoking is inversely associated with social class. Equally interesting is the statistic relating percentage of persons who are ex-smokers, which is very high among the college educated.

Overall, the prevalence of cigarette smoking is declining in the

United States. However, trends measured between 1977 and 1983 show that for the lowest income and educational groups, cigarette smoking is increasing (National Center for Health Statistics 1986).

Alcoholism and Social Class

Most Americans drink alcoholic beverages, but in widely different amounts, in widely different patterns of consumption, and for different reasons. Cultural factors, including ethnic values and social class, powerfully influence these patterns. Among Jews there is a very high proportion who drink at least some alcoholic beverage, but very few Jews get into trouble as a result of their drinking. Irish-Americans, on the other hand, have a lower proportion of drinkers but a fairly high proportion of these get into trouble because of their drinking. Surprisingly, there appears to be little correlation between amount of alcohol consumed and so-called problems. Why is this? One writer summarizes the literature as follows:

> When drinking is part of an institutionalized set of behaviors which include important other people in roles of authority and when drinking is part of ritualized or ceremonial activities, e.g. family meals, festivals, religious occasions, etc., as opposed to leisure time or private use, it is not likely to be associated with high individual variability (unpredictability, loss of control) in conduct nor with the growth of drug dependency nor with the judgement of observers of "abuse" or "alcoholism." [Blum 1967, p. 31]

Social class has an interesting relationship to alcohol. The higher the social class, the more frequent is the use of alcohol; however, problem drinking is more common among members of the lower social class. In a national study conducted by investigators at both the University of California in Berkeley, California, and at George Washington University in Washington, D.C., an Index of Problem Drinking was established for 1561 men aged twenty-one to fifty-nine (Cahalan and Cisin 1976). They defined "problems" as belonging to the following classes: frequent intoxication, binge drinking, symptomatic drinking, psychologic dependence, problems with spouse or relatives, problems with friends or neighbors, job problems, problems with police, accidents, health, financial problems, and belligerence associated with drinking. A group of men

163

TABLE 8.7

Drinking Problems (in Percent) for Men of Four Social Positions, Aged 21–59

Social Position	Non-Drinker	Drank, No Problems	High Consequence Score
Lowest	19	22	26
Lower Middle	17	38	17
Upper Middle	14	39	8
Highest Social Position	11	47	9

SOURCE: D. Cahalan and I. Cisin, "Drinking Behavior and Drinking Problems in the United States," in B. Kissin and H. Begleiter, eds., *Social Aspects of Alcoholism*, p. 99. New York: Plenum Press, 1976.

were identified who had a high score on this index, a so-called high-consequence score. Table 8.7 shows the results of this scoring by social class and drinking habits. Members of the lowest social class were found to be problem drinkers three times more commonly than those of the highest social position.

Not only is social pathology more frequent among the lowest social class, but there is also an increase in mortality associated with lower-class drinking behavior. The strong association of alcohol with accidental death and suicide is well known. There is also an increase in mortality from those diseases known to be a direct medical consequence of alcohol abuse. For example, cirrhosis of the liver is the eleventh leading cause of death in the United States. It is the fifth leading cause of death among men aged twenty-five to sixty-four. The disease is much more common among alcohol abusers than among moderate drinkers, but there is no consistent relationship between amount or duration of abuse and the subsequent development of cirrhosis. Mortality from cirrhosis is strongly associated with occupation (Sorenson et al. 1984) and with social class, the lowest class experiencing about twice that of other classes (Guralnick 1964; Terris 1967). From all causes of death combined, alcoholics' mortality rate is from two to four times that of nonalcoholics (de Lint and Schmidt 1976).

Obesity and Social Class

Although uncomplicated obesity does not in itself increase mortality rates, obesity does predispose to other medical conditions that do put persons at increased risk. Diabetes and high blood pressure are but two

TABLE 8.8

Prevalence of Obesity in Men and Women
of Different Social Classes in London

	Percent Obese[a] by Age			
	Men		Women	
Social Class	20–39	40–59	20–39	40–59
Upper	17	43	27	49
Middle	29	53	38	57
Lower	30	43	70	73

NOTE: Reprinted, by permission of the publisher, from J. Silverstone, "Obesity and Social Class," *The Practitioner* 202 (1969): 682.
[a] More than 120 percent of desirable weight for height.

examples. Obesity is associated with social class. Table 8.8 shows the distribution of obesity among a sample of the London population classified by age and social class. Working-class men and women have a higher prevalence of obesity than middle- and upper-class men and women, except among older men (aged forty to fifty-nine), where there is no social class gradient (Silverstone 1969). American studies show identical results, although the social class gradient for obesity appears more consistently for adult women than for men (National Center for Health Statistics 1975).

Why are some people obese and others not? Clearly we do not know the answer to this question. Amount of food consumption alone does not answer the question. Interestingly, the increased obesity among working-class people first appears early in childhood, suggesting that cultural patterns and possibly genetic factors, are important. A recent study was conducted among 1,505 Minneapolis schoolchildren (Gillum et al. 1986). Social status of the family was estimated by combining measures of the parents' educational and occupational status. The child's obesity was estimated by the use of body weight and the square of height, the body mass index. The finding of a strong influence of social class on obesity among children is consistent with other studies of obesity.

Diet is but one element in the obesity equation; what of exercise?

Exercise and Social Class

Those who exercise regularly are in better health than those who do not. In a study of the health of almost 17,000 Harvard graduates, men who regularly exercise experience reduced mortality from almost all causes, including accidents and suicide (Paffenbarger et al. 1984). Is this because healthy people exercise, or because exercise produces health, or both? Interpretation is complicated by the fact that several health behaviors are known to be associated. Men who jog regularly are also, among other things, much less likely to be heavy smokers, to drive after drinking, to be obese, and are more likely to use seat belts, take advantage of regular medical and dental checkups, and to engage in fewer risk-taking activities (Blair, Jacobs, and Powell 1985). What we need to better understand this are some good experimental studies in which persons are randomly assigned to exercise and nonexercise groups. One such study has been done; it showed that the mental health status of volunteers who were assigned to a program in which they received significant cardiovascular conditioning also improved (Goldwater and Collis 1985). This would support the conclusion that while healthier people may exercise, that regular exercise itself may contribute to better mental and physical health.

Studies have demonstrated reduced mortality rates and increased life expectancy among animals that are encouraged to exercise regularly. For example, in one study rats were permitted unrestricted access to food. Half of the animals were required to run ten minutes every twenty-four hours. The dietary intake in these animals increased by 13 percent, but their average life-span increased by two hundred days (Retzlaff, Fontaine, and Furuta 1966).

According to the evidence, people who voluntarily engage in regular exercise programs are those who like themselves, enjoy living the most, and are motivated to invest in their own health. Socioeconomic class is consistently the most potent predictor of exercise; blue-collar working men are consistently among those who engage least often in regular exercise programs (Carter 1977; Dishman, Sallis, and Orenstein 1985). Of the men entered in a recent Atlanta marathon race, 84 percent were college graduates (Koplan et al. 1982). Thirty-seven percent of members of the professional classes state that they exercise regularly, while only 8 percent of unskilled working persons say that they do so (Morris 1979).

166

Marital and Sexual Differences Among Social Classes

In chapter 7 it was noted that those who are married have lower rates of illness and mortality than those who are unmarried or divorced. As Stanford historian Carl Degler points out, throughout American history divorce has been more common among the working classes than among the middle and professional classes (Degler 1980). That relationship between social class and divorce persists today, in that social class has an inverse relationship to divorce—the higher the status, the less likely is the marriage to end in divorce (Kitson, Babri, and Roach 1985). Social class standing appears to be closely associated with the ability to form permanent commitments. Such commitments have important implications for health.

Just as marriage protects against illness and death, divorce predisposes to psychiatric illness, accident, and psychiatric hospitalization. Social class is also associated with venereal disease. Of the major venereal diseases, AIDS, syphilis, and gonorrhea, only the latter contributes little to mortality rates. While gonorrhea interferes with reproductive ability, particularly in the female, it rarely leads to death. Syphilis is not simply a nuisance; when untreated, syphilitic infection is associated with a 50 percent increase in mortality from all causes (Clark and Danbolt 1964) and a 30 percent mortality from late complications of the syphilitic infection itself.

Syphlitic infection is no longer an important cause of death. Not too long ago, however, the situation was considerably different. In the middle of the last century, it was estimated that 12 percent of the population of Berlin and 15 percent of the population of Paris were syphilitic. Since serologic tests for the disease were not available at the time, these estimates were based on overt evidence of disease. Undoubtedly, infection rates were considerably, possibly many times, higher. By the early part of this century, rates had begun to fall and by 1940, positive serologic tests of U.S. army recruits had fallen to 4.6 percent (Fleming 1964).

As with the infectious diseases generally, there was a distinct social class gradient in mortality from the venereal diseases. The best data are British, and figure 8.2A indicates social class mortality from syphilis. The rate for working-class males was twice that for professional males, and for females, there was almost a threefold difference between highest and lowest rates.

What explains the association of social class with venereal disease?

167

FIGURE 8.2.

Mortality from Syphilis, England and Wales, by Social Class, 1930–1932 (A), and Extramarital Intercourse among American Males Aged 16–20 (B)

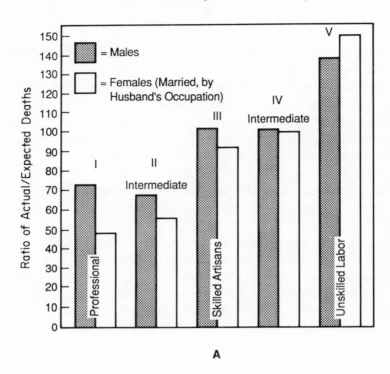

A

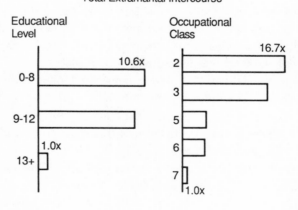

Total Extramarital Intercourse

B

NOTE: Figure 8.2A is reprinted by permission of the publisher, from W. Fleming, "Syphilis Through the Ages," *Medical Clinics of North America* 64 (1964): 604.

At least part of the explanation lies in social class patterns of sexual behavior, and particularly, differences in promiscuity. As shown in figure 8.2B, using either education or occupation as a measure of social class, extramarital intercourse appears to be far more common among lower classes than upper.

Promiscuity also appears to play a prominent role in the development of AIDS. In a study of sexual practices among San Francisco men, who are either homosexual or bisexual, 18 percent of those who had only one (or no) sexual partners in the previous two years were carriers of the virus, whereas 70 percent of those who had had fifty or more partners during two years (a quarter of the sample) were found to be carriers (Winkelstein et al. 1987).

Accidents and Social Class

Accidents kill more people in the United States between the ages of one and forty-four than all other causes of death combined. Trauma (physical injury) is the largest contributor to years of life lost before the age of sixty-five. The largest single cause of accidental death is the automobile.

Authorities are split as to those factors that are most important in explaining automobile accidents. Some attribute accidents to the engineering of the vehicle and the road. They see solutions as largely a matter of better engineering. Others see human behavior as the main culprit. The truth lies between these two. Improvements in both will help.

Social class is a good predictor of auto accident death rates. Is this because the poor have unsafe cars, or reckless driving, or both? Although one might argue that the poor have higher accident death rates because of older and less well-maintained vehicles, it is difficult to argue that the rich have even safer cars than the middle class. Figure 8.3 shows a consistent gradient among all income classes. Almost certainly some behavioral component can explain the social class gradient in accidental deaths. It is well known, for example, that alcohol plays an important role in accidents. Because of the social class gradient in problem drinking, it is plausible to conclude that alcohol plays some role in explaining the social class factor in accidental death rates.

169

FIGURE 8.3.
Deaths From Motor Vehicle Accidents:
By Per Capita Income Of Residence

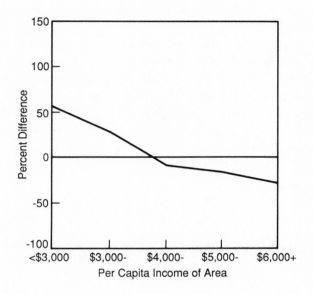

SOURCE: S. Baker, B. O'Neill, and R. Karpf, *The Injury Fact Book*, p. 53. Lexington, MA: Lexington Books, 1984.

There may be more than alcohol involved. It is sometimes said that "we drive the way we live," that those who have high self-esteem are more prudent, show concern for themselves and will drive more cautiously. Canadian psychiatrists William Tillman and George Hobbs (1949) noted that 10 percent of all drivers were responsible for 25 percent of all accidents, and these same drivers continued to be involved in accidents year after year. What is it about these few people that accounts for this? Are there patterns in their personal backgrounds that may help to explain this behavior? Are bad drivers different from good drivers in behavior other than in driving? Tillman and Hobbs set out to study forty taxi drivers—twenty of the best and twenty of the worst drivers, according to their accident records. Tillman sat with them as they waited for calls, talking with them about their childhood, school histories, criminal records, parents, and marital and sexual histories. He also checked these personal histories with the other drivers and with the police and other community agencies.

On the basis of these data, the authors drew the following profile of the high-accident drivers:

170

1. Family history: The parental divorce rate is high. Disharmony among the parents was common, with one or both parents being excessively strict. The father was often described as drinking excessively.

2. Childhood adjustment: Eleven gave a history of instability exhibiting behavior of an aggressive nature, such as frequent fights, and other delinquent acts. Neurotic behavior, such as enuresis and excessive daydreaming, were also common.

3. Academic work: Their school records were average. There was strong interest in body-building.

4. Work record: The work history showed frequent short-term employment, the driver stating that he had been discharged often.

5. Social adjustment: These were individuals with many acquaintances but few friends. Their main activities were in the fields of sports, drinking, and gambling.

6. Sexual adjustment: This group, if married, tended to be unfaithful to their wives and manifested little sense of responsibility to their families.

7. Previous health: Other than for injuries associated with accidents, their health was good.

8. Behavior patterns: Immature behavior was common. They were good conversationalists but took every opportunity to impress others.

9. Driving habits: As a group, they were easily distracted while driving. They tended to become annoyed with others while driving, often criticizing their own driving mistakes in others. Horn honking and racing away from stops were their specialty. They tended to be discourteous to their passengers.

10. Philosophical outlook: Their thinking was fatalistic and dominated by a materialistic interest in life. They disliked discipline, abhorred routine, and expressed a strong desire to be their own boss. They considered only the immediate future, thinking only of the satisfactions of each day.

The characteristics of the low-accident drivers were distinctly different. These observations have now been confirmed in many other studies. Although the studies differed in detail and design, the general conclusion that can be drawn is clear: characteristics such as low tension tolerance, immaturity, belligerence, and a tendency toward risk taking are all risk factors for accidents (Tsuang, Boor, and Fleming 1985). It seems likely, then, that the strong relationship of social class to accident experience may be, to a large extent, the consequence of social class differences in behavior.

The Influence of Medical Care

In chapter 4 I concluded that, as a whole, medical care has not made a significant contribution to a reduction in mortality rates. Much of that evidence is also applicable to a consideration of the influence of medical care in explaining social class differences in health. Briefly, the evidence is:

1. When barriers to medical care are removed by governmental subsidies, social class differences in morbidity and mortality persist unabated in both the United States and the United Kingdom.

2. When health outcomes, such as survival from cancer, are compared among members of different social classes treated at the same medical establishment, social class differences persist and are as great as those in the general population. In one study of breast cancer survival at the Medical College of Virginia, large differences in survival were found among members of different social classes with the same stage of disease and the same treatment regime. Five years after treatment, 50 percent of the high social class women survived, whereas only 10 percent of the women of low social class survived (Dayal, Power, and Chiu 1982).

3. Although the relative or proportional health advantage of the upper classes has persisted undiminished for several decades, the decline in absolute death rates of the lower classes has been more rapid. It is hardly plausible that those people with the least access to medical care, and presumably that of the lowest quality, would reap the greatest benefits if that care were effective in reducing death rates.

These comments on the inability of medical care to influence life expectancy should not be taken to mean that medical care is unimportant or that we need not be concerned about equal access to care. Besides the fact that some medical treatments are life saving (these are unfortunately uncommon), more important is the fact that much of medical care is effective in reducing pain and disability.

Summary

Social class is strongly associated with the morbidity and mortality rates of a broad range of diseases and accidents. These differences in health have been persistent throughout this century. They affect children as well as adults and are almost certainly not the result of differences in access to medical availability.

What public policy implications follow from these conclusions? Should we not divert resources and personnel from our expensive and often ineffective treatment efforts to conduct research and intervention into the social and psychological sources of illness-related behavior? I clearly favor this approach. Preventing alcoholism has to be more effective than treating cirrhosis. Sex education is clearly more effective than treating AIDS. Educational efforts and economic incentives directed toward the prevention of cigarette smoking has to be more effective than treating lung cancer. From 1953 to the present time, lung cancer has been the commonest fatal cancer among American males and is now rapidly becoming the most common cancer in females. The total number of lung cancers is now about 100,000 per year. The most optimistic estimate of the "cures" resulting from chemotherapy is 5,000 to 10,000. Clearly the problem is more amenable to education than to treatment.

While much of the difference in health outcomes that are associated with social class are the result of differences in health practices, such as drug, alcohol, and tobacco use, almost certainly there are more fundamental psychosocial forces operating. Social class differences in accident experience, divorce rates, manifestations of violence, and criminal behavior all suggest that differences in health are only partly explained by differences in the conventional health behaviors—they may also be related to basic personality patterns, for example, patterns of mitigating and coping with stress. Indeed, a study of the independent contributions of socioeconomic status and health practices to health demonstrate both to be important and interdependent (Slater, Lorimer, and Lairson 1985). In the next chapter I examine one difference in behavior among social classes that has a powerful influence on health—the demand for and consumption of education.

9   Education and
Life Expectancy

SOME YEARS AGO I had the good fortune to spend a year in a wonderful old Hapsburg palace poring over dusty tomes of data collected from almost 150 nations. These nations spanned the gamut from premodern to highly complex postmodern societies. My collaborator and I were searching for those statistical characteristics that would best predict life expectancy. The data we examined included demographic, social, and medical factors; religious preferences; distribution of wealth; urbanization; per-capita income; energy consumption; and many others. Each of these characteristics is related to modernization, and therefore demonstrates some association with mortality rates. Unraveling causation under such circumstances is tricky; one searches for consistency and uses statistical tests to determine which factor(s) appear to be causal. Applying such tests, we found that by far the most consistently powerful predictor of life expectancy was the prevalence of literacy.

Not only are literacy and education correlated with health among nations, but there is also a strong historical relationship between the growth of mass education and the fall in death rates. Reading and writing are so reflexive for us that we forget that mass literacy is still radically new in world history. William the Conqueror (1027–1087) was illiterate, as were most of his contemporaries; in fact, only 1 percent or so of the population at that time could read (Galbraith 1935).

In Europe, literacy grew at a rather slow and uneven rate. Historian Carlo Cipolla estimates that by 1700, 55 to 65 percent of Europeans were still illiterate, with England and possibly the Netherlands the most

174

advanced. By 1850, 90 percent of white U.S. males were literate. A high-school education, now the minimum educational requirement, is a more recent achievement among a large portion of American citizenry. In the United States, the percentage of people graduating from high school has grown from only a few percent in 1870 to over 80 percent today.

With increased educational achievement, there has also been a dramatic improvement in intellectual performance in modern populations. Soldiers drafted into the army in World War II performed much better on IQ tests than did draftees in World War I (Tuddenham 1948). Comparisons of test scores over these fifty years show "massive" gains in performance (Flynn 1984). Similar observations have been made elsewhere; two national surveys among Scottish schoolchildren using identical testing materials, the first carried out in 1932 and the second in 1947, demonstrate steadily rising scores on IQ tests. Other studies carried out in England, Sweden, and the United States also support these conclusions (Stein et al. 1975).

Given the uncontestable observation that education and intelligence have improved in modern populations, what evidence is there that these cognitive skills directly contribute to health? How can we test the existence of a causal relationship? One test would be the demonstration of a "graded response"—that is, a parallel relationship between the two variables; if a little (education) is good for you, is more even better? The data are shown in table 9.1. The mortality differences between those of the least and those of the highest achievement are very great, more so for women than for men, and are greatest among the middle-aged; females who have had four or more years of college have half the death rate experienced by those with little or no education. Differences in mortality among educational classes exist for a broad spectrum of diseases, the greatest differences occurring in deaths due to infectious diseases. Men with the least educational achievement experienced death from tuberculosis at a rate 776 percent higher than those with the highest educational level.

TABLE 9.1

Mortality Ratios, by Educational Achievement, United States,
for Sex and Specified Age Groups

| | Age Groups | | | | | |
| | Males 25–64 | | | Females 25–64 | | |
Years of Schooling	25 and Over		65 and Over	25 and Over		65 and Over
All Persons	1.00	1.00	1.00	1.00	1.00	1.00
0–4	1.02	1.15	1.02	1.27	1.60	1.17
5–7	1.04	1.14	1.00	1.08	1.18	1.04
8	1.02	1.07	1.00	1.05	1.08	1.03
High School						
1–3 yrs	1.01	1.03	0.99	0.87	0.91	
4 yrs	0.98	0.91	0.99	0.92	0.87	0.94
College						
1–3 yrs	0.98	0.85	0.98	0.73	0.82	
4 or more	0.80	0.70	0.98	0.71	0.78	0.70

NOTE: Reprinted, by permission of the publisher, from E. Kitagawa and P. Hauser, *Differential Mortality in the United States*, p. 12. Cambridge, MA: Harvard University Press, 1973.

Education and Morbidity

Death rates are clearly associated with educational achievement, but what of morbidity, disability, and the subjective quality of life? In the National Health Interview Survey, conducted by the National Center for Health Statistics (1983), people were asked to evaluate their health. Well-educated people reported themselves in excellent health far more often than those who were poorly educated (see table 9.2). To some extent, the greater income associated with higher education may account for this effect; at any given level of education, about 10 percent more people report themselves in excellent health than those in the lowest income group. That effect is small, however, compared with the effect of education; holding income level constant, about 30 percent more people with college educations report excellent health when compared with those without education.

One might reasonably question whether self-reported health has any validity, compared, for example, with a physician's assessment. Isn't self-reported health more likely to reflect attitudes than a more objective appraisal? The remarkable thing is, however, that self-reported health status is meaningful. In a large Canadian study, self-appraisal was a better predictor of mortality than was the assessment of the examining physician

176

Education and Life Expectancy

TABLE 9.2

*Percentage of People Reporting Themselves to be in Excellent Health, U.S. 1978,
by Income and Education*

Years of Education	Family Income			
	Under $5,000	$5,000–9,999	$10,000–14,999	$15,000–24,999
No Education	17.1	18.5	20.8	26.6
1–8 Years	18.5	21.2	25.9	30.4
9–11 Years	27.3	30.3	36.8	42.0
12 Years	34.5	37.4	46.7	49.9
13–15 Years	46.9	47.5	52.4	54.9
16 and Over	51.0	58.6	57.7	62.2

SOURCE: National Center for Health Statistics and P. W. Ries, *Americans Assess Their Health: United States, 1978.* Vital and Health Statistics, series 10, no. 142, p. 29. Washington, D.C.: U.S. Government Printing Office, 1983.

(Mossey and Shapiro 1982). This is not really surprising; most people are probably incorporating information from medical sources in their self-appraisal. Physicians, on the other hand, are likely to ignore psychosocial factors such as subjective well-being in appraising wealth.

A Proxy for Wealth?

Many people assume that the health benefits associated with education are but the consequence of greater economic advantage—more education begets affluence, better nutrition, better medical care, and so forth—all of those things that money can buy. But the evidence reviewed does not seem to support this view. For example, Samuel Preston finds that "factors exogenous to a country's current level of income probably account for 75–90 percent of the growth in life expectancy for the world as a whole between the 1930's and the 1960's. Income growth per se accounts for only 10–25 percent" (Preston 1976, p. 72). The studies seem to favor literacy as being *directly* linked to health rather than as a proxy for other variables. That is, the statistical association between literacy and health is consistently stronger than that between health and income, just as in the study of infant mortality rates among states of India shown in table 9.3. Infant mortality rates are compared with both the female literacy rates and mean income of the population. Increased literacy

TABLE 9.3

*Infant Mortality Rates, Female Literacy, and Output Per Capita in India,
Selected States*

State	*Infant Mortality Per 1,000 Births*	*Female Literacy (Percent of Population)*	*State Domestic Product Per Capita (in US dollars)*
Kerala	52	64	96
Karnataka	81	28	99
Maharashtra	94	35	139
Punjab	104	34	162
Tamil Nadu	108	34	95
Haryana	113	22	145
Himachal Pradesh	114	31	111
Andhra Pradesh	123	21	86
Assam	128	—	81
Orissa	141	21	80
Gujarat	146	32	118
Rajasthan	146	11	83
Madhya Pradesh	146	16	76
Uttar Pradesh	181	14	60

SOURCE: United Nations, *State of the World's Children, 1984*, p. 150. New York: Oxford University Press, 1983.

among women is inversely related to infant mortality rates (more education leads to less infant mortality). Per-capita output, a measure of wealth, has little apparent association with infant mortality. While all of the states have a low output, as judged by the standard of modern western countries—in other words, they are all essentially premodern—there is more than a threefold difference in infant mortality rates among the states. Kerala, with a female literacy rate of 64 percent, the highest of any state reported, has the lowest infant mortality rate.

I have examined literacy and death rates among the fifty American states. The data show the same thing—while the per-capita income of each state has no statistical relationship with infant mortality rates (for 1980), education as measured by the percent of residents who complete high school is highly significant statistically in predicting the infant mortality in that state (the probability of such a strong relationship occurring by chance is one in a thousand).

Acquisition of Health Knowledge

Why is it that education is so powerfully associated with health? Does education produce health? Does health somehow engender education? Are the two together the result of some third factor, or are all of these hypotheses valid?

One hypothesis is that education provides health benefits through the increased knowledge of health and health behaviors that are acquired. A simple example might be one related to cigarette smoking. If people were not informed of the existence of hazards to health, such as those from cigarette smoking (or dietary fats, or of obesity, and so forth), they would be at greater risk. As was noted in chapter 8, not only is there much lower tobacco usage among members of the highest educational and occupational categories, but these groups also show the influence of information regarding hazards; the highest percentages of ex-smokers are among the most educated (as measured by percent of college graduates).

This explanation of the relationship between education and smoking behavior has been challenged. Smoking habits are developed long before education is completed and therefore cannot be the result of education any more than smoking can be the cause of education (Farrell and Fuchs 1981).

Another example: the higher the educational level, the greater the likelihood that persons will wear seat belts; this could be interpreted as demonstrating that those with higher education have better information regarding the efficacy of seat belts in the prevention of injury (Goldbaum et al. 1986).

That the better educated are the better informed regarding health behavior is an explanation that must be at most a weak explanatory variable in determining the health gradient among educational categories. Most physicians—and most other people as well—know that the provision of information alone is a very weak stimulus to human behavior. Knowledge of the hazards associated with obesity, cigarette smoking, and alcohol and other drug abuse is widespread; yet the results of educational programs directed at these and other public health hazards have been disappointing.

Nor is it always clear that the health information disseminated in the interests of health promotion is efficacious. Many practices widely promoted by the health professions until recently are now viewed as useless or even harmful: tonsillectomies, restricted weight gain during

179

pregnancy, limitation of carbohydrates in the diet of diabetics, and the use of prolonged bed rest for a number of illnesses. None of these is generally recommended any longer.

Education as a Source of Coping Strategies

It has been thoroughly documented that stressful life events are damaging to health (see chapter 6). Although life in a highly productive society provides some protection against stressors (for example, against famine and other natural disasters), stressful events are an inevitable consequence of the human condition; adolescence, sexual development, career choices, and choice of a marriage partner are examples of those stressful life events. People have two strategies for confronting such events: anticipation and anticipatory decision making, so as to avoid or mitigate those stressful events (prevention), and the adoption and use of successful coping strategies for those stressors that cannot be avoided (mitigation). Education contributes skills that are useful for both of these strategies.

Coping means more than the development of strategies for reducing the impact of existing stressors. To cope effectively also implies the early recognition of future threats and the development of those actions necessary to avoid or mitigate the consequences of those threats. Competent people with strong coping skills, then, will be constantly searching horizons, watching for opportunities as well as storm clouds, and responding appropriately to both.

Are these coping abilities related to educational achievement? While formal schooling offers no courses in coping, per se, certainly such skills may be sharpened through the experience of formal schooling. The student who has mastered high school calculus, for example, is more likely to confront stressors with a greater sense of confidence and self-assurance than those who have not mastered such courses.

One likely mechanism, then, through which education leads to improved health and reduced death rates is through the enhanced life skills that education provides—the ability to plan, foresee, avoid, and/or mitigate stressors. There may well be many other mechanisms through which education leads to improved health. For example, in chapter 3 I mentioned the fact that educated people are more likely to exercise than those who are less educated. Having a higher level of self-esteem, they are likely to be more concerned with their appearance, to control obesity, and to concern themselves with the appearance of symptoms. In addition to these cognitive skills are those social skills that accrue to those who have participated in those group activities that are inevitably a part of the educational process.

Educational Achievement as a Proxy for Mental Health

If education does help us to avoid and mitigate stress, then one would expect that there would be an association between education and mental health status. There is a considerable literature on the association of educational level with mental health status, including depression (see chapter 8). Those with more education are less susceptible to depression. In a study conducted in Santa Clara County, California, a random sample of 1345 people were asked to participate in a telephone survey of depression. The validity of these psychiatric assessments had been corroborated independently by three psychiatrists who had, in a previous pilot study, interviewed and ranked people as to the degree of depressive symptoms. The study showed that of all of the variables tested, educational level was the strongest predictor of depression or its absence. In the entire sample, the group with a college education or more had 80 percent fewer people with evidence of depression than the group with 0 to 4 years of schooling. Among those in the study who were Mexican, the influence of education as a predictor of depression was even stronger. Sex, marital status, age, youth, and marital separation also influenced the prevalence of depression (Vega et al. 1984). These observations suggest that education reflects a profound change in the personality. Reading and writing are more than technical skills or tools; the ability to communicate provides an opportunity to be sensitive to one's own feelings, to communicate and relate with others in a meaningful way, to achieve a sense of competence that the illiterate can rarely gain.

Men enrolled in a health plan in New York were given routine examinations after having suffered a heart attack. Of those whose EKG revealed persistent signs of coronary disease, many died suddenly. How did those who died differ from those who survived? Educational records were examined. Sudden death occurred three times more frequently among men with less than five years of schooling than among men with nine or more years of schooling. Intrigued with this result, the investigators did a second study that provides an extremely useful insight. Suspecting that educational levels may be serving as a proxy for emotional factors in disease, the investigators studied psychosocial factors associated with death from myocardial infarction. They found that the risk of death was four to five times higher in men with high levels of stress and loneliness than in men with low scores. Furthermore, when these factors were accounted for, the influence of education on survival disappeared; these investigators concluded that the influence of education on survival was only a proxy for stress and loneliness; those men who were poorly educated suffered much more loneliness, and it was this that predisposed them to recurrence of illness and death (Ruberman et al. 1984).

Functional Illiteracy in the United States

What lessons can we draw from the foregoing with respect to health in the United States today? According to the conventional definition of literacy—the ability to read and write simple sentences—we are a highly literate nation. The truth is, however, that the number of people who are functionally illiterate is large, and, according to the U.S. Department of Education, that number is growing.

The most recent national assessment of the prevalence of illiteracy was conducted in 1975. The study, known as the Adult Performance Level Study (APL), was conducted for the Department of Education by the University of Texas. Literacy was defined as consisting of a variety of skills, including those related to communication, computation, government and law, health and safety, occupational knowledge, consumer economics, and use of community resources. Using this yardstick, 23 million American adults were found to be unable to function adequately in our society—they were functionally illiterate. These people cannot properly follow medical instructions, they cannot fill out job applications, they cannot manage a family budget or take advantage of community resources (Bell 1982). They are helpless.

A more recent California survey describes the problem of illiteracy as a "crisis." Twenty-five percent of adult Californians were found to be functionally illiterate, and the number is growing at a rate of 230,000 per year. In monetary terms, the costs of that burden of illiteracy, reflected in welfare payments, unemployment costs, and prison expenses, were estimated to be a billion dollars a year. No price can be put on the limitations to human fulfillment created by this tragedy. Each illiterate adult will be followed in the next generation by a larger number of illiterate children whom their parents are unable to educate properly (Connor 1986).

Of the nation's unemployed, 75 percent are functionally illiterate. Of those in prison, 80 percent are functionally illiterate. The great majority of those in mental institutions are also functionally illiterate. Of those with fewer than six grades of education, four times as many are on welfare as among those with nine to eleven years of schooling. The evidence linking mortality and lack of education was reviewed earlier in this chapter.

Clearly the most desirable approach would be preventive. In the early 1960s, many people became concerned that culturally deprived children who began school with little preparation became discouraged easily and gradually fell even farther behind, only to eventually drop out. The strategy adopted was to intervene at preschool ages, with the hope that preschool preparation would provide deprived children with the education nondeprived children receive within the family. The best known of these intervention programs was Head Start, but there were many other ones as well, all designed with a somewhat different curriculum.

Early evaluation of these programs was rather pessimistic. The initial beneficial effect appeared to be ephemeral, with children's intellectual improvement gradually declining to control levels within a few years after they left the program. More recent reevaluation indicates that these early intervention programs may indeed have had important behavioral effects, benefits not apparent in early test results. As these children were followed into high school, they experienced lower dropout rates, less delinquency, and lower rates of teenage pregnancy. The rates of employment and participation in college or vocational training were twice those seen among the controls. The magnitude of these effects was not small; 50 percent improvement was observed (Berrueta-Clement et al. 1984). These results suggest that intervention programs more than pay off their costs in social benefits, and we can reasonably assume that health benefits will accrue as well.

10 Reflections and Proposals

WHAT DO these observations of increasing life expectancy among modernized populations tell us about the dimensions of health? Why was it that death rates fell so steadily for so long, and why does the decline appear to be coming to an end in the United States? What should we, as individuals and as a nation, be doing about it?

In this search for the origins of health, I chose to examine modernization as a "case study" because its influence on health is so spectacular and because its history has been so badly neglected. For example, children born in the United States in the year 1900 had only a 75 percent chance of surviving to age twenty-five; today the chance is 98 percent. In 1900 a child had less than an even chance of living to age sixty-five; today there is a 78 percent chance.

The history of rapid health gains in the United States is not unique; the rate at which death rates have fallen is even more rapid in more recently modernizing countries. The usual explanations for this dramatic improvement—better medical care, nutrition, or clean water—provide only partial answers. More important in explaining the decline in death worldwide is the rise of hope and the decline in despair and hopelessness. As important as the introduction of vaccines and clean water supplies may be the introduction of the transistor radio and television, bringing into the huts and shanties of the world the message that progress is possible, that each individual is unique and of value, and that science and technology can provide the opportunity for fulfillment of these hopes. These revolutionary messages produce a radical transformation of the

184

individual's self-image and self-esteem, of relationships among individuals, and of the family unit, which transmits these messages to the next generation.

Figure 10.1 presents a bird's-eye view of the multiple factors that together represent sources of health. The figure emphasizes the interdependence of personal, social, and family factors, all of which are necessary to good health for the individual.

Under conditions of scarcity, the family serves primarily an economic function; with modernization, the family becomes a social support system that nurtures rather than exploits its members. As the grinding poverty of the premodern world fades, individuals gain the means—physical, intellectual, and emotional—with which to cope with the inevitable stressors of life. With modernization, then, we become "better animals," better able physically and emotionally to cope, and are at the same time confronted with fewer threats with which we must cope. Admittedly, this view of modernization as having a moderating influence on stress differs considerably from the more widely held and pessimistic view that life in modern communities resembles a pressure cooker. Such is the view of those who have no personal experience of scarcity and its psychological consequences.

Although we Americans appear to be in the midst of rapidly increasing concern for health, the concept of health that arises from the analysis in this book differs considerably from that which is being sold in "health food" stores, sun-tan parlors, and exercise studios. Those trendy activities implicitly define health as physical fitness, in contrast with a more global concept of health, which I view as largely cognitive and emotional. It is the brain that is the true health provider. I am not opposed to physical fitness; a sense of subjective well-being is often associated with improvements in fitness. But I am concerned that physical fitness is being equated with health to the neglect of mental health. Similarly, our overwhelming concern with environmental conditions, directed toward the physical-chemical environment, ignores the importance to health of family and other interpersonal relationships, i.e., the social environment.

FIGURE 10.1.
The Origins of Modern Health and Life Expectancy

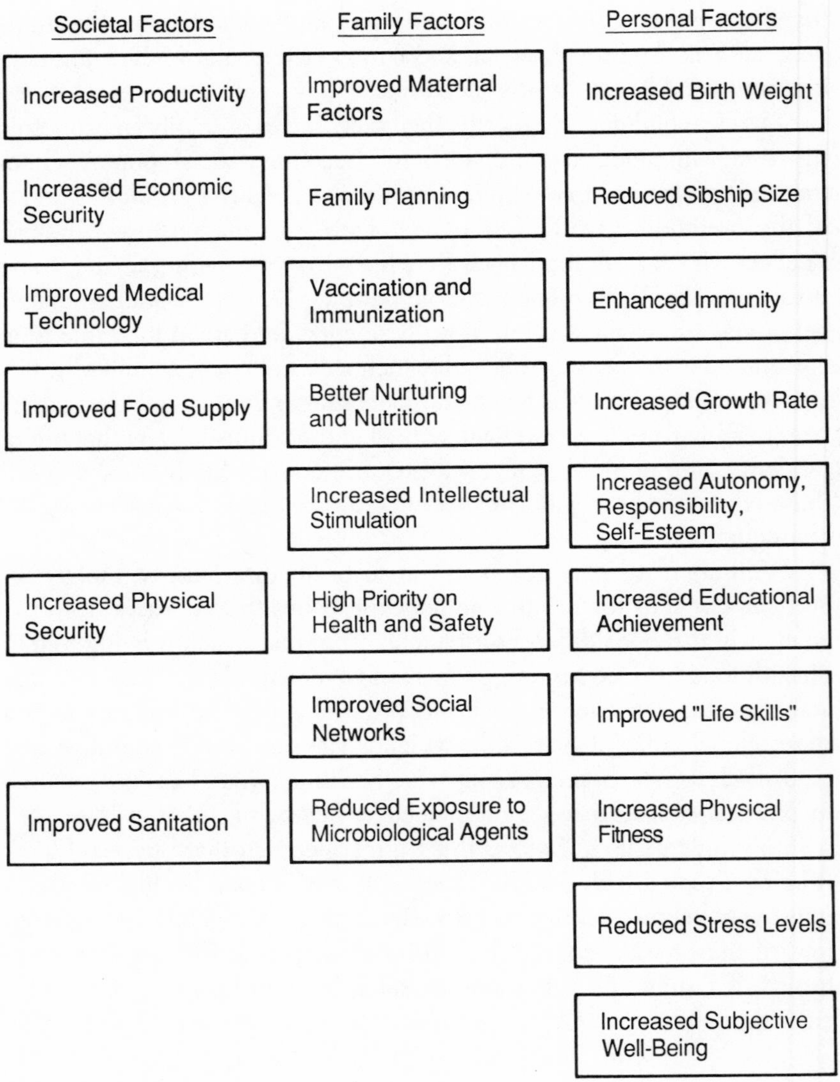

Societal Factors	Family Factors	Personal Factors
Increased Productivity	Improved Maternal Factors	Increased Birth Weight
Increased Economic Security	Family Planning	Reduced Sibship Size
Improved Medical Technology	Vaccination and Immunization	Enhanced Immunity
Improved Food Supply	Better Nurturing and Nutrition	Increased Growth Rate
	Increased Intellectual Stimulation	Increased Autonomy, Responsibility, Self-Esteem
Increased Physical Security	High Priority on Health and Safety	Increased Educational Achievement
	Improved Social Networks	Improved "Life Skills"
Improved Sanitation	Reduced Exposure to Microbiological Agents	Increased Physical Fitness
		Reduced Stress Levels
		Increased Subjective Well-Being

Psychological Characteristics of the Healthy Person

An important purpose of this study has been the search for a better definition of the healthy person. I believe that eight characteristics are common to healthy people.

First, they have a high level of self-esteem, an "inner locus of control." That is, they are confident of their ability to make competent decisions. They do not rely solely on traditional authority for guidance, but are able to acquire and evaluate information and make decisions independently (Rodin 1986). In contrast with traditional people who believe that outcomes are determined by gods, chance, or persons of influence, healthy people believe that their decisions can be efficacious in determining outcomes—that is, they believe that what they think and do will matter. Some call this quality "hardiness" (Kobasa, Maddi, and Kahn 1982).

Second, although healthy people have high regard for themselves, they are not self-indulgent or preoccupied with their personal identity or welfare. Rather they are committed to goals other than their own personal welfare. Goals may be global in scope or quite modest; most important, however, they are not egotistical in nature but will benefit others. Healthy people are compassionate, they have a strong sense of community. I believe that these qualities are in a state of decline in the United States—it may not be a coincidence that evidence of worsening health is appearing at the same time that Americans are preoccupied with "self-realization."

In his lifelong studies of psychologically healthy people, Abraham Maslow emphasized this quality of commitment (Maslow 1950). He describes healthy people as having a deep sense of identification with all of mankind, a sense of brotherhood, of affection, and of respect for each individual. Yet this affection does not obscure their basically clear vision of the defects of the world. Healthy people see warts as well as the beauty of humanity. Their perception is uncluttered.

Third, just as people living in premodern society place a low value on health and survival, healthy people place high values on these qualities. Although this is likely to result in certain behavior (such as exercise and diet), the high regard for health may itself be more important to health than the associated behavior. Jogging and vegetarianism may not be "causes" of good health so much as reflections of a healthy personality.

Fourth, healthy people are future-oriented—willing to delay immediate gratifications for future gains. They are willing to invest in themselves, particularly through education. Healthy people constantly collect information to improve decision making, to increase security and reduce uncertainty. They are generally well informed and consider it important to form opinions on affairs beyond those that touch solely on private interests.

Fifth, healthy people are trusting and easily enter into social networks, forming strong and persistent affectionate bonds. A strong and enduring marriage reflects the union of two healthy people. The well-known health advantage of married people is as much a reflection of the individual partners and their ability to make commitments as it is a result of the compatibility of the two partners.

Sixth, healthy people relish companionship. Yet, because they have a high regard for themselves, they are not uncomfortable when alone; indeed, periods of quiet contemplation and reflection are sought for their soul-nourishing value.

Seventh, beyond formal education, healthy people pursue knowledge, knowledge of themselves as well as knowledge of the world around them; to understand and find meaning is a basic human need. Although authoritarian societies provide meaning, they insist on conformity with their dogma. Modern society provides an environment in which individuals are free to creatively develop their own cosmologies.

Aaron Antonovsky (1984), a medical sociologist at Ben-Gurion University, has attemped a simple formulation of the healthy personality. He describes this person as having a "sense of coherence": "a global orientation that expresses the extent to which one has a pervasive, enduring though dynamic feeling of confidence that one's internal and external environments are predictable and that there is a high probability that things will work out as well as can reasonably be expected" (p. 41). Antonovsky feels, as I do, that far too much attention has been directed to study of the pathological personality to the neglect of an understanding of the healthy personality.

Revisiting the Biomedical Model

In chapter 1 I suggested that the medical model on which health policy is based is a set of arguable assumptions. One of these assumptions is the primary role of disease in determining health: we are assumed to be healthy until proven to be diseased. Another major assumption is that those diseases largely have their origin in the environment. Just as in the nineteenth century bacterial germs were accepted as the cause of disease, today we assume that chemical "germs" are a major cause of disease and death.

Still another assumption is that cultural and behavioral factors are relatively unimportant as determinants of health and disease. In this view diseases are largely explainable on the basis of chance encounters with environmental contaminants; the individual's predisposing characteristics are unimportant. Mental health is seen as important in determining the quality of life but not in determining the onset or outcome of the major causes of death.

Throughout history, prevailing attitudes toward individual responsibility for health maintenance have moved between extremes. Hippocrates and Galen believed that diet, exercise, and characteristics of good mental health were the primary determinants of physical health. Individuals were considered responsible for their own health. Throughout European history the human body was considered to be the seat of the soul. As the gift of God, it was the responsibility—a religious duty—of the individual to maintain health. American rugged individualism encouraged people to be responsible for their own medical care. Every family had its own self-help medical encyclopedia and homemade remedies—a collection of tonics, cathartics, and herbs.

With the recognition of the influence of environmental factors in disease at the end of the nineteenth century, there was a shift of responsibility for health from the individual to the physician and to public health authorities. At this time government was also assigned an important role in health protection (Reiser 1985). Since that time individuals' role as their own "health care provider" has contracted, and the government's responsibility to protect us against environmental sources of disease has expanded.

If, as I have proposed, health and life expectancy are as much, or more, a matter of psychosocial factors than of sanitation and medical care, then some important policy implications exist for us as individuals and for several of our institutions responsible for health. What, then, should be the new directions for individual and institutional reform?

Implications for the Individual

This is not a self-help book, and I shall not try to suggest simplistic schemes for acquiring good health, but readers might consider the following conclusions:

Self-esteem and a sense of personal competence as characteristics of healthy people should receive high priority as a national goal. The data reviewed throughout this book demonstrate that those who are competent and have confidence in themselves and in their ability to control their own lives will experience better health outcomes than those who do not. On the other hand, those who view themselves as passive victims helpless to determine outcomes will inevitably find themselves in stressful and difficult life situations. The sources of these personal qualities (or their absence) can be traced to the earliest family and social environment. It is here that the individual acquires life skills; such attitudes and values are difficult but not impossible for the adult to change.

In essence, the message is that in order to be healthy, people should not permit themselves the role of victim. Passive individuals often complain about being deprived of their rights, about how badly the world is treating them. As long as they complain and do nothing to improve the situation, nothing will happen, nothing will improve. Instead of brooding, people should allow feelings to surface. Anger may be justified; it is not a perfect world. Anger should be expressed not destructively but constructively. How did a particular situation or condition arise? What can be done to change those conditions? Only children and those who are greatly disabled are powerless. Mature adults take responsibility for surviving.

I have asserted that Americans' emphasis on physical fitness to the exclusion of behavioral components is misdirected. Rather than a national obsession with jogging, a campaign to improve self-fulfillment for oneself as well as for the disadvantaged, would likely prove much more beneficial to health. As I have stated, I am not opposed to regular exercise; indeed the evidence is that regular exercise is useful. Rather, it is a matter of priorities, of moderation in all things. Creating and improving relationships with others and learning to communicate effectively are as important as aerobics. Our lives may depend on both.

As a nation, we appear to be obsessed with stress and its consequences. I believe that the dangers of stress, while real, must be carefully

190

distinguished from the benefits of confronting challenge. It is as important to strengthen our coping skills as it is to reduce our exposure to excessive and unnecessary stressors. We should not allow our concern with stress to deter us from attempting to achieve excellence. The difference is a subtle one; while those with a low threshold for stress are likely to be impaired by stressful situations, those who possess robust coping mechanisms can tolerate and benefit from challenging experiences.

We also are obsessed with diet, vitamins, cholesterol and salt content, or whatever is the current trendy faddism in foods. Somehow little credit is given to good common sense in dietary choices. Beyond the necessity of maintaining reasonable body weight, there is little persuasive evidence that differences in diet are important to health, given a reasonably balanced diet. Furthermore, it must be recognized and remembered that eating should provide pleasure and be joyful, and not medicalized or viewed only as a means of beautifying the body. Recently I overheard teenagers discussing whether or not to eat ice-cream cones. They decided against it because of their concern with dieting and obesity although they were not obese.

We must accept responsibility for our own health. There is a widespread fear that minor symptoms should not be ignored lest some dreadful disease be overlooked and significant treatment deferred. Far more harm results from needless testing and medication than from neglect of symptoms. The average doctor rarely sees evidence of untreated disease that could have been aborted by earlier treatment. Preventive check-ups and screening of healthy populations for early disease detection have now been shown to be ineffective (Robin 1984).

Finally, we must not permit fear to dominate our concern with health. Many people become profoundly concerned with news of trace contamination of food, water, or air, particularly with industrial chemicals. There is no scientific evidence that justifies such concerns (see pp. 192–94).

Implications for Health Professionals

Patients consult physicians when they experience symptoms. Modern physicians are trained to analyze symptoms, to diagnose and treat disease. In China, however, physicians play a different role: they are expected to maintain the health of their patients, and when their patients become ill, physicians consider their efforts a failure.

If our extended live-span is, as I believe it to be, largely a result of an increase in resistance to and postponement of disease, rather than primarily a decline in disease incidence, then our health care system should change its emphasis from its current exclusive concern with *disease* care, to also encompass health care.

This is not to say that physicians should relinquish their treatment role in any way; rather they should stop treating their patients as "cases" and learn to evaluate and strengthen patients' health and resistance—the whole person. They must learn to enhance patients' sense of control and efficacy and not create a state of dependency. Journalist Norman Cousins (1983) has written that hospitals are operated in such a manner as to produce a state of total helplessness in their patients—just the opposite of what is most needed when a patient is experiencing a life crisis.

I saw this happen recently to my own father in one of San Francisco's finest hospitals. My father, who is a vigorous eighty-eight-year-old who spends part of each day working out in a gymnasium, entered the hospital for what should have been minor surgery. By being needlessly probed, x-rayed, neglected in drafty hallways, and left without information on what was happening, he quickly became depressed and developed a bleeding ulcer. Removal from the hospital environment was necessary to save his life. The physician had focused on my father's disease and ignored his health. Such things happen daily in any large hospital.

Far too much diagnostic testing is done. Physicians no longer seem to trust their own judgment. The practice is not harmless. Often, puzzling test results lead to more invasive and potentially harmful results without benefiting the patient. Every physician has seen many patients who have undergone unnecessary surgery due to suspicious and misleading test results. Physicians should adopt the rule that no test should be done unless the results will benefit the patient. Testing merely in order to gain information or to verify a diagnosis for which there is no effective treatment should not be condoned; it is often thoughtless, meddlesome, anxiety provoking, and costly for the patient.

The adoption of a resistance-oriented health model also implies that at every opportunity, physicians should be alert to evidence of a patient's poor or failing coping skills. They should routinely inquire about relationships at work, at home, and with friends. They should be as alert to symptoms of psychological decompensation as to signs of organ decompensation. This does not mean that each physician must be a skilled psychotherapist; the great majority of psychological problems do not require skilled or prolonged psychotherapy. Skilled and insightful grandmothers have been doing a good job of this for centuries.

Throughout this book I have repeatedly referred to behavioral patterns strongly associated with increased mortality: obesity, smoking, inactivity, abuse of alcohol. These too should alert physicians to important psychological issues that require investigation and counseling. Traumatic events, such as a death in the family, are also indications of an increased need for professional help and support. Physical evidence of distress, such as hypertension, angina, or ulcers, should not be treated only with drugs, but should indicate to alert physicians that their patient is confronting a level of stress with which he or she cannot easily cope. These are problems for which a drug prescription is not sufficient. While many good physicians do all of these things now, most do not.

Still another reason that medical consultations so often neglect the patient's psychological needs is that the patient may be unready to accept psychosocial explanations for illness and disease. It is convenient for patients to accept the thesis that the disease has its origins in environmental or genetic sources, thus relieving them of the need to reassess their own health and behavior. It is comfortable to shift responsibility for bad outcomes to others—to society, to physicians. It is also self-defeating.

One reason that the recognition and treatment of emotional disorders does not now occur as frequently as it should is that many physicians are not well trained *or* psychologically prepared to do so. Medical schools must change. They must alter both their curriculum and their staffs to provide new generations of physicians who will promote health and be sensitive to the whole person rather than only treating diseases.

Medical professionals and their patients must stop considering that every medical problem has a "technical fix." Many members of the public are appalled by the unnecessary and dehumanizing efforts to prolong the life of elderly and chronically ill patients during their terminal illness. The use of surgical procedures as treatment for mental illness has been an example of our proclivity to treat emotional problems with mechanical means. More than ten thousand psychotic people were tragically subjected to destruction of the frontal part of their brain—prefrontal lobotomies—before the practice was abolished (Valenstein 1985). I am afraid that we are approaching coronary artery disease in the same way—with a technical fix (coronary bypass surgery).

Leading educators are beginning to recognize these defects in medical education and to call for reform. Derek Bok, the president of Harvard University, points to the inadequacy of science alone to deal with disease (Bok 1984). He urged the Harvard Medical School to adopt as a goal the need "to understand the emotional, psychological and cultural underpinnings of human behavior, including the interweaving of mind and body in health" (p. 11).

I do not mean to encourage people to become their own physicians or to abandon the assistance of physicians. Laypeople, however, should be able to recognize the symptoms of common viral illnesses and know their effective treatment. They should also recognize the uselessness of such unnecessary physician visits as the annual physical examination when there are no symptoms. But when significant symptoms occur— and intelligent adults can certainly learn to recognize these—then by all means a physician should be consulted and advice obtained.

Under these circumstances, patients should treat their physician as a source of expert information; patients themselves should make final decisions regarding treatment; it is their body, their health is at stake. Therefore, after the physician has made a diagnosis and recommended treatment, patients should not be reluctant to inquire as to the basis for the diagnosis. What is the natural course of this disease? What complications can be expected? What is the rationale for the prescribed treatment and what benefits can be expected? Is it likely to relieve symptoms? Is treatment likely to prolong life? Some more curious patients may want to review the studies on which the doctor's judgments are based. If the diagnosis and treatment are life-threatening, the patient may want to visit the local medical library and, with the physician's guidance, do some reading. What are the possible risks and complications of the treatment? If drugs have been prescribed, what side effects might be expected? Are there interactions between this drug and others the patient may be taking? In pursuing these issues, patients are not challenging the physician's authority; the physician is performing as teacher, not as authority figure. The patient is student and ultimate decision maker. If a bad outcome results, it is not the physician who is at fault (unless there was negligence or the physician provided misleading information), it is the patient who made the decision leading to that outcome. Healthy people readily accept responsibility for their own lives.

Why Is the United States Faltering
in its Health Experience?

As I have emphasized, many people believe that American medical care is largely responsible for the spectacular increase in life expectancy that has been achieved in the United States in the past century. They also believe that U.S. life expectancy exceeds that of most other post-modern countries. Both of these assumptions are simply wrong. During the recent period of rapidly rising consumption of medical services, the United States ranked eighteenth in the world in life expectancy from birth; although the life-span continues to rise, the United States has nevertheless fallen among the modernized nations of the world, and now lags behind such countries as Greece, Spain, and Italy, countries whose per-capita health expenditures are a fraction of ours. Furthermore, as I noted in the introductory chapter, while death rates are still falling, measures of morbidity and disability, particularly among the young, demonstrate increases, not decreases.

Until now, these disturbing signs of increasing ill health in the United States have not been brought to the public's attention. Nor have goals for our health care system been well articulated. Should the United States be first in the world in life expectancy? Is that a worthwhile national goal? Is it reasonable to expect that a nation that includes numerous newly arrived immigrants to experience the same health as those countries whose populations are socially homogeneous and highly educated, such as Sweden? Why not? In the earlier part of this century when the United States was even more of a "melting pot," we were among the leaders in world health. Why are we slipping now? Earlier I pointed out many of the social problems that I believe provide answers to this question. The most important of these by far is the decline of the family. If the growth of the caring and nurturing modern family has played a key role in the development of modern health, then is it not likely that this decline in the strength of the family unit plays an important role in explaining the decline of American health in the postmodern period? I believe it does. This is as much a social as a medical problem. It can be attacked by educational means. Why are we not doing so? Dollars invested in sex education and community programs to encourage stronger family relationships will be far more conducive to health improvement than will

195

dollars spent for the intensive care of the medical problems to which these children and their mothers are so vulnerable.

There are other neglected subpopulations whose serious health problems contribute to our declining national health, including the homeless (particularly, the homeless and mentally ill), the illiterates and the hopeless, i.e. "the underclass." This population has grown in the very period during which American health has been declining, the last three decades. While applauding those who are helping, those efforts are largely directed toward providing care, rather than directed toward the source of this growing problem—the dissolution of the family.

It is not known with any certainty whether mental illness is increasing in the United States. The difficulty is that we have no consistently applied measures of mental illness in the American population. We also know that most cases of mental illness, even severe cases, do not come to medical attention. A door-to-door survey recently conducted by the National Institutes of Mental Health in three different communities (New Haven, Baltimore, and St. Louis) has produced some reliable information. Data were collected to provide evidence on prevalence during the current six-month period as well as to provide an estimate of lifetime prevalence (Glass and Freedman 1985). The most common single disorder found was alcoholism, which had a six-month prevalence of 5 percent and a lifetime prevalence of 12 to 16 percent. In other words, more than one out of every ten Americans will be incapacitated by alcoholism at sometime during their lifetimes. Five percent of Americans will have a major depressive disorder during their lifetimes. As many as a quarter of all medical visits are occasioned by mental health problems, but these are not always recognized as such either by the patient or the physician. Most people with even severe mental disorders are not treated. Yet the evidence is that these illnesses have a very high national cost; one estimate is $185 billion per year (Glass and Freedman 1985). More than economic losses are the enormous pain and suffering among patients as well as their families. In chapter 8 I reviewed the data on increased mortality rates among the mentally ill. Given the known contribution of family instability to the children of such families, this problem is likely to grow, as evidenced by the growing rates of suicide and drug addiction.

In still another area of American life we also see evidence of decline—education. In chapter 9, while stressing the strong relationships that exist between educational achievement and health, I also emphasized that there is a growing number of functionally illiterate Americans, those who can read and write but who do not have the skills necessary to acquire and keep jobs in a highly technologically advanced society. Is it

196

irrelevant that a recent study in Japan, which leads the world in health, shows that by fifth grade, the worst Japanese math class studied did better than the highest-performing American math class (Stevenson, Lee, and Stigler 1986)? Our high-school graduation rate is 75 percent. The Japanese rate is 90 percent! According to Diane Ravitch (1985), the average Japanese high-school graduate is as well educated as the average American college graduate!

We are becoming an increasingly service-oriented society. The number of jobs for those who are functionally illiterate is declining. The alienation and frustration of those who will be unemployed and dependent in such a postaffluent society bodes ill for the future health of the United States.

Implications for Public Health Policy

Public health policy in the United States is based on a biomedical model that assumes that disease, both acute and chronic, results largely from environmental agents and that, just as infectious disease was "conquered" during the past century through improvements in sanitation, the future of disease eradication in this century and the next will also result from improvements in the environment rather than changes in human behavior. We annually spend tens of billions of dollars on environmental improvement based largely on the hope that through such means we shall reduce cancer and other chronic diseases thought to result from contamination of the environment. Such a strategy ignores the fact that life expectancy rose in the United States most rapidly during the early decades of this century, when environmental contamination was most intense. In fact, just as with the medical care system, the enormously expensive environmental movement of the past few decades was initiated largely after the major improvement in American health had begun to plateau.

The evidence of hazard from these exposures derives from observations in highly susceptible laboratory animals exposed to unrealistically high doses throughout their lives. Rarely are estimates of health hazards based on observations of human populations and when they are, they are experiences with accidental or prolonged occupational exposures to very high concentrations. Nevertheless, because of those associations, it is assumed that even the briefest exposure to even very small concentrations is hazardous.

When estimates of risk are based on "hard" evidence—on reliable observations in human populations—then only a very small percentage—less than 1 percent—of all mortality can be traced to such exposures. Consider as examples the cases of diethylstilbestrol (DES), vinyl chloride, and ionizing radiation, three of the small group of agents known to be carcinogenic to humans.

During the 1950s, DES was routinely prescribed to women early in their pregnancy when there was a history of habitual abortion. Although the drug was effective in preventing abortion, it was later found that female children who had been exposed to the drug as a fetus were at increased risk of vaginal cancer. Millions of women had thus been exposed, yet the total number of such cancers worldwide is less than five hundred. Even this number is tragic, but the point is that even with the very high doses of DES that were used, only rarely did the woman's offspring develop cancer. One estimate is that one cancer resulted in the daughter of each thousand women for whom the drug was prescribed (Melnick 1987).

Vinyl chloride is the basic material from which one of the commonest of all plastic materials, poly vinyl chloride, is made. Vinyl chloride is now known to produce an unusual cancer of the liver, hemangioendothelioma. In spite of the extensive industrial use of this plastic, less than one hundred cases of this disease are cited in the world literature.

Ionizing radiation is established as a carcinogenic agent, yet, like the other agents just described, its effects are not terribly potent. For example, among the 285,000 persons who survived the atomic bombings in Japan, there have now been 67,660 deaths. Of these, it is estimated that 526 were from cancers that were the result of weapons-produced radiation (Kato and Schull 1982). This represents an increase of about 5 percent in cancer risk in a population that was exposed to massive radiation exposure.

The exception to the observation that human populations are generally highly resistant to the toxic effects of harmful agents is cigarette smoking; the combustion products of tobacco are powerful carcinogens, but several daily inhalations directly into the lungs over many years in high concentration are required to produce cancer or other health hazards.

All of these examples relate to cancer. Although we do know something of the ability of certain agents to increase the incidence of particular cancers, our knowledge is fragmentary. We often assume that contami-

198

nation with traces of these agents are harmful; yet, we still know precious little about the processes through which a cancer is initiated or promoted. We do know that many, if not most, of the natural plant substances found in our diet, as well as many of the hormones in our bodies, can be carcinogenic under certain conditions. Almost certainly, the role of exogenous agents in the origin of human cancer has been exaggerated.

Other than for cancer, we have little evidence that other diseases are related to exposure to environmental agents (except microorganisms). Why is it, then, that the public holds such an exaggerated view of the influence of environmental agents on health and has so little concern about personal or psychosocial factors as determinants of disease? Why is it that we divert enormous resources to study* and/or remove unproven sources of disease in the environment while ignoring obvious human problems of neglect, brutality, loneliness, and ignorance? Certainly the explanations are complex, but at least part of the blame lies in our faith in our theoretical model of the origins of disease and our ignorance of health. While I endorse a thoughtful environmental improvement, I also feel that the promise that such improvement will alone contribute to health in an important way is badly misguided. If the intent is to improve health, there are clearly better ways to expend those funds. Throughout this book I have identified a number of social problems for which investment of resources is much more likely to contribute to improved health. The homeless could be housed, more attractive conditions could be created for the elderly and disabled, and the illiterate could be rehabilitated. Recognizing the devastating effects to health that follow psychologically traumatizing events such as rape, we must create the social support mechanisms necessary to support victims and mitigate the health consequences. Rape, for example, is extremely common and growing rapidly. Rape is said to be the fastest growing of the violent crimes. It is estimated that one in six women will be raped during her lifetime (Martin, Warfield, and Braen 1983). We must recognize these events as being just as much public health problems as are smallpox epidemics.

---

* It is estimated that more than a billion dollars have been spent in researching possible biological effects of dioxins, yet not a single human death has been attributed to exposure to these substances (Tschirley 1986).

Implications for Research

There are enough unproven assertions in this volume to provide material for hundreds of Ph.D. candidates for several decades. Yet I insisted from the very beginning that in complex systems such as those represented by human health, proof in the usual legal sense is too high a standard. If the assertions presented here are not provable, neither are those held by the more conventional majority. If not provable, there are nevertheless many areas of investigation that could throw further light on the issues raised here. Some are:

1. An assumption important for my basic conclusion is that those living in premodern societies experience more stressors than those living in modern societies, that their greater exposure to family death and catastrophe, to natural disasters and to scarcity take a large toll in their health. While this appears plausible, even likely, it deserves study.

2. I have asserted that those living in premodern societies are less resilient, less able to cope, and therefore more vulnerable to stress, helplessness, and death. People living in premodern societies, then, experience a "double whammy"—they are exposed to more frequent stressors and are less well equipped, both psychologically and otherwise, to cope with those stressors. I believe that the evidence supporting this conclusion is substantial, but the question also deserves considerably more investigation by anthropologists and sociologists.

3. I have asserted that the underlying basis for these differences in behavior are to be found in different parenting behavior among modern and premodern societies. Although much evidence cited in previous chapters supports this view, more research is clearly needed.

4. Although there has been considerable study of the health consequences to the child of loss of the mother, little attention has been paid to the importance to the child of the complete family unit, which of course includes the father or father surrogate. Given the rapidly rising prevalence of single-parent families in the United States, the need for this information is acute.

5. There is much to learn about human response to stressors. What are the predisposing characteristics of those who are vulnerable, as contrasted with those who are not? I have suggested some factors that appear to be important: education, social support systems, well-developed coping mechanisms. How important are they?

200

6. If social support systems protect against hopelessness and disease, how do they do this? Are such networks effective before the occurrence of stress, during the episode of stress, afterward, or all of these?

7. The relative roles of education, nutrition, and medical care in the improvement of health deserve more attention. My own belief is that investments in education are more likely to pay off in improved health, dollar for dollar, than are investments in either of the other areas. The conditions under which this may not be true need consideration.

8. I have emphasized the importance of response to stressors as a factor that explains survival differences between healthy and unhealthy people. I also believe that this explanation alone is unsatisfactory, and that there also exists among healthy people a sense of fulfillment, of personal growth, of joy, of creativity, that contributes in an important way to survival. Because of their obsession with disease, scientists have neglected to study persons of robust psychological health. We need to examine, for example, not only the immune mechanisms of those who are depressed or otherwise under stress but also mechanisms of disease resistance of people who display evidence of superior psychological health and creativity.

One study of such people was conducted on 6,329 distinguished men, chosen randomly from men cited in *Who's Who in America* (Quint and Cody 1970). When compared with other men of an identical age distribution, the risk of death to the *Who's Who* sample was about 57 percent of that experienced by other men in similar occupations. There were also wide differences among the professional groups; of persons listed in the volume, journalists had a mortality rate twice that of all others, whereas scientists had a mortality rate 20 percent less than the remainder of the study population. Why are these accomplished people so long-lived? Abraham Maslow suggests that human beings have innate needs that exist in hierarchical form. When the basic needs of physical and nutritional security are satisfied, he says, then the drive for intellectual growth, for "self-actualization," becomes preeminent (Maslow 1950). If people denied adequate nutrition and security experience increased vulnerability to disease and death, are those whose needs for full intellectual growth also at increased risk, and are those with the opportunity for full emotional and cognitive growth able to live to the biological limits of life expectancy?

9. I have suggested that many common medical procedures are ineffective in prolonging life. The wide geographic variability in the consumption of medical diagnostic and therapeutic procedures provides ample evidence that there are not well-considered or well-agreed-upon

standards among physicians as to when they use these procedures (Chassin et al. 1986). Since all medical and surgical procedures impose some risk as well as financial cost, there is a need to conduct experiments that will demonstrate the efficacy of medical procedures. Such studies are expensive and difficult; nevertheless, ignoring the need for such studies is almost certainly more wasteful of human lives and resources. There are too many procedures that have become part of commonly accepted practices, only later to be abandoned as ineffective, to rely on traditional authority for judgment on the matter.

10. There is also a desperate need to examine the social condition that, for want of a better term, I shall call the decline in American character, as well as the means for reversing this condition. Why is the American family disintegrating? Why are young people no longer willing to make a permanent commitment to family? Why is there a drug epidemic? Such questions are asked not out of any sense of offended morality, but rather because their answers appear to be closely related to the increasing failure of American health.

The welfare programs initiated by the past generation were reflections of a compassionate desire to help. Yet evidence is now accumulating that those programs also contribute to dependency and reduce health, rather than assisting the helpless to regain their pride and help themselves. The means with which to do this better are desperately needed. How to achieve these ends are not obvious, but neither are the causes of other diseases. Once we recognize that health is more closely related to pride and self-sufficiency than to trace contaminants in the environment, then the resources and imagination to achieve improved health will become available.

While results of this proposed research will be useful to future health planning, the health of Americans will depend upon more than good research and information. Improvements in health will fundamentally depend upon a new vision of human health and its determinants. That new vision of health will have far broader dimensions than the present narrow concept. The unit of health must be broadened beyond the individual to include the entire social network on which the health of the individual depends; a healthy nation is more than a collection of healthy individuals. Just as no person is entirely self-contained ("no man is an island"), so too does the health of each of us depend upon those around us, upon the family, and also upon the larger network of a caring and nurturing community. Both the family and the caring community appear to be in decline in the United States; that trend must be reversed.

Reflections and Proposals

Another dimension that must be incorporated into our notion of health is an understanding and appreciation for the preeminent role of early childhood in forming the attitudes and values that are fundamental to the formation of a healthy personality. Our current biomedical paradigm focuses attention narrowly on adult behavior, on diet and particularly on physical fitness as the primary determinant of health, and largely ignores the fundamental role of our self-esteem, and our ability to form affectionate relationships with others, and finally, to feel ourselves to be in charge of our own lives. It is in these qualities that true health lies.

References

Aaby, P. "Overcrowding and Intensive Exposure as Determinants of Measles Mortality." *American Journal of Epidemiology* 120 (1984):49–63.

Acheson, R., and Williams, D. "Does Consumption of Fruit and Vegetables Protect Against Stroke?" *Lancet* I (1983): 1191–1194.

Adam, K. S. "Loss, Suicide and Attachment." In *The Place of Attachment in Human Behavior*, ed. C. Parkes and J. Stevenson-Hinde, pp. 269–294. New York: Basic Books, 1982.

Ader, R. "Behavioral Influences on Immune Responses." In *Perspectives on Behavioral Medicine*, ed. S. Weiss, J. Herd, and B. Fox, pp. 163–182. New York: Academic Press, 1979.

Antonovsky, A. "Social Class, Life Expectancy and Overall Mortality." *Millbank Memorial Fund Quarterly* 45 (1967):31–73.

———. "The Sense of Coherence as a Determinant of Health Advances." *Advances; Institute for the Advancement of Health* 1 (1984):37–50.

Arieff, A. "Hyponatremia, Convulsions, Respiratory Arrest, and Permanent Brain Damage After Elective Surgery in Healthy Women." *New England Journal of Medicine* 314 (1986):1529–1535.

Aries, P. *Centuries of Childhood*. New York: Vintage Books, 1962.

Arneil, G., et al. "National Post-perinatal Infant Mortality and Cot Death Study, Scotland, 1981–2." *Lancet* I (1985):740–743.

Axtell, J. *The Educational Writings of John Locke*. London: Cambridge University Press, 1968.

Babigian, H. M., and Odoroff, C. "The Mortality Experience of a Population with Psychiatric Illness." *American Journal of Psychiatry* 126 (1960):470–480.

Bailar, J., and Smith, E. "Progress Against Cancer?" *New England Journal of Medicine* 314 (1986):1226–1323.

Baird, D. "Social Class and Fetal Mortality." *Lancet* II (1947):531–535.

Banfield, E. *The Moral Basis of a Backward Society*. New York: Free Press, 1958.

Barlow, K. "Bread, Diet and Health: A Plea for Policy." *Science and Public Policy* (1984, February):47–51.

Bartrop, R., et al. "Depressed Lymphocyte Function After Bereavement." *Lancet* I (1977):834–836.

Baruffi, G., et al. "A Study of Pregnancy Outcomes in a Maternity Center and a Tertiary Care Hospital." *American Journal of Public Health* 74 (1984):974–978.

Bassuk, E., quoted in C. Holdren, "Homelessness: Experts Differ on Root Causes." *Science* 232 (1986):569–570.

Behbehani, A. "The Smallpox Story: Life and Death of an Old Disease." *Microbiological Reviews* 47 (1983):455–509.

Bell, T. "Illiteracy and the Scope of the Problem in This Country." Testimony in hearing before the House Subcommittee on Postsecondary Education of the Committee on Education and Labor, September 21, 1982. Washington, D.C.: U.S. Government Printing Office, 1984, p. 10.

Benham, L., and Benham, A. "The Impact of Incremental Medical Services on Health Status, 1963–1970." In *Equity in Health Services: Empirical Analysis of Social Policy,* ed. R. Anderson, J. Kravetz, and O. Anderson, pp. 217–228. Cambridge, MA: Ballinger, 1975.

Bennett, J. "Human Infections: Economic Implications and Prevention." *Annals of Internal Medicine* 89 (pt. 2) (1978):761–763.

Bergsjo, P., Schmidt, E., and Pusch, D. "Differences in the Reported Frequencies of Some Obstetrical Interventions in Europe." *British Journal of Obstetrics and Gynecology* 90 (1983):628–632.

Berkman, L. "Assessing the Physical Health Effects of Social Networks and Social Support." *Annual Review of Public Health* 5 (1984):413–432.

Berkman, L., and Syme, S. "Social Networks, Host Resistance, and Mortality: A Nine-Year Follow-up Study of Alameda County Residents." *American Journal of Epidemiology* 109 (1979):186–204.

Berlin, N., Buncher, C., and Fontana, R. "The National Cancer Institute Cooperative Early Lung Cancer Detection Program: Results of the Initial Screen (Prevalence)." *American Review of Respiratory Disease* 130 (1984):545–570.

Bernstein, L., and Elrick, H. "The Handling of Experimental Animals as a Control Factor in Animal Research—A Review." *Metabolism* 6 (1957):479–482.

Berrueta-Clement, J., et al. *Changed Lives: The Effects of the Perry Preschool Program on Youths Through Age 19.* Ypsilanti, MI: High/Scope Press, 1984.

Bettelheim, B. *Surviving and Other Essays.* New York: Knopf, 1979.

Birdsall, N. "Fertility and Economic Change in Eighteenth and Nineteenth Century Europe." *Population and Development Review* 9 (1960):111–123.

Black, D., Morris, J., Smith, C., and Townsend, P. *Inequalities in Health: The Black Report.* New York: Penguin Books, 1982.

Blair, S., Jacobs, D., and Powell, K. "Relationships Between Exercise or Physical Activity and Other Health Behaviors." *Public Health Reports* 100 (1985):172–180.

Block, G., et al. "Nutrient Sources in the American Diet: Quantitative Data from the NHANES Dietary Survey." *American Journal of Epidemiology* 122 (1985):27–40.

Blum, H. "Mind Altering Drugs and Dangerous Behavior: Alcohol." In *Task Force Report: Drunkenness* (app. B), President's Commission on Law Enforcement and Administration of Justice, pp. 29–49. Washington, D.C.: U.S. Government Printing Office, 1967.

Blythe, R. *Akenfield: Portrait of an English Village.* New York: Pantheon, 1959.

Boffey, P. "Cancer Progress: Are the Statistics Telling the Truth?" *New York Times,* 18 Sept. 1984.

Bok, D. *The President's Report to the Board of Overseer's, 1982–3.* Cambridge, MA: Harvard University, 1984.

Bottoms, S., Rosen, M., and Sokol, R. "The Increase in the Cesarean Birth Rate." *New England Journal of Medicine* 302 (1980):559–563.

Bowlby, J. *Young Children in Hospitals.* New York: Basic Books, 1958.

Bradburn, N., and Noll, C. *The Structure of Psychological Well-Being.* Chicago: Aldine, 1969.

Braitman, L., Adlin, E., and Stanton, J. "Obesity and Caloric Intake: The National Health and Nutrition Examination." Survey of 1971–75 (HANES I). *Journal of Chronic Diseases* 38 (1985):727–732.

Branden, N. *The Psychology of Romantic Love.* Los Angeles: Tarcher, 1980.

References

Braunwald, E. "Effects of Coronary-artery Bypass Grafting on Survival." *New England Journal of Medicine* 309 (1983):1181–1184.

Brenner, M. *Estimating the Effects of Economic Change on National Health and Social Well-being.* Study prepared for the Subcommittee on Economic Goals and Intergovernmental Policy of the Joint Economic Committee Congress of the United States. Washington, D.C.: U.S. Government Printing Office, 1984.

Breslow, L., and Endstrom, J. "Persistence of Health Habits and Their Relationship to Mortality." *Preventive Medicine* 9 (1980):469–483.

Britten, R. "The Incidence of Epidemic Influenza, 1918–19. A Further Analysis According to Age, Sex, and Color of the Records of Morbidity and Mortality Obtained in Surveys of 12 Localities." *Public Health Reports* 47 (1932):303–339.

Brown, G. W., and Harris, T. O. *Social Origins of Depression.* New York: The Free Press, 1978.

Brozek, J., and Keys, A. "Drastic Food Restriction: Effect on Cardiovascular Dynamics in Normotensive and Hypertensive Conditions." *Journal of the American Medical Association* 137 (1948):1569–1574.

Bureau of the Census. *Historical Statistics of the United States, Colonial Times to 1970.* Bicentennial edition, part 2. Washington, D.C.: U.S. Government Printing Office, 1975.

Burgess, A., and Holmstrom, L. "Rape Trauma Syndrome." *American Journal of Psychiatry* 131 (1974):981–986.

Bustad, L. *Animals, Aging and the Aged.* Minneapolis: University of Minnesota Press, 1980.

Calabrese, E. *Toxic Susceptibility: Male/Female Differences.* New York: Wiley Interscience, 1985.

Cahalan, D., and Cisin, I. "Drinking Behavior and Drinking Problems in the United States." In *Social Aspects of Alcoholism*, ed. B. Kissin and H. Begleiter, pp. 77–115. New York: Plenum Press, 1976.

Caplan, G. "The Family as a Support System." In *Support Systems and Mutual Help: Multidisciplinary Explorations*, ed. G. Caplan and M. Killilea, pp. 19–36. New York: Grune & Stratton, 1976.

Caplan, G. "Mastery of Stress: Psychosocial Aspects." *American Journal of Psychiatry* 138 (1981):413–420.

Carter, R. "Exercise and Happiness." *Journal of Sports Medicine and Physical Fitness* 17 (1977):307–313.

Centers, R. *The Psychology of Social Classes.* Princeton, N.J.: Princeton University Press, 1949.

Chase, H. *International Comparisons of Perinatal and Infant Mortality: The United States and Six West European Countries.* Public Health Service Publication no. 1000, series 3, no. 6. Washington, D.C.: U.S. Government Printing Office, 1967.

Chassin, M., et al. "Variations in the Use of Medical and Surgical Services by the Medicare Population." *New England Journal of Medicine* 314 (1986):285–289.

Chen, E., and Cobb, S. "Family Structure in Relation to Health and Disease." *Journal of Chronic Diseases* 12 (1960):544–567.

Chief Medical Officer. Report of Chief Medical Officer of the Ministry of Health: The State of Public Health During Six Years of War, 1946. (Cited in Barlow.)

Cipolla, C. M. *Before the Industrial Revolution: European Society and Economy, 1000–1700.* New York: W. W. Norton, 1975.

———. *Literacy and Development in the West.* Middlesex, England: Penguin Books, 1969.

Clark, E., and Danbolt, N. "The Oslo Study of the Natural Course of Untreated Syphilis." *Medical Clinics of North America* 64 (1964):613–624.

Cohen, S., and Wils, T. "Stress, Social Support, and the Buffering Hypothesis." *Psychological Bulletin* 98 (1985):310–357.

Coleman, J. *Abnormal Psychology and Modern Life*. Chicago: Scott-Foresman, 1964.

Comstock, G., and Partridge, K. "Church Attendance and Health." *Journal of Chronic Diseases* 25 (1972):665–672.

Connor, K. "Invisible Citizenship: Adult Illiteracy in California." A Special Report on Adult Illiteracy to Senator David Roberti. Sacramento, CA: Senate Office of Research, 1986.

Consensus Conference. "Limb-sparing Treatment of Adult Soft-tissue Sarcomas and Osteosarcomas." *Journal of the American Medical Association* 254 (1985):1791–1794.

Cornfeld, D., and Hubbard, J. "A Four-year Study of the Occurrence of Beta-hemolytic Streptococci in 64 School Children." *New England Journal of Medicine* 264 (1961): 211.

Corson, S., and Corson, E. "Pet Animals as Non-Verbal Communication Mediators in Psychotherapy in Institutional Settings." In *Ethology and Non-verbal Communication in Mental Health*, ed. S. Corson and E. Corson, pp. 83–110. New York: Pergamon Press, 1980.

Cousins, N. "Anatomy of an Illness (as Perceived by the Patient)." *New England Journal of Medicine* 295 (1976):1458–1463.

———. *The Healing Heart*. New York: W. W. Norton, 1983.

Covey, L., and Wynder, E. "Smoking Habits and Occupational Status." *Journal of Occupational Medicine* 23 (1981):537–542.

Cyeyinka, G. "Age and Sex Differences in Immunocompetence." *Gerontology* 30 (1984): 188–195.

Daly, M., and Wilson, M. "Child Abuse and Other Risks of Not Living with Both Parents." *Ethnology and Sociobiology* 6 (1985):197–210.

Danforth, D. "Cesarean Section." *Journal of the American Medical Association* 253 (1985):811–817.

Darcy, C., and Siddique, C. "Marital Status and Psychological Well Being: A Cross-National Comparative Analysis." *International Journal of Comparative Sociology* 26 (1985):146–166.

Dayal, H., Power, R., and Chiu, C. "Race and Socioeconomic Status in Survival from Breast Cancer." *Journal of Chronic Diseases* 35 (1982):675–683.

Degler, C. *At Odds: Women and the Family in America from the Revolution to the Present*. New York: Oxford University Press, 1980.

de Lint, J., and Schmidt, W. "Alcoholism and Mortality." In *Social Aspects of Alcoholism*, ed. B. Kissin and H. Begleiter, pp. 275–305. New York: Plenum Press, 1976.

Demos, J. "Demography and Psychology in the Historical Study of Family Life: A Personal Report." In *Household and Family in Past Time*, ed. P. Laslett and R. Wall, pp. 561–569. New York: Cambridge University Press, 1972.

DeRegt, R., et al. "Relation of Private or Clinic Care to the Caesarean Birth Rate." *New England Journal of Medicine* 315 (1986):619–624.

DeVos, S. "An Old Age Security Incentive for Children in the Philippines and Taiwan." *Economic Development and Cultural Change* 33 (1985):793–814.

Dishman, R., Sallis, J., and Orenstein, D. "The Determinants of Physical Activity and Exercise." *Public Health Reports* 100 (1985):158–170.

Divale, W. "Systemic Population Control in the Middle and Upper Paleolithic: Inferences Based on Contemporary Hunters and Gatherers." *World Archeology* 4 (1972): 222–243.

References

Dohrenwend, B., and Dohrenwend, B. *Social Status and Psychological Disorder: A Causal Inquiry*. New York: Wiley, 1969.

Drabek, T., and Key, W. *Conquering Disaster: Family Recovery and Long-term Consequences*. New York: Irvington, 1984.

Dublin, L., Lotka, A., and Spiegelman, M. *Length of Life*. New York: Ronald Press, 1949 (rev. ed.).

Duff, R., and Campbell, M. "Medical and Ethical Issues in the Special Care Nursery." *New England Journal of Medicine* 289 (1973):890–894.

Easterlin, R. "Does Economic Growth Improve the Human Lot? Some Empirical Evidence." In *Nations and Households in Economic Growth*, ed. P. David and M. Reder, pp. 89–125. New York: Academic Press, 1974.

Eaton, J., and Weil, R. *Culture and Mental Disorders*. Glencoe, IL: Free Press, 1955.

Editorial. "Why Has Stroke Mortality Declined?" *Lancet* I (1983):1195–1196.

Eggertsen, S., and Berg, A. "Is It Good Practice to Treat Patients with Uncomplicated Myocardial Infarction at Home?" *Journal of the American Medical Association* 251 (1984):349–350.

Eickhoff, T. "Antibiotics and Nosocomial Infections." In *Hospital Infections*, ed. J. Bennett and P. Brachman, pp. 171–192. Boston: Little, Brown, 1986.

Eisenstadt, R., and Schoenborn, C. "Basic Data from Wave II of the National Survey of Personal Health Practices and Consequences: United States, 1980." Working Paper series no. 13, National Center for Health Statistics, U.S. Dept of Health and Human Services, October 1982.

Epstein, L., and Wing, R. "Aerobic Exercise and Weight." *Addictive Behavior* 5 (1980): 371–388.

Erikson, K. "Loss of Community at Buffalo Creek." *American Journal of Psychiatry* 133 (1976):302–305.

Farrell, P., and Fuchs, V. "Schooling and Health: The Cigarette Connection." Working Paper no. 768, National Bureau of Economic Research, Cambridge, MA, 1981.

Fawcett, J., and Bornstein, M. "Modernization, Individual Modernity, and Fertility." In *Psychological Perspectives on Population*, ed. J. Fawcett, pp. 106–131. New York: Basic Books, 1973.

Feachem, R., et al. *Water, Health, and Development: An Interdisciplinary Evaluation*. London: Tri-Med Books, 1978.

Feinleib, M., and Wilson, R. "Trends in Health in the United States." *Environmental Health Perspectives* 62 (1985):267–276.

Feinstein, A., Sosin, D., and Wells, C. "The Will Rogers Phenomenon: Stage Migration and New Diagnostic Technique Source of Misleading Statistics for Survival of Cancer." *New England Journal of Medicine* 312 (1985):1604–1608.

Finland, M. "Emergence of Antibiotic Resistance in Hospitals, 1935–1975." *Review of Infectious Diseases* 1 (1979):4–21.

Fisher, B., et al. "Five Year Results of a Randomized Clinical Trial Comparing Total Mastectomy and Segmental Mastectomy With or Without Radiation in the Treatment of Breast Cancer." *New England Journal of Medicine* 312 (1985):665–673.

Fleming, W. "Syphilis Through the Ages." *Medical Clinics of North America* 64 (1964): 587–612.

Flynn, J. "The Mean IQ of Americans: Massive Gains 1932 to 1978." *Psychological Bulletin* 95 (1984):29–51.

Fogle, B., ed. *Interrelations Between People and Animals*. Springfield, IL: Charles C Thomas, 1981.

Fouriaud, C., et al. "Influence of Socioprofessional Conditions on Blood Pressure Levels and Hypertension Control." *American Journal of Epidemiology* 120 (1984):72–86.

Frazier, S. "Responding to the Needs of the Homeless Mentally Ill." *Public Health Reports* 100 (1985):452–469.

Freedman, D. "Psychiatric Epidemiology Counts." *Archives of General Psychiatry* 41 (1984):931–933.

Frerichs, R., Chapman, J., and Maes, E. "Mortality Due to All Causes and to Cardiovascular Diseases Among Seven Race-Ethnic Populations in Los Angeles County, 1980." *International Journal of Epidemiology* 13 (1984):291–298.

Friedman, E., et al. "Animal Companions: One-Year Survival After Discharge from a Coronary Care Unit." *Public Health Reports* 95 (1980):307–312.

Fromm, E. *The Art of Loving.* New York: Harper & Row, 1956.

Fuchs, R. *Abandoned Children: Foundlings and Child Welfare in Nineteenth Century France.* New York: State University of New York Press, 1984.

Galbraith, V. H. "The Literacy of Medieval Kings." *Proceedings of the British Academy* 21 (1935):204.

Garrow, J. "Weight Penalties." *British Medical Journal* 2 (1979):1171–1172.

Gavin, H. *Sanitary Ramblings.* London: J. Churchill, 1848.

Gelles, R. "Family Violence." *Annual Review of Sociology* 11 (1985):347–367.

Gille, H. "The Demographic History of the Northern European Countries in the Eighteenth Century." *Population Studies* 34 (1949):3–65.

Gillum, R., et al. "Personality, Behavior, Family Environment, Family Social Status and Hypertension Risk Factors in Children." *Journal of Chronic Diseases* 38 (1985): 187–194.

Glass, R., and Freedman, D. "Psychiatry." *Journal of the American Medical Association* 254 (1985):2282–2283.

Glenn, N., and Kramer, K. "The Psychological Well-being of Adult Children of Divorce." *Journal of Marriage and the Family* November (1985):905–912.

Goedert, J., et al. "Decreased Helper T Lymphocytes in Homosexual Men: I. Sexual Contact in High-incidence Areas for the Acquired Immune Deficiency Syndrome." *American Journal of Epidemiology* 121 (1985):629–636.

Goldbaum, G., Remington, P., Powell, K., et al. "Failure to Use Seat Belts in the United States." *Journal of the American Medical Association* 255 (1986):2459–2462.

Goldwater, B., and Collis, M. "Psychologic Effects of Cardiovascular Conditioning: A Controlled Experiment." *Psychosomatic Medicine* 47 (1985):174–181.

Graham, G. "Searching for Hunger in America." *The Public Interest* 78 (1985):3–17.

Guidubaldi, J., and Perry, J. "Divorce and Mental Health Sequelae for Children: A Two Year Follow-up of a Nationwide Sample." *Journal of the American Academy of Child Psychology* 24 (1985):531–537.

Guralnick, L. "Socioeconomic Differences in Mortality by Cause of Death: United States, 1950, and England and Wales, 1949–53." Paper presented at the International Population Congress, Ottawa, August 1963. Liege: International Union for the Scientific Study of Population, 1964.

Haenzel, W., and Tauber, L. "Lung Cancer Mortality as Related to Residence and Smoking Histories: II. White Females." *Journal of the National Cancer Institute* 32 (1964):803–838.

Hagerty, R. "Life Stress, Illness and Social Supports." *Developmental Medicine and Child Neurology* 22 (1980):391–400.

Haggard, H. *Devils, Drugs, and Doctors.* New York: Harper, 1929.

Haley, R., et al. "The Nationwide Nosocomial Infection Rate." *American Journal of Epidemiology* 121 (1985):159–167.

References

Hamburg, B., and Killea, M. *Relation of Social Support, Stress, and Use of Health Services.* In "Healthy People." Background Papers (USDHEW) DHEW Publ. No. 79-550/1A. Washington, D.C.: U.S. Government Printing Office, 1979.

Hamilton, J. "The Role of Testicular Secretions as Indicated by the Effects of Castration in Man and by Studies of Pathological Conditions and the Short Lifespan Associated with Maleness." *Recent Progress in Hormone Research* 3 (1948):257-324.

Hampton, R., and Newberger, E. "Child Abuse and Reporting by Hospitals: Significance of Severity, Class and Race." *American Journal of Public Health* 75 (1985):56-60.

Hanson, S., and Sporokowski, M. "Single Parent Families." *Family Relations* 35 (1986): 3-8.

Harrington, P. "Mary and Femininity: A Psychological Critique." *Journal of Religion and Health* 23 (1984):204-217.

Hauser, W., and Remington, J. "Effect of Antibiotics on the Immune Response." *American Journal of Medicine* 72 (1982):711-716.

Hawthorn, G. *The Sociology of Fertility.* London: Collier-McMillan, 1970.

Healthy People: The Surgeon General's Report on Health Promotion and Disease Prevention. U.S. Dept. of Health, Education and Welfare. DHEW (PHS) Publication No. 79-55071, 1979.

Hedrich, A. W. "Monthly Estimates of the Child Population 'Susceptible' to Measles, 1900-1931." *American Journal of Hygiene* 17 (1933):613-636.

Hendershot, G. "Domestic Review: Trends in Breast Feeding." *Pediatrics* 74, Supplement (1984):591-602. (Report of the Task Force on the Assessment of the Scientific Evidence Relating to Infant-Feeding Practices and Infant Health.)

Henry, J., and Henry, Z. *Doll Play of Pilaga Indian Children.* New York: Vintage Books, 1944.

Herberman, R. "Immune Surveillance Hypothesis: Updated Formulation and Possible Effector Mechanisms Progress." In *Immunology V*, Yamamuray, Y. and Tada, T., pp. 1157-1167. New York: Academic Press, 1984.

Heron, W. "Cognitive and Psychological Effects of Perceptual Isolation." In *Sensory Deprivation*, ed. P. Solomon et al., pp. 6-33. Cambridge, MA: Harvard University Press, 1961.

Hersher, L., Moore, A., and Richmond, J. "Effect of Postpartum Separation of Mother and Kid on Maternal Care in the Domestic Goat." *Science* 128 (1958):1342-1343.

Herzog D., and Copeland, P. "Eating Disorders." *New England Journal of Medicine* 313 (1985):295-303.

Hess, R., and Shipman, V. "Early Experience and the Socialization of Cognitive Modes in Children." *Child Development* 36 (1965):869-886.

Holland, J. "ICU Syndrome: Fact or Fancy?" *Psychiatry in Medicine* 4 (1973):241-249.

Hollingshead, A., and Redlich, F. *Social Class and Mental Illness: A Community Study.* New York: Wiley, 1958.

Hollingsworth, T. "Mortality in the British Peerage Families Since 1600." *Population* 32 (1977):323-325.

House, J., Robbins, C., and Metzner, H. "The Association of Social Relationships and Activities with Mortality: Prospective Evidence from the Tecumseh Study." *American Journal of Epidemiology* 116 (1982):123-140.

Huntington, S. "The Change to Change: Modernization, Development and Politics." In *Comparative Modernization*, ed. C. Black, pp. 25-61. New York: Free Press, 1976.

References

Huxley, E. "Science, Psychiatry—or Witchcraft?" *New York Times Magazine* (May 31, 1959):17–19.

Imhof, A. "Man and Body in the History of the Modern Age." *Medical History* 27 (1983):394–496.

Inkeles, A., and Smith, D. *Becoming Modern: Individual Change In Six Developing Countries*. Cambridge: Harvard University Press, 1974.

Institute of Medicine, Committee for the Study of Health Consequences of the Stress of Bereavement. *Bereavement: Reactions, Consequences, and Care*. Washington, D.C.: National Academy Press, 1984.

Jelliffe, D. "Infant Nutrition in the Subtropics and Tropics." World Health Organisation, Geneva, 1968 (second edition). *Journal of the National Cancer Institute* 65 (1980): 1097–1107.

Jemmot, J., and Locke, S. "Psychosocial Factors, Immunologic Mediation, and Human Susceptibility to Infectious Disease: How Much Do We Know?" *Psychological Bulletin* 95 (1984):78–107.

Jenkins, D. "Social Environment and Cancer Mortality in Men." *New England Journal of Medicine* 308 (1983):395–398.

Jones, E., et al. "Teenage Pregnancy in Developed Countries: Determinants and Policy Implications." *Family Planning Perspectives* 17 (1985):53–63.

Jones, W., Carpenter, B., and Quintana, D. "Personality and Interpersonal Predictors of Loneliness in Two Cultures." *Journal of Personality and Social Psychology* 6 (1985):1–9.

Kasarda, J., and Billy, J. "Social Mobility and Fertility." *Annual Review of Sociology* 11 (1985):305–328.

Kass, E. "Infectious Disease and Social Change." *Journal of Infectious Diseases* 123 (1971):1–14.

Kato, H., and Schull, W. "Studies of the Mortality of A-bomb Survivors. 7. Mortality, 1950–1978: Part 1, Cancer Mortality." *Radiation Research* 90 (1982):395–432.

Kaye, K. *The Mental and Social Life of Babies: How Parents Create Persons*. Chicago: University of Chicago Press, 1983.

Kettering Foundation report, 1980. *The Most Significant Minority: One-Parent Children in the Schools*. Quoted in D. P. Moynihan, *Family and Nation*, pp.92–93. New York: Harcourt Brace Jovanovich, 1986.

Kessel, S., et al. "The Changing Pattern of Low Birth Weight in the United States." *Journal of the American Medical Association* 251 (1984):1978–1982.

Keys, A. "Coronary Heart Disease in Seven Countries." *Circulation* supp. to 41 (1970): 1–198.

Kiecolt-Glaser, J., et al. "Psychosomatic Modifiers of Immunocompetence in Medical Students." *Psychosomatic Medicine* 46 (1984):7–14.

———. "Distress and DNA Repair in Human Lymphocytes." *Journal of Behavioral Medicine* 8 (1985):311–320.

King, Martin Luther. Speech delivered at Abbott House, Westchester County, New York, October, 1965.

Kirby, B., et al. "Legionnaires' Disease: Report of 65 Nosocomially Acquired Cases and Review of the Literature." *Medicine* 59 (1980):188–205.

Kitagawa, E. M., and Hauser, P. M. *Differential Mortality in the United States*. Cambridge, MA: Harvard University Press, 1973.

Kitson, G., Babri, K., and Roach, M. "Who Divorces and Why." *Journal of Family Issues* 6 (1985):255–293.

212

References

Klaus, M., and Kennell, J. *Maternal-Infant Bonding*. St Louis: C. V. Mosby Co., 1982.

Knodel, J. "Breast-feeding and Population Growth." *Science* 198 (1977):1111–1115.

Kobasa, S., Maddi, S., and Kahn, S. "Hardiness and Health: A Prospective Study." *Journal of Personality and Social Psychology* 42 (1982):168–177.

Koenig, M., and D'Souza, S. "Sex Differences in Childhood Mortality in Rural Bangladesh." *Social Sciences and Medicine* 22 (1986):15–22.

Kohn, M. *Class and Conformity: A Study in Values*. Homewood, IL: Dorsey Press, 1969.

Kolata, G. "Studying Learning in the Womb." *Science* 225 (1984):302–303.

———. "Is the War on Cancer Being Won?" *Science* 229 (1985):543–544.

Koplan, J., et al. "An Epidemiologic Study of the Benefits and Risks of Running." *Journal of the American Medical Association* 248 (1982):3118–3121.

Kreger, B., et al. "Gram Negative Bacteremia III. Reassessment of Etiology, Epidemiology and Ecology in 612 Patients." *American Journal of Medicine* 68 (1980):332–343.

Kristal, A. "The Impact of the Acquired Immunodeficiency Syndrome on Patterns of Premature Death in New York City." *Journal of the American Medical Society* 255 (1986):2306–2310.

Kunin, C., Tupasi, T., and Craig, W. "Use of Antibiotics: A Brief Exposition of the Problem and Some Tentative Solutions." *Annals of Internal Medicine* 79 (1973): 555–560.

Lamb, H., ed. *The Homeless Mentally Ill: A Task Force Report of the American Psychiatric Association*. Washington, D.C.: American Psychiatric Association, 1984.

Latham, M. "Nutrition and Infection in National Development." *Science* 188 (1975): 561–565.

Lazarus, R. *Psychological Stress and the Coping Process*. New York: McGraw-Hill, 1966.

———. *Patterns of Adjustment*. New York: McGraw-Hill, 1976.

Lefcourt, H. *Locus of Control*. Hillsdale, NJ: Lawrence Erlbaum Associates, 1976.

Lerner, D. *Passing of Traditional Society: Modernizing the Middle East*. Glenco, IL: The Free Press, 1958.

Lesser, A. "The Origin and Development of Child Health Programs in the United States." *American Journal of Public Health* 75 (1985):590–598.

LeShan, L. "An Emotional Life-History Pattern Associated with Neoplastic Disease." *Annals of the New York Academy of Science* 125 (1966):780–793.

Levine, R., et al. "Failure of Sanitary Wells to Protect Against Cholera and Other Diarrheas in Bangladesh." *Lancet* II (1976):86–89.

LeVine, S., and LeVine, R. "Child Abuse and Neglect in Sub-Saharan Africa." In *Child Abuse and Neglect*, ed. J. Korbin, pp. 35–55. Berkeley: University of California Press, 1981.

Leyvraz, S., et al. "Association of Epstein-Barr Virus with Thymic Lymphoma." *New England Journal of Medicine* 312 (1985):1296–1299.

Lipset, S. "Working Class Authoritarianism." In *Political Man*, ed. S. Lipset, pp. 79–103. New York: Doubleday, 1960.

———. *The Confidence Gap: Business, Labor and Government in the Public Mind*. Baltimore, MD: Johns Hopkins Press, 1983.

Lipton, E., Steinschneider, A., and Richmond, J. "Swaddling, a Child Care Practice: Historical, Cultural and Experimental Observations." *Pediatrics* supp. to 35 (1965): 521–565.

Lipworth, L., Abelin, T., and Connely, R. R. "Socioeconomic Factors in the Prognosis of Cancer Patients." *Journal of Chronic Diseases* 23 (1970):105–166.

Livi-Bacci, M. "Fertility, Nutrition, and Pellagra." *Journal of Interdisciplinary History* 16 (1986):431–454.

Lynch, J. J. *The Broken Heart*. New York: Basic Books, 1977.

McCollum, E. "Response." In *The Nutritional Ages of Man: Proceedings of the Borden Centennial Symposium on Nutrition*, pp. 123–126. New York: The Borden Foundation, 1958.

McCormick, M., Shapiro, S., and Starfield, B. "The Regionalization of Perinatal Services." *Journal of the American Medical Association* 253 (1985):799–804.

McDermott, W., Deuschle, K., and Barnett, C. "Health Care Experiment at Many Farms." *Science* 175 (1972):23–31.

Mcdonald, D. "Drugs, Drinking and Adolescents." *American Journal of Diseases of Children* 138 (1984):117–125.

Macdonald, L., et al. "Hypertension: The Effects of Labelling on Behavior." *Quality of Life and Cardiovascular Care* Jan./Feb. (1985):129–139.

McCay, C. M., et al. "Retarded Growth, Life Span, Ultimate Body Size and Age Changes in the Albino Rat After Feeding Diets Restricted in Calories." *Journal of Nutrition* 18 (1939):1–15.

McKeown, T. *The Modern Rise of Population*. New York: Academic Press, 1976.

McKinlay, J., and McKinlay, S. "The Questionable Contribution of Medical Measures to the Decline of Mortality in the Twentieth Century." *Milbank Memorial Fund Quarterly* 55 (1977):405–428.

MacMahon, B., and Pugh, T. *Epidemiology: Principles and Methods*. Boston: Little, Brown and Co., 1970.

McManners, J. *Death and the Enlightenment: Changing Attitudes to Death Among Christians and Unbelievers in Eighteenth Century France*. New York: Oxford University Press, 1981.

Mare, R. D. "Socioeconomic Effects on Child Mortality in the United States." *American Journal of Public Health* 72 (1982):539–547.

Marmot, M., and McDowall, M. "Mortality Decline and Widening Social Inequalities." *Lancet* II (1986):274–275.

Marmot, M., Shipley, M., and Rose, G. "Inequalities in Death—Specific Explanations of a General Pattern?" *Lancet* I (May 5, 1984):1003–1006.

Martin, C., Warfield, M., and Braen, G. "Physician's Management of the Psychological Aspects of Rape." *Journal of the American Medical Association* 249 (1983):501–3.

Martin, J. "Neural Regulation of Growth Hormone." *New England Journal of Medicine* 288 (1973):1384–1393.

Maslow, A. "Self-actualizing People: A Study of Psychological Health." In *Personality Symposia: Symposium No. 1 on Values*, pp. 11–34. New York: Grune & Stratton, 1950.

Medalie, J., and Goldbourt, U. "Angina Pectoris Among 10,000 Men: II. Psychosocial and Other Risk Factors as Evidenced by a Multivariate Analysis of a Five-year Incidence Study." *American Journal of Medicine* 60 (1976):910–921.

Melnick, S., Cole, P., Andersen, D., and Herbst, A. "Rates and Risks of Diethylstilbestrol-Related Clear-Cell Adenocarcinoma of the Vagina and Cervix." *New England Journal of Medicine* 316 (1987):514–16.

Mercer, A. "Smallpox and Epidemiological-Demographic Change in Europe: The Role of Vaccination." *Population Studies* 39 (1985):287–307.

214

References

Merrick, T. "The Effect of Piped Water on Early Childhood Mortality in Urban Brazil 1970 to 1976." *Demography* 22 (1985):1–23.

Metropolitan Life Insurance Company. "Socioeconomic Differentials in Morbidity." *Statistical Bulletin* June (1972):10–11.

————. "Mortality Among United States Service Personnel." *Statistical Bulletin* 63 (1982):8–12.

————. "Gains in U.S. Life Expectancy." *Statistical Bulletin* 65 July-Sept. (1984):18–23.

————. "The Risky First Years of Life." *Statistical Bulletin* 66 Jan.-Mar. (1985):2–8.

Meuret, J. "Demographic Crisis in France from the Sixteenth Century to the Eighteenth Century." In *Population in History*, ed. D. Glass and D. Eversley, pp. 507–522. London: Edward Arnold, 1965.

Millard, A. "Child Mortality and Economic Variation Among Rural Mexican Households." *Social Sciences and Medicine* 20 (1985):589–599.

Miller, D., Alderslade, R., and Ross, E. "Whooping Cough and Whooping Cough Vaccine: The Risks and Benefits Debate." *Epidemiologic Reviews* 4 (1982):1–24.

Minuchin, S., Rosman, B., and Baker, L. *Psychosomatic Families*. Cambridge, MA: Harvard University Press, 1978.

Moffet, H. "Common Infections in Ambulatory Patients." *Annals of Internal Medicine* 89 (pt. 2) (1978):743–745.

Mohl, R. *Poverty in New York, 1783–1825*. New York: Oxford University Press, 1971.

Morris, J. "Social Inequalities Undiminished." *Lancet* I (1979):87–90.

Morris, N., Udry, J. R., and Chase, C. L. "Shifting Age Parity Distribution of Births and the Decrease in Infant Mortality." *American Journal of Public Health* no. 4 65 (1975):359–362.

Mossey, J., and Shapiro, E. "Self-rated Health: A Predictor of Mortality Among the Elderly." *American Journal of Public Health* 72 (1982):800–808.

"Multiple Risk Factor Intervention Trial." *Journal of the American Medical Association* 248 (1982):1465–1477.

Myers, J., Lindenthal, J., and Pepper, M. "Social Class, Life Events, and Psychiatric Symptoms: A Longitudinal Study." In *Stressful Life Events*, ed. B. Dohrenwend and B. Dohrenwend, pp. 191–205. New York: Wiley, 1974.

Nardini, J. E. "Survival Factors in American Prisoners of War of the Japanese." *American Journal of Psychiatry* 109 (1952):241–248.

National Center for Health Statistics. "Preliminary Findings of the First Health and Nutrition Examination Survey, United States, 1971–72, Anthropomorphic and Clinical Findings." DHEW Pub. no. (HRA) 74–1229. Washington, D.C.: U.S. Government Printing Office, 1975.

————. "Trends in Smoking, Alcohol Consumption, and Other Health Practices Among U.S. Adults, 1977 and 1983." Advanced Data no. 118. Washington, D.C.: U.S. Government Printing Office, 30 June 1986.

————. "Health, United States, 1985." DHHS Pub. no. (PHS) 86–1232. Washington, D.C.: U.S. Government Printing Office, December 1985.

National Center for Health Statistics and P. W. Ries. "Americans Assess Their Health: United States, 1978." *Vital and Health Statistics*, series ten, no. 142. DHHS Pub. no. (PHS) 83–1570. Washington, D.C.: U.S. Government Printing Office, March 1983.

Neu, H., and Howrey, S. "Testing the Physician's Knowledge of Antibiotic Use." *New England Journal of Medicine* 293 (1975):1291–1295.

Newachek, P., Budetti, P., and McManus, P. "Trends in Childhood Disability." *American Journal of Public Health* 74 (1984):232–236.

Newman, J. "Children of Disaster: Clinical Observations at Buffalo Creek." *American Journal of Psychiatry* 133 (1976):306–312.

O'Connell, M. "Comparative Estimates of Teenage Illegitimacy in the United States, 1940–44 to1970–74." *Demography* 17 (1980):13–23.

O'Conner, S., Vietze, P., Hopkins, J., et al. "Postpartum Extended Maternal-Infant Contact: Subsequent Mothering and Child Health." *Pediatric Research* 11 (1977): 380.

Oliver, J. "The Epidemiology of Child Abuse." In *The Maltreatment of Children*, ed. S. Smith, pp. 95–119. Baltimore: University Park Press, 1978.

Oliver, M. "Should We Not Forget About Mass Control of Coronary Risk Factors?" *Lancet* II (1983):37–38.

Olson, E. "Socioeconomic and Psychocultural Contexts of Child Abuse and Neglect in Turkey." In *Child Abuse and Neglect: Cross-Cultural Perspectives*, ed. J. Korbin, pp. 96–119. Berkeley: University of California Press, 1981.

Ounsted, C., Oppenheimer, R., and Lindsay, J. "Aspects of Bonding Failure: The Psychopathology and Psychotherapeutic Treatment of Battered Children." *Developmental Medicine and Child Neurology* 16 (1974):447–456.

Paffenbarger, R., et al. "A Natural History of Athleticism and Cardiovascular Health." *Journal of the American Medical Association* 252 (1984):491–495.

Pell, S., and Fayerweather, W. "Trends in the Incidence of Myocardial Infarction and in Associated Mortality and Morbidity in a Large Employed Population, 1957–1983." *New England Journal of Medicine* 312 (1985):1005–1011.

Peller, S. "Births and Deaths Among Europe's Ruling Families Since 1500." In *Population in History: Essays in Historical Demography*, ed. D. Glass and D. Eversley, pp. 87–100. London: Edward Arnold, 1965.

Peltola, H., et al. "Prevention of Hemophilus Influenza Type B Polysaccharide Vaccine." *New England Journal of Medicine* 310 (1984):1561–1566.

Pelton, L. "Child Abuse and Neglect: The Myth of Classlessness." *American Journal of Orthopsychiatry* 48 (1978):175–183.

Pendleton, B., and Yang, S. "Socioeconomic and Health Effects on Mortality Declines in Developing Countries." *Social Science and Medicine* 20 (1985):453–459.

Peplau, L., and Perlman, D. "Perspectives on Loneliness." In *Loneliness: A Sourcebook of Current Theory, Research and Therapy*, ed. L. Peplau and D. Perlman, pp. 1–20. New York: Wiley Interscience, 1982.

Phillips, R., et al. "Mortality Among California Seventh Day Adventists for Selected Cancer Sites." *Journal of the National Cancer Institute* 65 (1980):1097–1107.

Pixley, F., et al. "Effect of Vegetarianism on Development of Gallstones in Women." *British Medical Journal* 291 (1985):11–12.

Pocincki, L., Dogger, S., and Schwartz, B. *The Incidence of Iatrogenic Injuries*. Report prepared for the Secretary's Commission on Medical Malpractice, U.S. Dept. of Health, Education and Welfare, under contract no. HEW OS 73–22, with Geomet, Inc. report no. SCMM–ER–GE–11 (1973):50–70.

Poffenberger, T. "Child Rearing and Social Structure in Rural India: Toward a Cross-Cultural Definition of Child Abuse and Neglect." In *Child Abuse and Neglect*, ed. J. Korbin, pp. 71–95. Berkeley, CA: University of California Press, 1981.

Preston, S. *Mortality Patterns in National Populations*. New York: Academic Press, 1976.

References

Provence, S., and Lipton, R. *Infants in Institutions.* New York: International Universities Press, 1962.

Quint, J., and Cody, B. "Preeminence and Mortality: Longevity of Prominent Men." *American Journal of Public Health* 60 (1970):118–24.

Radbill, S. "A History of Child Abuse and Infanticide." In *The Battered Child*, 2nd ed., ed. R. Helfer and C. Kempe, pp. 3–21. Chicago: University of Chicago Press, 1974.

Ravitch, D. "Japan's Smart Schools." *New Republic* (6 Jan. 1985):13–15.

Reiser, S. "Responsibility for Personal Health: A Historical Perspective." *Journal of Medicine and Philosophy* 10 (1985):717.

Retzlaff, E., Fontaine, J., and Furuta, W. "Effects of Daily Exercise on Life Span of Albino Rats." *Geriatrics* 21 (1966):171–177.

Reuler, B., Broudy, V., and Cooney, T. "Adult Scurvy." *Journal of the American Medical Association* 253 (1985):805–807.

Reves, R. "Declining Fertility in England and Wales as a Major Cause of the Twentieth Century Decline in Mortality." *American Journal of Epidemiology* 122 (1985): 112–126.

Richter, C. "On the Phenomenon of Sudden Death in Animals and Man." *Psychosomatic Medicine* 19 (1957):191–198.

Robin, E. *Matters of Life and Death: Risks vs. Benefits of Medical Care.* San Francisco, CA: W. H. Freeman, 1984.

Robins, L., et al. "Lifetime Prevalence of Specific Psychiatric Disorders in Three Sites." *Archives of General Psychiatry* 41 (1984):949–958.

Rode, A., and Shepard, R. "Growth, Development and Acculturation—A Ten-Year Comparison of Canadian Inuit Children." *Human Biology* 56 (1984): 217–230.

Rodin, J. "Health, Control, and Aging." In *The Psychology of Control and Aging*, ed. M. Baltes and P. Baltes, pp. 139–165. Hillsdale, N.J.: L. Erlbaum, 1986.

Rosenberg, C. *The Cholera Years: The United States in 1832, 1849, and 1866.* Chicago: University of Chicago Press, 1962.

Ross, M., and Bras, G. "Food Preference and Length of Life." *Science* 190 (1975): 165–167.

Roth, D., and Holmes, D. "Influence of Physical Fitness in Determining the Impact of Stressful Life Events on Physical and Psychologic Health." *Psychomatic Medicine* 47 (1985):164–173.

Rousseau, J. *Emile: Or, On Education.* Translated by Alan Bloom. New York: Basic Books, 1979.

Ruberman, W., et al. "Psychosocial Influences on Mortality After Myocardial Infarction." *New England Journal of Medicine* 311 (1984):552–559.

Ruegamer, L., Bernstein, C., and Benjamin, J. "Growth, Food Utilization, and Thyroid Activity in the Albino Rat as a Function of Extra Handling." *Science* 120 (1954): 184–195.

Russin, D., et al. "Incidence of Breast-feeding in a Low Socioeconomic Group of Mothers in the United States: Ethnic Patterns." *Pediatrics* 73 (1984):132–137.

Sabbeth, B., and Leventhal, J. "Marital Adjustment to Chronic Childhood Illness: A Critique of the Literature." *Pediatrics* 73 (1984):762–768.

Sachs, J., et al. "Epidemiology of a Tuberculosis Outbreak in a South Carolina Junior High School." *American Journal of Public Health* 75 (1985):361–365.

Safe Drinking Water Committee. *Drinking Water and Health.* Washington, D.C.: National Academy of Sciences, 1977, 1982.

St. Leger, A., Cochrane, A., and Moore, F. "The Anomaly That Wouldn't Go Away." *Lancet* II (1978):1153.

Salimbine. "The Emperor Frederick II." In *A Portable Medieval Reader*, ed. J. Ross and M. McLaughlin, pp. 362–368. New York: Viking Press, 1949.

Salonen, I. Puska, P., and Mustaniemi, H. "Changes in Morbidity and Mortality During Comprehensive Community Programme to Control Cardiovascular Diseases During 1972–1977 in North Karelia." *British Medical Journal* IV (1979):1178–83.

Sarason, B., et al. "Concomitants of Social Support: Social Skills, Physical Attractiveness, and Gender." *Journal of Personality and Social Psychology* 49 (1985):469–480.

Sarason, I., et al. "Life Events, Social Support, and Illness." *Psychosomatic Medicine* 47 (1985):156–163.

Sarrazin, D., Dewar, J., Arriagada, R., et al. "Conservative Management of Breast Cancer," *British Journal of Surgery* 73 (1986):604–606.

Savage, D., et al. "Race, Poverty and Survival in Multiple Myeloma." *International Journal of Health Services* 15 (1985):321–338.

Schleifer, S., Keller, S., Camarino, M., et al. "Suppression of Lymphocyte Stimulation Following Bereavement." *Journal of the American Medical Association* 250 (1984): 374–377.

Schleifer, S., et al. "Depression and Immunity." *Archives of General Psychiatry* 42 (1985):129–133.

Schmale, A. H. "Giving Up as a Final Common Pathway to Changes in Health." *Advances in Psychosomatic Medicine* 8 (1972):20–40.

Schneider, R., Schiffman, M., and Faigenblum, J. "The Potential Effect of Water on Gastrointestinal Infections Prevalent in Developing Countries." *American Journal of Clinical Nutrition* 31 (1978):2089–2099.

Schoenborn, C., and Cohen, B. "Trends in Smoking, Alcohol Consumption, and Other Health Practices Among U.S. Adults, 1977 and 1983." National Center for Health Statistics, Advanced Data no. 118. Washington, D.C.: U.S. Government Printing Office, 30 June 1986.

Scrimshaw, S. "Infant Mortality and Behavior on the Regulation of Family Size." *Population and Development Review* 4 (1978):383–403.

Seligman, M. *Helplessness: On Depression, Development and Death*. San Francisco: W. H. Freeman, 1975.

Seltzer, C., and Jablon, S. "Army Rank and Subsequent Mortality by Cause: 23-year Follow-up." *American Journal of Epidemiology* 105 (1977):559–566.

Selye, H. "The Stress Concept." In *Stress Research*, ed. C. Cooper, pp. 1–20. New York: John Wiley, 1983.

Shapiro, S. *Infant, Perinatal, Maternal and Childhood Mortality in the United States*. Cambridge, MA: Harvard University Press, 1968.

Shorter. E. *A History of Women's Bodies*. New York: Basic Books, 1982.

———. "Female Emancipation, Birth Control, and Fertility in European History." *American Historical Review* 78 (1973):605–640.

———. *The Making of the Modern Family*. New York: Basic Books, 1975.

Shryock, R. *Medicine and Society in America: 1660–1860*. Ithaca, NY: Cornell University Press, 1960.

Siegel, E., et al. "A Controlled Evaluation of Rural Regional Perinatal Care: Impact on Mortality and Morbidity." *American Journal of Public Health* 75 (1985):246–253.

Silverstone, J. "Obesity and Social Class." *The Practitioner* 202 (1969):682.

Skeels, H., and Dye, H. "Adult Status of Children with Contrasting Early Life Expe-

References

riences." *Child Development Monograph*. The Society for Research in Child Development, Series 31, p. 3, 1966.

Slater, C., Lorimer, R., and Lairson, D. "The Independent Contributions of Socioeconomic Status and Health Practices to Health Status." *Preventive Medicine* 14 (1985): 372–378.

Smith, D. "Breastfeeding in the United States." *Social Biology* 32 (1985):53–60.

Social Class Indicators III. U.S. Dept. of Commerce, Bureau of the Census. Washington, D.C.: U.S. Government Printing Office, 1980.

Solomon, G., Levine, S., and Kraft, J. "Early Experiences and Immunity." *Nature* 220 (1968):821–822.

Sorenson, T., et al. "Prospective Evaluation of Alcohol Abuse and Alcoholic Liver Injury as Predictors of Development of Cirrhosis." *Lancet* II (1984):241–244.

Spitz, R. "Hospitalism: An Inquiry into the Genesis of Psychiatric Conditions in Early Childhood." *Child* 1 (1945):53.

Stallones, R. "Mortality and the Multiple Risk Factor Intervention Trial." *American Journal of Epidemiology* 117 (1983):647–650.

———. "The Rise and Fall of Ischemic-Heart Disease." *Scientific American* 243 (1980): 53–59.

Stamler, J. "Coronary Heart Disease: Doing the 'Right Things.' " *New England Journal of Medicine* 312 (1985):1053–1055.

Stanbury, J., Wyngarden, J., and Frederickson, D. *The Metabolic Basis of Inherited Disease*. New York: McGraw-Hill, 1983.

Starfield, B. H. "Child Health and Socioeconomic Status." *American Journal of Public Health* 72 (1982):532–533.

Starr, P. *The Social Transformation of American Medicine*. New York: Basic Books, 1982.

Stein, Z., et al. *Famine and Human Development: The Dutch Hunger Winter of 1944–1945*. New York: Oxford University Press, 1975.

Stern, M. "The Recent Decline in Ischemic Heart Disease Mortality." *Annals of Internal Medicine* 91 (1979):630–640.

Stevenson, H., Lee, S., and Stigler, J. "Mathematics Achievement of Chinese, Japanese, and American Children." *Science* 231 (1986):693–699.

Stone, L. *The Family, Sex and Marriage in England 1500–1800*. London: Weidenfeld and Nicolson, 1977.

Strassman, H., Thaler, M., and Schein, E. "A Prisoner of War Syndrome: Apathy as a Reaction to Severe Stress." *American Journal of Psychiatry* 113 (1956):998–1003.

Straus, M., Gelles, R., and Steinmetz, S. *Behind Closed Doors: Violence in the American Family*. Garden City, NY: Anchor Doubleday, 1980.

Stunkard, A., et al. "An Adoption Study of Human Obesity." *New England Journal of Medicine* 314 (1986):193–198.

Surgeon General. *The Surgeon General's Report on Health Promotion and Disease Prevention*. Background Papers, U.S. Dept. of Health, Education and Welfare, PHS 79-55071A. Washington, D.C.: U.S. Government Printing Office, 1979.

Susser, M., Watson, W., and Hopper, K. "Sociology in Medicine," 3rd ed. New York: Oxford University Press, 1985.

Sussman, M., and Burchinal, L. "Kin Family Network: Unheralded Structure in Current Conceptualizations of Family Functioning." *Marriage and Family Living* 24 (1962): 231–240.

Sydenstricker, E. "The Declining Death Rate from Tuberculosis." In *The Challenge*

219

of Facts: Selected Public Health Papers, ed. E. Sydenstricker, pp. 345–369. New York: Prodist, 1974.

Syme, L., et al. "Social Class and Racial Differences in Blood Pressure." *American Journal of Public Health* 64 (1974):619–620.

Tanner, J. *Growth at Adolescence*, 2nd ed. New York: Oxford University Press, 1961.

———. "Earlier Maturation in Man." *Scientific American* 218 (1968):21–27.

Teitelbaum, M., and Mantel, N. "Socio-economic Factors and the Sex Ratio at Birth." *Journal of Biosocial Science* 3 (1971):23–41.

Terr, L. "Chowchilla Revisited: The Effects of Psychic Trauma Four Years After a School Bus Kidnapping." *American Journal of Psychiatry* 140 (1983):1543–1550.

Terris, M. "Epidemiology of Cirrhosis of the Liver." *American Journal of Public Health* 57 (1967):2076–2088.

Thomas, C., and Duszynski, K. "Closeness to Parents and the Family Constellation in a Prospective Study of Five Disease States: Suicide, Mental Illness, Malignant Tumor, Hypertension, and Coronary Heart Disease." *Johns Hopkins Medical Journal* 129 (1974):251–270.

Thompson, J., Jarvie, G., Lahey, B., and Cureton, K. "Exercise and Obesity: Etiology, Physiology, and Intervention." *Psychological Bulletin* 91 (1982):55–79.

Tillman, W. A., and Hobbs, G. E. "The Accident-prone Driver: A Study of the Psychiatric and Social Background." *American Journal of Psychiatry* 100 (1949):321–331.

Torrance, E. "Comparative Studies of Stress-seeking in the Imaginative Stories of Pre-adolescents in Twelve Different Subcultures." In *Why Man Takes Chances: Studies in Stress-Seeking*, ed. S. Klausner, pp. 195–233. New York: Anchor Books, 1968.

Travis, R. "On Powerlessness and Meaninglessness." *British Journal of Sociology* 37 (1986):61–73.

Tschirley, F. "Dioxin." *Scientific American* 254 (1986):2935.

Tsuang, M., Boor, M., and Fleming, J. "Psychiatric Aspects of Traffic Accidents." *American Journal of Psychiatry* 142 (1985):538–546.

Tuddenham, R. "Soldier Intelligence in World Wars I and II." *American Psychologist* 3 (1948):54–56.

Uhlenberg, P. "Death and the Family." In *Growing Up in America*, ed. N. Hiner and J. Hawes, pp. 244–252. Urbana, Ill.: University of Illinois Press, 1985.

Uhlenberg, P., and Eggebeen, D. "The Declining Well-Being of American Adolescents." *The Public Interest*, Winter (1986):25–38.

United Nations Children's Fund. *The State of the World's Children, 1984*. New York: Oxford University Press, 1983.

Ursano, R. "The Vietnam Era Prisoner of War. Precaptivity Personality and the Development of Psychiatric Illness." *American Journal of Psychiatry* 138 (1981):315–318.

Vaillant, G. "Natural History of Male Psychologic Health: Effects of Mental Health on Physical Health." *New England Journal of Medicine* 301 (1979):1249–1254.

Valenstein, E. *Great and Desperate Cures: The Rise and Decline of Psychosurgery and Other Radical Treatments for Mental Illness*. New York: Basic Books, 1985.

Vandenbroucke, J. "Survival and Expectation of Life from the 1400's to the Present." *American Journal of Epidemiology* 122 (1985):1007–1016.

Vega, W., et al. "The Prevalence of Depressive Symptoms Among Americans and Anglos." *American Journal of Epidemiology* 120 (1984):592–607.

Verbrugge, L. "Marital Status and Health." *Journal of Marriage and the Family* 41 (1979):267–285.

———. "Longer Life but Worsening Health? Trends in Health and Mortality of Middle-

References

Aged and Older Persons." *Millbank Memorial Fund Quarterly* 62 (1984):475–519.

——. "Gender and Health: An Update on Hypotheses and Evidence." *Journal of Health and Behavior* 26 (1985):156–182.

Veronesi, U., Seccozzi, R., Del Vecchio, M., et al. "Comparing Radical Mastectomy with Quadrantectomy, Axillary Dissection, and Radiotherapy in Patients with Small Cancers of the Breast." *New England Journal of Medicine* 305 (1981):6–11.

Viorst, J. *Necessary Losses*. New York: Simon and Schuster, 1986.

Viste, A., et al. "Risk of Carcinoma Following Gastric Operations for Benign Disease." *Lancet* II (1986):502–504.

Waaler, H. "Height, Weight, and Mortality." *Acta Medica Scandinavica* Supplement 679 (1984).

Wallerstein, J., and Kelly, J. *Surviving the Breakup: How Children and Parents Cope with Divorce*. New York: Basic Books, 1980.

Washburn, T., Medearais, D., and Childs, B. "Sex Differences in Susceptibility to Infections." *Pediatrics* 35 (1965):57–64.

Watt, N., and Lubensky, A. "Childhood Roots of Schizophrenia." *Journal of Consulting Clinical Psychology* 44 (1976):363–375.

Weininger, O., McClelland, W., and Arima, R. "Gentling and Weight Gain in the Albino Rat." *Canadian Journal of Psychology* 8 (1954):147–151.

Weir, R., *Selective Nontreatment of Handicapped Newborns*. New York: Oxford University Press, 1984.

Weitzman, L. *The Divorce Revolution: The Unexpected Social and Economic Consequences for Women and Children in America*. New York: The Free Press, 1985.

Wertheimer, M., et al. "Increasing the Effort Toward Breast Cancer Detection." *Journal of the American Medical Association* 255 (1986):1311.

Wickes, I. "A History of Infant Feeding: Part II: Seventeenth and Eighteenth Centuries." *Archives of Diseases of Children* 28 (1953):232–240.

Wicklund, K., Moss, S., and Frost, F. "Effects of Maternal Education, Age, and Parity on Fatal Infant Accidents." *American Journal of Public Health* 74 (1984):1150–1152.

Widdowson, E. "Mental Contentment and Physical Growth." *Lancet* 1 (1951):1316–1318.

Wilson, J. "The Rediscovery of Character: Private Virtue and Public Policy." *The Public Interest* 81 (1984):3–16.

Wilson, W. "On Mortality Trends by Occupation and Social Class." Paper presented at the Council of Europe, European Population Conference, Strasbourg, 30 Aug.–6 Sept. 1966.

Wing, J. *Reasoning About Madness*. New York: Oxford University Press, 1978.

Wingard, D. "The Sex Differential in Morbidity, Mortality, and Lifestyle." *Annual Review of Public Health* 5 (1984):433–458.

Winkelstein, W., Lyman, D., Padian, N., et al. "Sexual Practices and Risk of Infection by the Human Immunodeficiency Virus: The San Francisco Men's Health Study." *Journal of the American Medical Association* 257 (1987):321–325.

Winn, M. *Children Without Childhood*. New York: Pantheon Books, 1983.

Winslow, C. *The Conquest of Epidemic Disease*. Madison, WI: University of Wisconsin Press, 1980.

Wohl, A. *Endangered Lives: Public Health in Victorian England*. London: J. M. Dent, 1983.

Wolfe, T. *The Pump House Gang*. New York: Farrar, Straus & Giroux, 1968.

Woodbury, R. *Infant Mortality and Its Causes*. Baltimore: Williams & Wilkins, 1926.

World Health Organization. "The First Ten Years of the World Health Organization." Geneva: WHO, 1958.

World Health Organization and the European Collaborative Group. "Multifactorial Trial in the Prevention of Coronary Heart Disease: 3. Incidence and Mortality Results." *European Heart Journal* 4 (1983):141–47.

Wray, J. "Population Pressures on Families: Family Size and Child Spacing." In *Rapid Population Growth: Consequences and Policy Implications*, ed. National Academy of Sciences, pp. 403–461. Baltimore: Johns Hopkins Press, 1971.

Wrench, G. *The Wheel of Health*. New York: Schocken Books, 1972.

Wylie, L. *Village in the Vaucluse*, Cambridge, MA: Harvard University Press, 1957.

Zinsser, H. *Rats, Lice and History*. New York: Little, Brown, 1935.

Zweig, S. *Mental Healers*. New York: Viking Press, 1962. (Originally published 1932.)

Index

Index

Tuberculosis, 6, 11n, 67, 83, 153, 175; death rates from, 28–29, 33–34; drugs for, 64; and stress, 40; transmission of, 32
Tuddenham, R., 175
Tupasi, T., 66
Typhoid, 32, 35, 36, 67
Typhus, 12

Uhlenberg, P., 105, 119
Ulcers, 58, 193
United Nations Children's Fund, 178
U.S. Public Health Service, 83

Vaginal cancer, 198
Vaillant, G., 121, 122
Valenstein, E., 193
Vandenbroucke, J., 15
Vega, W., 181
Venereal disease, 65, 167–69
Verbrugge, L., 4, 21
Veronesi, U., 74
Vinyl chloride, 198
Viorst, Judith, 133
Viral infections, 65–66
Viste, A., 58
Vitamin deficiencies, 43
Voodoo death, 117

Waaler, H., 100
Wallerstein, J., 104
Warfield, M., 101, 199
Wartime deprivation, 51–53
Washburn, T., 20
Watson, W., 154
Watt, N., 158
Weil, R., 7
Weininger, O., 102

Weir, R., 108n
Weitzman, L., 105
Welfare programs, 202
Wells, C., 75
Wertheimer, M., 74
Wet nursing, 46, 47, 49
White blood cells, 38
Whooping cough, 68
Wickes, I., 46–48
Wicklund, K., 156
Widdowson, Elsie, 101, 102
William the Conqueror, 174
Wils, T., 136
Wilson, M., 109
Wilson, R., 4
Wilson, W., 151, 152
Wing, J., 158
Wing, R., 55
Wingard, D., 21, 22
Winkelstein, W., 169
Winn, M., 106
Winslow, C., 28, 32
Wohl, A., 33
Wolfe, Tom, 111–13
World Health Organization (WHO), 8, 9, 60
World War I, 51–52, 175; influenza epidemic after, 35, 45
World War II, 52, 68, 132, 175
Wray, J., 96, 97
Wrench, G., 52
Wylie, Laurence, 143–44
Wynder, E., 162
Wyngarden, J., 52

Yale-New Haven Hospital, 75
Yang, S., 44

Zinsser, H., 12
Zweig, Stefan, 139

233